SARA WHEELER

Travels in a
Thin Country

A Journey through Chile

LITTLE, BROWN AND COMPANY
Boston New York Toronto London

ISBN 0–316–93257–4

10 9 8 7 6 5 4 3 2

Printed in England

For Mathew Wheeler

PERU

Parinacota
Lake Chungará
Arica
Poconchile
Azapa
Surire Salt Lake
Nama
Isluga
Colchane
Camiña
Chusmiza
Pisagua
Huara
Humberstone
Iquique
Pica
Pintados
Salt Lake

BOLIVIA

Pampa del Tamarugal

Tocopilla

Chuquicamata
Lasana
Calama
Chiu Chiu
Tatío Geysers
San Pedro
de Atacama
Toconao
Atacama
Salt Lake
Lake Lejía
TROPIC OF CAPRICORN

PACIFIC
OCEAN

Antofagasta

PANAMERICAN HIGHWAY

Taltal

Atacama Desert

Pan de Azúcar
National Park
Chañaral
El Salvador Mine

Caldera
Bahía Inglesa
Copiapó

ARGENTINA

Inca
Site

Vallenar

Isla Choros
Choros

La Serena
Coquimbo
Vicuña
El Tololo Observatory
Peralillo
Monte Grande

Miles
0   50   100

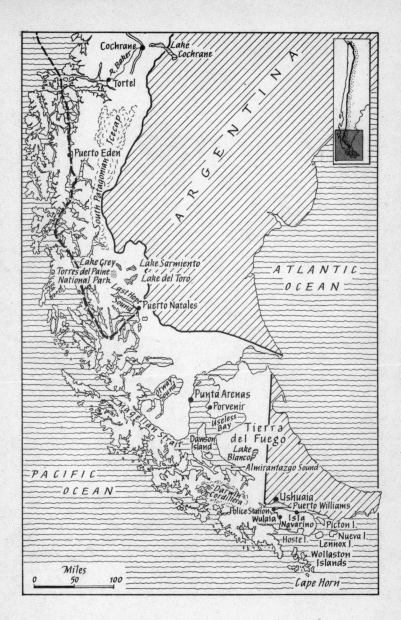

Acknowledgements

I owe a great debt to many people in both Chile and England. In the former I must single out first Germán Claro Lyon, who gave of his lovable and irascible self unstintingly and unlocked many doors, real and imaginary. Simon Milner and Rowena Brown provided the home base in Santiago and rich friendship; Ken Forder and Sylvie Bujon opened their apartment to me as well as their generous hearts. José (Pepe) Gomez was a bountiful companion, and a true teacher. The Columban Sisters furnished me with hospitality, wisdom and an insight into a side of Chile I would not otherwise have discovered. Eugenio Yunis and his henchpeople at Sernatur, the National Tourist Board, indulged me deliciously and solved several of my more intractable problems, especially in Magallanes. Roberto Olivos and his team at Hertz always came up with a jeep when I needed one and watched me disappear up scarcely travelled Andean passes without flinching. The Chilean Air Force flew me to Antarctica in a Hercules: it was one of the greatest experiences, and I shall never forget it. I am grateful to the Santiago-based Patagonia Connection for conveying me to the San Rafael glacier in high style. Chris Sainsbury more than doubled the fun I had on Chiloé. Down in the wild country Mark Surtees and Alex Prior provided me with an unrivalled base camp, moral support, advice and many of my most memorable hangovers.

Back at home I wish to thank my editor, Alan Samson, who made me believe I could do it, and Gillon Aitken, a literary agent perfectly shaped for a book on Chile and the only person whose confidence truly inspires me.

Timberland were generous with their unbeatable outdoor gear and Damart kept me warm in Antarctica. Linguaphone taught me South American Spanish: I recommend their excellent course to anyone considering travel in South America.[1] Andy Rattue provided comparative historical material on Victorian England.

It took me about a year to write *Travels in a Thin Country*, and during that time I fled Mornington Crescent three times in order to work in peace: I was lent an old farmhouse in the heart of the Auvergne by Jane Walker and Lyn Parker, Chris Coles created a study for me in a medieval hill fort in Roccatederighi, Tuscany, and Bruce Clark invited me to The Lookout in Fahan, County Donegal, where we both wrote all day and tried not to drink afterwards and still managed to stay reasonably sane. These three places are very special, and I am grateful to have been given the privilege of working in them.

As for readers, I was outrageously fortunate. Professor Victor Bulmer-Thomas looked at my work from a great height and Professor Robin Humphreys scrutinized it close up: both contributed to my capacity to keep going. Jane Walker read portions of the typescript and commented with great lucidity. Sabine Gardener also provided a cogent reading. Two people stand out for their commitment to my task. Phil Kolvin, who read doggedly on, is a brilliant critic. Cindy Riches read many drafts. What she gave, while herself moving continents, was of simply incalculable value.

---

[1] Linguaphone UK can be found at St Giles House, 50 Poland Street, London W1V 4AX; tel. 071 287 4050.

Introduction

Hard work and geographical isolation once earnt the Chileans the epithet 'the English of South America'. A dubious distinction, perhaps; but anyway, I went and lived among them for six months and I found them delightfully un-English.

You will see from the first chapter why I went to Chile rather than any other place. What I fear I cannot do is convey to you adequately at the beginning of the book how passionately I felt about the country at the end of the journey. I had never been there before. I set off with two carpetbags and a desire to find out what Chile was about, and I carried all three for thousands of miles, from the desert to the glaciated south. The book which has emerged is offered as a subjective and impressionistic portrait; painting it was a rich and joyful experience.

It was not one long idyll. I struggled to understand a society which had been so deeply divided by fear and hatred that in some circles human rights still means the same as Marxism. The extraordinary polarization of politics confused me: people were always eager to tell me what was black and what was white, but very few shaded in any grey. I have done my best to make some sense of it.

Although I made several visits to offshore Chilean territory, and these were among the most revelatory and entertaining episodes of the journey, I did not visit Easter Island. Rapa Nui, as it is called by its own people, does belong to Chile, but its culture is Polynesian, and as it really has nothing to do with anything else in the thin country I decided it would distract me from the task I had set myself. I was game for distraction – but not if I had to travel 2500 miles for it.

People often ask whom among the many travellers who have boldly gone before me I would cite as my heroes. Let me pay homage to one by using his words to cast some more light on the genesis of my journey. I have said that the primary reason I went to Chile was to paint a personal portrait of a country. Peter Fleming set down a similarly sober motive for travelling 3500 miles through Tartary with a stranger in 1935, and then he said, 'The second [reason], which was far more cogent than the first, was because we wanted to travel – because we believed, in the light of previous experience, that we should enjoy it. It turned out that we were right. We enjoyed it very much indeed.'

Chapter One

Noche, nieve y arena hacen la forma
de mi delgada patria,
todo el silencio está en su larga línea

Night, snow, and sand make up the form
of my thin country
all silence lies in its long line

Pablo Neruda, from '*Descubridores de Chile*'
('Discoverers of Chile'), 1950

I was sitting on the cracked flagstones of our lido and squinting at the Hockney blue water, a novel with an uncreased spine at my side. It was an ordinary August afternoon in north London. A man with dark curly hair, toasted skin and only one front tooth laid his towel next to mine, and after a few minutes he asked me if the water was as cold as usual. Later, the novel still unopened, I learnt that he was Chilean, and that he had left not in the political upheavals of the 1970s when everyone else had left, but in 1990; he had felt compelled to stay during the dictatorship, to do what he could, but once it was over he wanted space to breathe. He came from the Azapa valley, one of the hottest places on earth, yet he said he felt a bond as strong as iron with every Chilean he had ever met, even those from the brutally cold settlements around the Beagle Channel over 2500 miles to the south.

I told him that I had just finished writing a book about a Greek island – I had posted the typescript off two days previously. I explained that I had lived in Greece, that I had studied ancient and modern Greek, and all that.

The next day, at the lido, Salvador said:

'Why don't you write a book about my country now?'

I had wanted to go back to South America ever since I paddled a canoe up the Amazon in 1985. The shape of the emaciated strip of land west of the Andes in particular had caught my imagination, and I often found myself looking at it on the globe on my desk, tracing my finger (it was thinner and longer than my finger) from an inch above the red line marking the Tropic of Capricorn down almost to the cold steel rod at the bottom axis. Chile took in the driest desert in the world, a glaciated archipelago of a thousand islands and most of the things you can imagine in between.

After Salvador had planted his idea, I sought out people who knew about the thin country.

'In Chile,' a Bolivian doctor told me, 'they used to have a saying, "*En Chile no pasa nada*" – nothing happens in Chile.'

He paused, and bit a fingernail.

'But I haven't heard it for a few years.'

I went to the Chilean Embassy in Devonshire Street and looked at thousands of transparencies through a light box. The Andes were in every picture, from the brittle landscape of the Atacama desert to the sepulchral wastes of Tierra del Fuego. I took a slow train to Cambridge and watched footage of Chilean Antarctica in the offices of the British Antarctic Survey; the pilots, who came home during austral winters, told me stories about leave in what they described as 'the Patagonian Wild West'.

I was utterly beguiled by the shape of Chile (Jung would have said it was because I wanted to be long and thin myself). I wondered how a country twenty-five times longer than it is wide could possibly function. When I conducted a survey among friends and acquaintances I discovered that hardly anyone knew anything about Chile. Pinochet always came up first ('Is he gone, or what?'), then they usually groped around their memories and alighted on Costa-Gavras' film *Missing*. The third thing they thought of was wine; they all liked the wine. Most people knew it was a Spanish-speaking country. That was about it. Our collective ignorance appealed to my curiosity.

I told Salvador that my Spanish had gone rusty, and that anyway it was the Spanish spoken in Spain.

'Well, you must learn a new Spanish! Do you want everything to be easy?'

Duly chastened, I persuaded Linguaphone to sponsor the project by donating a Latin American Spanish course and shut myself away with it for three hours a day for the first month. One afternoon, at the lido, I surprised Salvador with it.

'You have to go and see for yourself now,' he said.

I left three months later, to the day. I was anxious that the trip should be a natural progression from one end of the country to the other, but I was obliged to fly to Santiago, the capital, which was unhelpfully situated in the middle.

'Make it your base camp!' said an enthusiastic adviser, so I did.

I had been invited, via a mutual friend in London, to stay with Simon Milner and Rowena Brown of the British Council. They met me at the airport, she sitting on the barrier and smiling, holding a sign with my name on, and as we walked together through the harshly lit hall and the automatic glass doors and into the soft, warm air, fragrant with bougainvillea, she put her arm around my shoulder and her face close to mine and she said:

'Your Chile begins here. Welcome.'

Simon and Rowena were about my age, and had been in Santiago for a year, living in a penthouse on the thirteenth floor of a well-kept block of flats set among manicured lawns and acacia trees in the north of the city. It wasn't really their style – I had the idea that they thought it was quite a joke – but it was clear that they loved their Chilean posting, and their enthusiasm steadied my wobbling courage. I nurtured a sense of arrival for a day or two, contemplating the Andes on one side and the urban maw on the other from their spacious and safe balconies. When I did venture out I found a city discharging the usual international urban effluents – exhaust fumes to McDonald's hamburgers – though it had a delightful insouciance about it which was quintessentially South American, and it was impossible to imagine I was in Rome or Amsterdam or Chicago. I badly wanted to explore, but I was too impatient for the journey to begin; the city would wait.

I was going to save Santiago until its proper place, half-way down the country, so after two indolent days I bought a bus ticket to the far north. The plan was to travel up to the Peruvian border straightaway, in one leap, and then work my way south, leaving the continent right at the bottom and crossing over to the slice of Antarctica claimed by Chile – though I had no idea how I was going to do that. I was also determined to visit the small Chilean archipelago called Juan Fernández, half-way down, four hundred miles out in the Pacific and the prison-home of the original Robinson Crusoe. I had two arrangements to meet up with people from London, one in the north, which would coincide with Christmas, and one in the south, and these I saw as punctuation marks on the journey.

The only big decision I had made – to leave Santiago immediately – was almost instantly overturned. A South-African photographer called Rhonda telephoned to say that she was working on a feature about a sex hotel for a London magazine and had been let down by the journalist doing the words: could I step in? The subject was irresistible, though a bizarre introduction to the complex and apparently paradoxical Catholic moral code, so I changed my ticket and stayed an extra day.

Alongside the shifting sands of Santiago's public and private lives stands an institution of such permanence that it is difficult to imagine the city without it. Inscrutable and silent, its patrons anonymous but its services widely appreciated, the Hotel Valdivia is the example *par excellence* of what is inaccurately known as a love hotel, a concept inured in Japan but perfected west of the Andes. Rhonda had made an appointment with the manager of the Valdivia at ten the next morning, and she told me that I would have to pose as her assistant, as the man had specified photographs only; he didn't want anybody writing anything. She had only wheedled her way that far round him by promising she would never sell the pictures to any paper or magazine within Chile.

The hotel was disguised as a discreet private mansion, and I was obliged to ask a man in a kiosk for directions. He winked at me, and leered a spooky leer. I met Rhonda in the street outside the hotel. She was about my age, was wearing army fatigues, and she gave me an affectionate slap on the back. At ten o'clock exactly a young woman scuttled out of the hotel, sideways, like a cockroach, and hustled us in.

'We don't like people waiting in the street,' she said. 'It attracts attention.'

She showed us into a small, windowless office where a man in his mid-thirties wearing a dark suit and a herbaceous tie stood up to shake our hands and introduce himself as Señor

5

Flores. He didn't look like a sleazebag at all; I was disappointed. His hair was neatly parted, and he had frilled the edge of a silk hanky half an inch above the lip of his breast pocket. He reminded me of an insurance salesman who used to live next door to us in Bristol. There were two photographs of brightly dressed children and a smiling wife on his desk, and four enthusiastically executed oil paintings of rural scenes hanging behind him which I feared were his own work. A VDU stood on one side of the desk, and neatly stacked piles of paper on the other.

I was introduced as Rhonda's assistant, and Señor Flores meticulously copied down the details on our presscards. Rhonda asked a question. Señor Flores clasped his hands in front of him, narrowed his eyes and looked earnest.

'We take a great pride in the authenticity of our rooms', he said. 'We have fifty-four, each a different theme. We have to get it right – I mean, we might get an Egyptologist here, and he could complain or not come back if he noticed that the hieroglyphics in the Egyptian Suite were wrong.

'We employ indoor gardeners to get the flora right and landscape designers for the waterfalls,' he continued confidently, 'and we have created a microclimate in each suite.'

When Rhonda suggested a tour, Señor Flores led us through an open courtyard to a series of drive-in cubicles. 'A curtain is drawn behind each car,' he explained, 'so that the driver cannot be seen when he gets out. Our main aim is to protect the privacy of our clients.'

Most of them checked in as Juan Peres, the Hispanic John Smith. The cubicles opened onto booths upholstered in grey velour, whence a corridor of straw-matting partitions led to the rooms. The whole complex was covered with a perspex dome.

The lobby of the Egyptian Suite revealed a flight of stairs with a banister inlaid with bronze, and alongside it a ten-foot waterfall sprayed a fine mist over tropical vegetation. Señor Flores hurried ahead to turn on the dimmed lights and Egyptian music. The room had a sauna off one side (saunas, I would learn, are closely associated with sex in the Chilean mind), a minibar cunningly concealed in a Sphinx, and, past the huge bed, a jacuzzi with little Pharaoh heads on the taps. Behind the jacuzzi someone had painted an elaborate mural of feluccas sailing down a river in front of a sandy landscape dotted with pyramids. The standard of workmanship was excellent; I had expected a plastic tack-palace.

I had forgotten that I was a photographer's assistant. I thought Señor Flores might be suspicious, so I fiddled with a tripod leg. Later I asked Rhonda if she would like me to go out and get her a coffee. She looked at me as if I were barking mad.

The jacuzzi and waterfall in the Blue Lagoon Room had been niftily fused together, and two digital light panels were set into industrial-sized ceramic butterflies. The sound of parrots chattering emanated from a speaker disguised as a banana tree, and a stained-glass parrot panel concealed a bidet. This was the only room offering a vibrating bed, and Señor Flores switched it on and sat on it. He told us that it also lifted up at the top, and at the bottom, and demonstrated by zapping both ends up at once. The movement reminded me of a dentist's chair. I wondered why anyone would pay money for the use of a V-shaped bed, but Rhonda told me later that the idea was to raise either one end or the other, and that Señor Flores had only put both up at once to show us the range of options. She seemed to know a lot about it.

The Indianapolis Room had a car in it. The Arabian Room had a minaret above the bed. The Inside of a Snail Suite (an oblique appeal, I thought) was spotted with flashing red lights and furnished with gold sofas and so many mirrors that I had to lie on the floor holding the flashgun. I got a headache.

Back in the office Señor Flores spoke authoritatively about cleanliness, even describing the special fungal cleaner run through the jacuzzi pipes. The hotel employed eighty full-time staff as well as a phalanx of freelance workmen, and the busiest periods were lunchtimes and Friday nights.

Señor Flores took a clear moral position. Pornographic videos were off-limits, no one under twenty-one was admitted and the only combination allowed in each room was one man and one woman. He claimed that many clients were married to each other.

'The subterfuge and excitement inject new life into their marriage,' he said, 'especially for the women.'

Dream on, I thought. I must have begun to think aloud, because Rhonda stood on my foot. He used the phrase 'Disneyworld for couples'.

'What we are trying to do,' he continued, now in full throttle, 'is create the right atmosphere between a man and a woman. We employ a psychologist for this purpose in the design of each room.'

This was a man with a social mission, the Mother Teresa of the mattress.

When we stood up to go he produced two black carrier bags from behind his desk.

'Souvenirs for you,' he beamed.

He escorted us to the door, shook our hands and kissed our cheeks; I thought he might invite us home for tea to meet the family.

We couldn't wait to see what was in the bags. As soon as we got round the corner, blinking in the glare of a Santiago noon, we unwrapped the long thin objects sticking out of the top. They were porcelain vases. Each bag also contained a cigarette lighter, ashtray, pen, keyring and even a T-shirt, all tastefully proclaiming 'Hotel Valdivia'.

It was an odd marketing concept, that people would display

their allegiance to a knocking-shop, even if it was a high-class one.

I spent one more day in Santiago before starting my journey, as I remembered that I had to buy a camera. I had achieved the feat of having all my valuables stolen before my plane landed in Chile. Air Portugal had been kind enough to upgrade me from London to Rio; there we parted company, I to pass eight hours in a champagne-induced fog of misery waiting for a connection. An hour before my plane was scheduled to leave for Santiago I tried to elicit information as to how I might check in. Nobody knew anything about the flight. Then someone started paging me. I could hear my name being repeated, followed by a jabber of Brazilian Portuguese, so I approached random officials and said, 'I am Sara Wheeler', pointing at the air to make a connection with the announcement. A woman directed me to the Ladies.

I got on the plane in the end. There was a doctor next to me, the second Chilean I had ever talked to properly. He was very short and stout, and I was surprised; subconsciously I must have been expecting them all to be tall and thin. He turned out to be a weatherman with the national television company. I wondered what he told his viewers each day. 'Tomorrow it will be cold in the south, much, much hotter in the north, and warm in the middle'? He pointed down to the corrugated brown Andes and took a slug of Scotch.

'Look. The mountains cut us off, like a sea. My country is an island!'

My luggage appeared in Santiago, which was a pleasant surprise, and within an hour of arrival I was sitting on a balcony in Las Condes with a gin in my hand. Very late that night, after Simon and Rowena had gone to bed, I opened the carpetbags and discovered that my camera, flash unit, short-wave radio, dictaphone and minicassettes had been stolen –

presumably while the bags languished on some runway in Rio. I felt stricken with loss by the disappearance of the radio; the patrician voices of the World Service had often sustained me in places that felt a long way from home.

Lying in bed I remembered that the cassettes were old ones I had been planning on recording over. They had on them a series of interviews with Tory ministers' wives I had done for a newspaper. I wondered what the robbers would make of them.

The night before I finally left town I met Germán Claro Lyon for the first time. Two separate people in London had put me in touch with him; he was a renegade mover and shaker from one of the most august Chilean families. I had sent him a fax before I left London, and he had replied immediately telling me to call him when I arrived. I didn't get round to it until I was about to go north, and I told him I'd ring when I was next in the city. But he wasn't having any of that: he came to pick me up at nine that evening and took me on a tour of drinking dens.

Most of the places we visited were chic, North American style bars in the fashionable and rich districts. The barmen nodded at Germán. He was in his mid-thirties, over six feet tall (rare for a Chilean) and quite handsome, in a raddled kind of way. For ten years he had been running his family's sixteenth-century hacienda as a luxurious country house hotel; it was an hour or two south of Santiago, but he lived in the city and had an office on Providencia, one of the main streets. He had never married. Once, immediately after a characteristic volley of laughter, he said, looking very serious, 'I don't have many friends. I prefer that.' He was outspoken, and not very tolerant, and had some unfortunate habits, like always quarrelling with waiters and not listening to what other people said. Germán loathed small talk. He was insecure about his

10

lack of formal education, and didn't realise what a good mind he had and how effectively he applied it to his work. He was difficult, there was no doubt about that, and badly stressed all the time, which often made him over-critical; it was a great tragedy, as really he was as soft as a marshmallow.

We ended up sitting in a restaurant next to a large pig on a spit at four in the morning, out of cigarettes (he chain-smoked). I remember him signing the cheque for dinner with an oversize Mont Blanc fountain pen. By the time I woke the doorman to let me into Simon and Rowena's block of flats it was five o'clock, and my bus left at eight.

The ever-gracious Rowena drove me to the bus station, making a spirited attempt at conversation despite my semi-comatose condition. When we got there I bought a bottle of water from a stall, and noted that the souvenir industry was not trying to flog ashtrays fashioned in its country's eccentric image: it had hit on bookmarks. They were made of copper, and I bought one to replace the boarding card sticking out of Darwin's *Voyage of the Beagle*.

As it was a thirty-hour trip up to the northern border I had allowed myself to buy a ticket on one of the more comfortable buses. The couple in front of me boarded in their best clothes and asked me to take a picture of them posing in front of their seat. It transpired that the husband was a second-hand car dealer called Jesus.

The driver crossed himself as we pulled out of the bus station. I dozed fitfully for an hour, then tried to keep my eyes open as we travelled along the Panamerican highway through the central valley. It was curious to see horses pulling ploughs and women crouched in the fields so near the urban sprawl of Santiago. The yellow foothills of the Andes, wobbling in the heat, were stained with olive green blotches. When we stopped, people rushed on to the bus selling avocados, conserved papaya, savoury pastries and sweeties.

11

The Panamerican is the only longitudinal road in Chile. It runs up the country like a spine, with two lanes and a tarmac surface all the way. It simply goes north. If it weren't for a few stretches of jungle higher up you could probably keep driving until you hit Vancouver.

The price of the bus ticket included meals, and we parked outside a café on a featureless plain for lunch, which consisted of watery chicken broth and a chunk of meat of uncertain origin with boiled rice and a flaccid salad. In the early afternoon the central valley melted away and the landscape became scrubbier, the road following a depression between mountain ranges, at one point so narrow that it was like travelling through a tunnel. The coastal mountains vanished sometimes, leaving a thin strip of plain next to the ocean: that was Chile. But the Andes were always there, the one constant in the landscape. They were going to be the constant in every Chilean landscape.

I was trying to follow our route on a map. Chilean cartographers are still grappling with the problem of representing something very long and thin in a user-friendly format. They should go back to the old system of rolling them out on a spool like a toilet roll. I had three maps, and after two of them had brought me to the verge of a breakdown I gave up and looked out of the window. After several hours of scrub it got dark. The musak stopped, but respite was denied us as the television was switched on in its place, delivering interminable North American soaps in washed-out colour. At midnight the steward pressed a plastic token into my hand 'for dinner', and when the bus stopped we trooped into a noisy diner. In the centre of the room they had put up a ten-foot high perfectly conical Christmas tree made out of fluorescent green wire; I realized that it was already the middle of December. Dinner was the same as lunch.

I fell asleep almost as soon as we set off again, and I dreamt that I was back at home, at my leaving party. In contrast with the uncharted territory outside the bus, the familiar faces and furniture appeared in brighter colours. In this dream I was standing in my kitchen and a friend asked me if I was frightened. I laughed and said no. (It was true that I wasn't a bit afraid of what the friend was asking me about: bandits, rapists, illness and thieves. I was more likely to confront those hazards in Mornington Crescent, where I live, than in the Atacama desert.) Then someone else, whom I didn't recognize, appeared in the kitchen and said, 'She's not going to South America really. It's all a joke. She's only going on a journey inside her own head.'

I woke up with a start, feeling cross, and hit my elbow on the window.

When I next woke up it was light. Every molecule of air was pulsating with bright, clean desert light. The sky was blanched, and the naked sand was broken only by one long, straight road. Desert Chile, called the *norte grande*, the big north, covers approximately a quarter of the country (excluding what they refer to as Chilean Antarctica). It embraces the driest places on the planet, and much of it is lifeless. The transition zone between the central valley and the desert is called the *norte chico*, the little north, or the northlet, and I had slept through most of that.

After several unpunctuated hours of that featureless landscape, travelling in suspended animation, we pulled in at a customs post (Chileans, I was to learn, are fond of internal customs posts) which consisted of two or three hardboard shacks, two pairs of goalposts, a three-legged dog and six women in cerise ponchos picking the pellets off corncobs.

Halfway through the morning the ground fell away to our right, revealing a deep valley. A green ribbon appeared at the bottom of the valley, but the rest was smooth toffee brown, and the opposite rim was straight, flat and bare. The distance between the rims widened, perhaps to two, even three miles. Later, proximity to Arica, the most northerly Chilean town, almost at the Peruvian border, was signalled by a Coca-Cola logo carved into the hillside, and as if it knew it had almost made it, the refrigeration system cooling our oversweetened drinks broke down.

Thirty hours is long enough on a bus. Four rows ahead of me a Chilean emigré from Miami had found out I was foreign and kept shouting, 'How are you, darling?'

My spirits rose as shacks became bungalows and bungalows three-storey blocks, and we lumbered into Arica bus station. The station clock had stopped.

Arica is the unofficial headquarters of the north Chilean *gringo* trail. (Although the word *gringo* simply means 'foreigner' – similarly *gringa* for the female of the species – it is usually perceived to have negative connotations. I even saw it translated in a book once as 'foreign asshole'. In Chile *gringo* and *gringa* are regularly deployed as affectionate and humorous terms of abuse. Foreigners who use the word about themselves are seen to display a healthy sense of self-deprecation.) I had scarcely put my bags down when an anxious young Dutchwoman picked me out of the crowd of Chileans struggling to reunite themselves with their luggage.

'Shall we share a room? You are alone too? It is much cheaper, I think.'

Bemused by this presumptive strike, I allowed myself to be led to a *colectivo* (clapped-out cars that run regular routes like buses and charge a flat fee) and we were driven into the centre of town.

Heeta found us a tiny room overlooking a courtyard full of pink flowers, and after taking a shower she went to the beach. I tried to have a shower, but unlike Heeta I failed to master the controls, which were positioned on a large brown box resembling a pre-war wireless. My efforts produced only scalding or freezing jets, and caused a small but alarming flood.

When Heeta returned she said:

'I have met a Canadian boy and an Australian boy. They are picking us up for dinner at eight, yes?'

Heeta, the two men and I loitered in Arica for a few days, meeting up with and parting from other foreigners like ants in a colony. I hadn't planned to hang out with backpackers, and I didn't intend to continue, but I enjoyed doing so for that brief period, and it was a way of beginning.

Arica felt like the frontier town that it is. Seamen eddied around in little gangs. Cooling ocean breezes just didn't exist up there, and it was always hot, so dry you expected the brittle buildings to crumble. There were a lot of people on the streets, even at two in the morning, and they were either eating outside cafés or purposefully going somewhere. The pavements revealed an amalgam of cultures: sleek-haired indigenous women wearing bowler hats carried babies and shopping on their backs in bright pink woven slings, yet most of the food we ate was in the shape of a burger.

The whole town was overlooked by the *morro*, a pale cliff where Chilean troops defeated the Peruvians in the War of the Pacific in 1880. They were fighting, basically, over the nitrate- and guano-rich territories to the south; at that time they belonged to Peru and Bolivia (both of which share a border with Chile). During a particularly tense period in the triangular relationship Peru had entered into a secret alliance with Bolivia, effectively ganging up on Chile, and when it was exposed Chile declared war on both of them. In the treaties and agreements which followed Chilean territory was enlarged by one-third. The nitrates of the Atacama desert were to shape the country's socio-economic development, in the process transforming the labour movement, realigning the class structure, facilitating industrial expansion and, ominously, creating an export-dependent economy. Bolivia and Peru sorely resented their loss, and still do. One of my predecessors, a travel writer in the 1920s called Earl Chapin May, noted, 'Signs have appeared in Arica such as, "No dogs or Peruvians wanted". President Leguia [of Peru] once issued an order prohibiting the entry into his country of "Russians, Chileans and prostitutes".'

They had set up a life-sized nativity scene in the palmy *Plaza de Armas*. The flat-faced Mary was wearing a traditional Andean bowler hat, and there was an alpaca at the crib. We had been brought up to expect holy figures who looked like us.

'Those must be the three wise dudes,' said Colin, a tough Canadian engineer who had packed in his job to spend six months in South America.

The square also had an open-air hairdressing salon where a middle-aged woman was having thin curlers put in her glossy hair. It was overlooked by a strange, multi-coloured church designed by Gustav Eiffel in 1875 and brought from Peru block by block after all the churches in Arica were destroyed by a tidal wave. They had a lot of tidal waves; a US steamer was once carried a mile inland. It was impossible to refloat it, so they turned it into a hotel.

One day I took a *colectivo* to the Azapa valley. It was where Salvador came from, my friend from the lido. Two llamas were grazing in a quiet, sunny cul-de-sac opposite the sand-polished ruins of an Inca fort, and a woman was pushing a wheelbarrow containing a baby and a gas canister. A small archaeological museum behind a fence traced local habitation back 10,000 years. There was a sixteenth-century hat in one of the glass cases, woven in stripes.

Outside in the road again I asked the wheelbarrow-pusher,

on her way back, minus canister, if she knew Salvador's grandmother; he had made me promise I would find her. She pushed a small curtain of hair from her eyes and pointed to a diminutive house at the top of the road, square on.

Before I reached this house I saw her, stooped outside, fiddling with a plant, and as I got closer I could see that she was picking leaves off it. She was wearing a hat exactly like the one in the museum. She stood up and looked at me, shading her eyes with a hand. I thought I could see something of him in her, an echo of his face. When I reached the gate I introduced myself, and said that I knew her grandson, Salvador, that we were friends in London, that I was travelling in Chile and he had asked me to find her and send his love.

'Is he coming home?'

I looked down at the gatepost.

'Not yet. But he will one day. And he's very well.'

She gestured for me to enter, and I sat on a wooden stool in the shade of a banana tree while she brought two glasses of a bitter herbal infusion from the adobe kitchen. I told her about Salvador's life in London, describing the city in as much detail as I could, and she kept her eyes on mine, interrupting with questions. When I had finished she looked in the direction of the mountains, lifted her hands in the air and raised her eyebrows, as if to say, that's all very well, *but where is he?*

She softened a little, then, and talked about other members of the family, and the llamas, who had recovered from a long viral infection, and the problems she was experiencing irrigating her small plot that year. After an hour I stood up to leave, and she embraced me, but it was only when I was on my way down the road that she called out,

'Don't forget to tell him about the llamas.'

Chapter Two

Years of dictatorship by the last Prussian army in the world have not separated Chileans from Chile. The military rulers have prevented them from living like human beings, but they have not been able to prevent them from surviving like Chileans.

Chileans say that life goes on in the churches, the courtrooms, and the cemeteries. The rest is survival. They will survive General Pinochet and the dictatorship, because on the other side of their bondage is Chile.

Jacobo Timerman, *Chile*, 1987

Back in Arica Santa pranced around on street corners and sweated to the tune of 'White Christmas' while gruff money-changers cruised the gringo hangouts and wherever we were a succession of hawkers importuned us with anything from counterfeit Rolex watches to live furry spiders. One evening, in a café near the port, we were offered coloured condoms a year past their sell-by date. We were talking, at the time, about the worst truck journeys we had ever endured.

'I sat on the top of twenty crates of uncovered wet fish for four hours in Greece once,' contributed an Italian art student.

'Well I', said Paul from Tucson, Arizona, whom nobody

liked, 'hopped into the back of a lorry in Kurdistan carrying frozen pigs' trotters.'

I persuaded myself to stir from this easy and agreeably indolent life and start doing things properly. I wanted to move east, right up into the Andes, to the oxygen-starved volcanoes, cold lakes, strange lichen, green peat bogs and abundant camelids. Only one bus a week went up there. The day before the next one left I bought candles, food, water and a bus ticket, said goodbye to the others and went to bed early.

The bus pulled out of the station before dawn. Later, in the half-light, we passed geoglyphs of men and animals, carved into the hillsides by some wandering tribe, centuries before the accursed Spaniards appeared on the continent. We stopped among the alfalfa fields at a village called Poconchile, at a customs post; I rested my head on the dirty bus window and missed the gringos. They had been my transition zone.

There was a valley with a wide green floor. As we travelled higher, above the valley and past a borax mine, the wrinkled hills transmogrified into brown shale pierced with candelabra cacti. The landscape was oppressively arid, and the contrast between the fecund valley floor and the rough brown cliffs and slopes seemed shockingly stark. The dreamy light of dawn had quickly sharpened into desert glare, and static on my sunglasses attracted a filmy layer of dust which re-appeared almost as soon as I had wiped it off. At the Restaurante Internacional, where erratically tufted dogs limped around the baked mud floor, we ate dry biscuits and drank coca-leaf tea, an infusion often prescribed to combat altitude sickness. I learnt – months later – that you need a catalyst for this brew to have any effect at all.

Three men we had passed working on the road came in. They were wearing all-in-one garments resembling snow-suits, as well as cotton hats and goggles. I thought, What are they hiding from?, and I looked outside again, and realized they were hiding from everything – sun, wind, cold, dust. It was as harsh as another planet up there.

The vegetation changed again after the oregano and potato fields of Socoroma, a typical Andean village where Aymára and *mestizos* (Chileans of mixed indigenous and European descent) had built their abode houses around a crooked white church. The bus stopped, and the driver got out to hand a package to an Aymára man who took it and turned away, without a smile.

Groups of Aymára entered Chile centuries ago, probably from the Titicaca basin, and their existence has been an unrelieved struggle against the brutal conditions of the high Andes. Nobody knows a great deal about them; the written history of most of the indigenous peoples west of the Andes before the Spanish conquest is sketchy, at least compared with that of the high cultures of more northerly Latin American countries. It wasn't until I got home and historically minded friends asked me about 'sites' that I realized there weren't any – or very few. Chile didn't breed any great empires and civilizations like the famous cultures of Mexico, Central America and Peru; it was frugally peopled by a heterogeneous (though often related) collection of tribes, each rich in its own particular areas of development. Most of them subsequently melted into oblivion. There was one exceptionally strong culture to the south, the Mapuche, which continues, but even they never had a centralized government. The other indigenous peoples were too fragmented to present a united opposition to the Spaniards. With the exception of the Mapuche, small groups of other Araucanians (of which the Mapuche are a branch) and the northern Aymára, miscegenation assimilated the original Chileans fairly swiftly.

The racial mix of the nation therefore settled at an early stage, compared with other territories of the Spanish empire. Relatively few black slaves were brought in. Approximately 65 per cent of the thirteen million contemporary Chileans are *mestizos*, 30 per cent are white and 5 per cent indigenous (this latter concentrated at the bottom of the social scale). I remembered what a salient feature racial differences had been in Brazil. They barely exist in Chile, which enjoys an ethnic uniformity almost unique on the continent.

The rolling high plains of the central Andes above about 12,000 feet are called the altiplano, a word which has worked its way into the English language; it refers to the entire discontinuous series of plateaux and basins extending from southern Colombia to northern Chile. The high desert around the intersection of Chile, Peru and Bolivia is also known as the Puna, and it is the largest tableland outside of Tibet.

When we reached this territory we found long-necked vicuñas (close but wild relations of the llama) grazing on bunchgrass, and rocks covered with the rare llareta (*laretia compacta*), a dense and bright green lichen-like plant which only needs a twentieth of an inch of water a year and which protects itself from the environment by turning hard and gathering into dome shapes. I glimpsed a mountain vizcacha – a furry grey rodent which resembles a long-tailed rabbit – sunbathing on a rock near a cushion bog. Spangled volcanoes overlooked lakes skimmed by black-headed Andean gulls and giant coots, and on the shore of Lake Chungará, at 14,800 feet probably the highest lake in the world, I got out of the bus and waved goodbye as it trundled towards Bolivia.

Deep silence. I walked across to a tiny wooden refuge pointed out by the bus driver. It was run by a genial employee of Conaf, the national forestry service; he was called Umberto, and he said I could sleep on the floor of what purported to be an office. I sat talking to him outside the hut, and almost immediately the salmon pink streak of a flamingo curved above the lake.

The change in air pressure had caused my fountain pen to

21

leak over my clothes. I wondered what it was doing to my body. I drank a lot of water, didn't move much for twenty-four hours, and watched the vicuñas next to the hut. They were eating bunchgrass as hard as granite and spikier than a gorse bush. Umberto knew them all personally. He told me that they were much nicer than their relations the guanacos, who live at lower altitudes; guanacos spit.

As the sun prepared to set, delicate pink fingers curled around the volcano in front of us.

On the second day Umberto unfurled a Chilean flag on the flagpole.

'What's that for?' I asked.

'We like to put one up because we're so near Bolivia,' he said. 'The last one got ripped in the wind. Besides, the boss is coming up tomorrow.'

The next morning he scrubbed the hut, shaved and put on a clean shirt, tie, pressed trousers and regulation Conaf sweater. We sat outside watching white-throated sierra finches hopping in the shale. The boss never turned up. This didn't bother Umberto. It was difficult to imagine anything ever bothering him; he was so laid back I wondered if he was on anything, and if he was, I wanted some. His maternal grandmother was pure Aymára, his other three grandparents *mestizos*; he had been brought up in a valley not far off. He was diffident when he spoke, but apparently completely at ease with himself and his isolation. I asked him how he liked living alone so far from anyone else, and he laughed.

'It's better than the town! Pure air!'

'Thin air!' I said.

'Thin for you, not for me. My lungs are used to it.'

'Do you like it best when there are people staying at the refuge, or when you're alone?'

'Alone! I like peace. I like my thoughts. I like to write poetry.'

22

I walked to the shore of the lake, and counted the giant coots' nests floating on the water.

When I woke up on the fifth morning I surprised myself by feeling stirrings of desire to move on; I was uncontrollably eager to grasp more of the country. Inconveniently positioned mountains meant that I was obliged to go back before I could go forward, so I decided to leave for Arica. After packing my bag, however, I had an attack of altitude sickness, called *soroche* in South America. I threw up my breakfast, had a tight headache that aspirins wouldn't dislodge, and felt weak. It wasn't only oxygen deprivation which made life punishing up there: it was viciously cold at night, too. I had worn all my clothes to bed, including hat and gloves, and in the morning there was always ice in front of the hut. But during the day the sun was remorseless. I sat still inside the hut, recovering, and in an attempt to entertain me Umberto turned to Princess Anne's signature in the visitors' book, and asked me if I knew her. I wondered if she had suffered from altitude sickness.

By early afternoon I felt better, and decided to return to Arica after all. I said goodbye to Umberto and walked down the road, reasonably confident of picking up a ride down to the coast. Umberto was singing. I sat on a rock and looked back, so I could see the volcanoes behind the lake for a little longer. One of them was the highest volcano in the world. Chile has over 2000 volcanoes, and about fifty of them are active; they were all gods to the early peoples, many with names and personalities. Two of them were reflected in unbroken lines on the waters of the lake. Agents of the Pinochet regime had tried to drain that lake once, claiming they were going to pipe the water to the people of Arica. As it is salt water and they were apparently not building any desalination plants this was not very plausible. It was eventually revealed that the object was to increase the water supply to a hydroelectric plant

23

which they were about to privatise. The project was dropped.

The wind whipped up little typhoons of brown dust. After an hour a juggernaut crawled over the ridge. I knew it was Bolivian, as virtually all road traffic over that section of the Andes carries freight from landlocked Bolivia to Chilean ports. Bolivia lost its coastal territory in the War of the Pacific, and is obliged to station its navy on Lake Titicaca. Over a century after the war, its demands for free and full access to the coast continue to poison bilateral relations. I had already been told a laboured joke three times about Bolivian representations at the UN, which for some reason, according to the Chileans, were expressed in English ('We want sea'). Turned around ('Sea, we want'), this allegedly sounds very much like 'Yes, bollocks' (*Sí, huevón*) in Chilean Spanish.

The lorry skidded to a halt a few yards ahead of me, causing a minor cyclone, and I climbed up into the grimy cab, greeted by two sweaty and smiling dark brown faces. I reckoned the journey back down to Arica would take about eight hours. It was to turn out rather differently.

The truck was loaded with 34 tons of timber on its way to the United States. Simón and Rodríguez sat a couple of feet apart in the front seats and I perched on the narrow wooden bed behind them. A large plastic model of the Virgin in prayer, her body wreathed in fluorescent roses, was swinging violently from the mirror. (This, the South American equivalent of the furry dice, was to become a familiar sight on my trip.) Most of the metal in the cab was exposed and dented, and wherever possible it had been decorated with circular stickers printed with pithy Bolivian aphorisms such as 'Virginity kills – inoculate yourself'. Every few minutes the two men dipped their stubby fingers into crumpled paper bags on the dashboard and took out lurid jellyish sweeties. I ate one of these later. It tasted of Swarfega.

I had underestimated the capacity of 34 tons of wood to

slow a vehicle down. In addition, the height of the cab magnified the bumps (there were many bumps) and I often clenched my eyes in pain as *soroche* flooded back. When the sun began to set I made a headrest out of my sleeping bag, and then the pink and orange liquid Andean sky turned my torture chamber into a palace.

I began to realize that there was more to the extraordinary slowness of the truck than was immediately apparent. It was slowest when we went downhill. Whenever we confronted a sweeping slope downwards, beads of sweat appeared on Simón's brow and he rammed his foot on the brake and changed down to first gear.

We passed two other Bolivian juggernauts parked on a verge, and pulled over. It appeared that each truck needed a tyre change – an astonishing coincidence – and a team effort was required. This took two hours. I sat on a rock trying to be patient and finished Gavin Young's *Slow Boats Home*.

We set off again, and I estimated that we could still make Arica by midnight. I asked Simón when we would be arriving. '*En un ratito,*' he said, a phrase I had already heard many times in Chile. It had the same connotations as *mañana* in Spain (without the sense of urgency, as the old but reliable joke goes). It was the first of many journeys which took far longer than it would ever have been possible to imagine at the outset, and by the end of my six months in Chile I experienced a sense of achievement whenever I actually arrived anywhere.

When we pulled over again, at ten o'clock, a building materialized in the blackness, and it was surrounded by Bolivian trucks. Simón hustled me inside, where an Aymára family was watching television behind a straw screen. In the front portion of the building Simón and Rodríguez greeted about fifteen of their compatriots and we joined them at a long table.

Thus it was, then, that at 13,000 feet on a cold night in the heart of the Andes I had dinner with seventeen Bolivian truckers. They all had masses of glossy, straight black hair, dark skin, thin moustaches, high cheekbones and large, straight white teeth. We ate *cazuela*, a staple Chilean dish I became very fond of comprising potato, corn and a chunk of meat in tasty brown broth. The truckers were in high spirits (though they didn't touch alcohol) and graciously tried to include their strange dinner guest in the conversation, but I had just about got my ear around the Chilean idiom, and this Bolivian Spanish defeated me. The volume, inflection and accompanying gestures indicated that they were not discussing the finer points of the Bolivian constitution.

As we left the building Rodríguez cheerfully announced that we still had four hours to go. This was depressing news, as the boarding-house where I had left my bags only received its guests until two o'clock. I fidgeted on my wooden bed. After a couple of hours we reached a section of road allowing one-way traffic only, and had to wait in a line of trucks for half an hour until we were mysteriously waved through. And then, at one o'clock, we drove into a lorry park where Simón announced that we were to snatch 'a couple of hours' sleep'. Rodríguez, whose sole role was apparently to allow Simón to boss him around, was dispatched into the back of the truck with blankets. I was motioned forwards while Simón made up the bed behind the seats. He lay down, breathing heavily. I sat rigid in the passenger seat.

'Why don't you come back here?' he said alluringly. 'It's much more comfortable.' After two or three further attempts at persuasion he fell asleep. I tried to do the same in the passenger seat, but the man could have snored for Bolivia, so I put my thermal gloves on and watched the stars until the sky transformed itself from deep black to the pale pearly shades of an oyster, and sunlight leaked from the east.

A cockerel crowed, but it was a very old cockerel, and half way through his wheezy crow collapsed into a rasping cough. A small dairy farm coalesced out of the gloom. A man was chasing cows around a pen. Simón woke up with a snort, cross at having slept too long. He shouted at Rodríguez, spat on the floor of the cab, got out and stumbled around outside in the cold, climbing into the adjacent trucks and waking his colleagues. We left in a hurry with a lot of loud farting, past the man who had been chasing cows, standing now in the sunlight concentrating on a mirror hanging on a gatepost and working at his chin with a cutthroat razor.

It was no surprise when the three trucks pulled over half a mile further on. Everyone got out and started shouting. I learnt a few Bolivian swear words and figured out that the Chileans operated a weighbridge at the Poconchile customs post. Any Bolivian truck over a certain tonnage was required to pay stiff excess charges. The lumber trucks were way off-limits, and had no means of paying the charges – the plan had been to pass Poconchile before the weighbridge operators arrived at work. But the truckers had overslept, and were going to have to idle on the side of the road until nightfall, and cross the customs post in the dark, when it was unmanned.

It was tacitly and mutually understood that we had to part company. I reckoned we were about twenty-five miles from Arica. Despite the fact that I had a hard slog ahead of me to any kind of settlement, with only a brief period of pleasant air temperature between extreme cold and extreme heat, I couldn't tolerate another stultifying day getting nowhere with the Bolivians. Simón was displaying pointed indifference towards me. He felt the rebuff of the previous night, and the delay meant that he had a problem with his schedule, so didn't want to be bothered fussing around a gringa. My bag wasn't very heavy, and I was fairly confident that another, better organized Bolivian truck would pass, and pick me up. If it didn't, I could probably break the journey at Poconchile.

As I left, Simón belched loudly. I set off along the deserted road through the Lluta valley, returning the occasional wave from straw-hatted figures intent on their fields. It was warm by the time I reached the weighbridge five or six miles further on, but the pale light of morning still hung over the valley. The weighers waved me through, grinning, and soon another Bolivian stopped for me, smirking with delight that cunning redistribution of his load of timber a hundred yards up the road had secured him a clear passage over the rudimentary Chilean weighbridge.

The remoter reaches of the north Chilean Andes require a four-wheel drive jeep, and Hertz produced one for me for the next leg of the journey, the first of many of their vehicles which conveyed me to the more difficult areas of the incontiguous Chilean landscape. My plan was to go inland again before I left the far north, which meant I was descending the country in a zigzag. There were tracts of volcanic land near the Bolivian border post of Colchane which people told me were inaccessible. That was like catnip to me.

Another gringo was heading south, so I asked him if he wanted to join me on the mountain trip. Matthew was a tall, skinny Australian in his mid-thirties who worked as a computer programmer when he wasn't travelling, and we had shared a meal together three or four times in Arica. He was quick-witted, with a touch of pedantry about him, and always knew exactly what he thought, a trait which makes me cautious. But he was open and friendly, with a highly developed sense of humour, and he was game for anything. His Spanish was good, and he made a great effort with the Chileans. Whenever someone asked him where he was from, he used to put his hands in the begging dog position, crouch over and hop around impersonating a kangaroo.

We loaded up with essentials such as water, emergency provisions and ten gallons of spare fuel, and set out down an empty Panamerican, windows down and a dubious Australian cassette marked 'various artists' batting out of the speakers. We travelled at our own pace on a good road through trembling mauve mountains, smooth caramel desert and swathes of red and brown pampa, at one point required to abandon the fruit in our bags at a pest control 'fruit check'. Matthew was handed a receipt for an orange, and wondered whether it would enable him to claim the fruit back on a return trip. Passports, driving licences and sundry documents were pored over. In the police room they had erected a board displaying photos of smashed cars and corpses.

We stopped to climb in the crispy heat to the human geoglyph at Chiza, picking among limbs like Gulliver on Brobdingnag. The hot wind stuck in our throats. When we got back in the jeep I put on a Ry Cooder tape: it was perfect desert music. Time dissolved in those empty spaces, and hours passed that afternoon without us noticing them go. Later we searched a valley below the road for a nineteenth-century British cemetery, a lonely memorial to the families who came out to make their fortunes from Chilean nitrates. Invisible dogs started barking when we drew up outside a solitary house, and an old man standing on the porch squinted at us. He guessed what we wanted, waving in the direction of the mountains, and beyond a small oasis, on the opposite side of a sandy wasteland, we found an arched iron gate.

Little children called Amy and Hubert had died before they had learnt their own names. The climate had killed off most of the settlers' children; on one porous headstone I read the names of four brothers under two years old. They must have hated it there, those Victorians, with their layers of clothes and their inhibiting Britishness, and at that moment, the sun high and the tall tombstones casting no shadow, I hated it too; it was murderous. I put a desert flower on a cracked flagstone, and as I turned to leave I saw an inscription. It was from the sixteenth chapter of Numbers. It said, 'Is it a small thing that thou hast brought us up out of a land that floweth with milk and honey, to kill us in the wilderness, except thou make thyself altogether a prince over us?'

The owner of the house was waiting when we returned to the jeep, and he introduced himself as Señor Keith, the Chilean grandson of an Irishman and his Scottish wife who had pitched up in 1875. His great uncle had been big in nitrates, and the pine walls of the house were hung with dusty photographs of flourishing mines. Señor Keith, who couldn't speak a word of English but referred to me as his *compatriota*, said I looked like Jackie Kennedy, and called me Jackie while we drank tea; she wouldn't have been very flattered by the comparison, and Matthew laughed immoderately.

We pressed on down the Panamerican, past the turning to Pisagua, where mass graves, dug during the dictatorship, were discovered in 1990. The uncovering of mass graves became a fairly common occurrence after democracy was restored in March of that year. Following one such discovery, Pinochet was asked what he thought of the fact that several unidentified corpses had been found stuffed into one grave. He said, 'What economy!'

Turning inland, we tackled forty-three miles of poor road, hoping to end up at Camiña, a mountain village which one of the maps confidently told us offered accommodation. 'Turning off the Panamerican' was to become as much of a concept as a road direction. It meant starting to travel, rather than simply getting from somewhere to somewhere else; it meant being free to move as slowly as I wanted (or constrained to move much slower than I would have liked), and it meant a dramatic deterioration in the quality of the road. Nowhere was it more apparent than up there in the baked, dead desert that the Panamerican was the umbilicus of Chile, and you strayed from it at your peril.

We picked up a farmer and his wife, walking from their square of land on the valley floor to a meeting at a Seventh Day Adventist church. I was amazed to find this church in what I had thought were the Catholic heartlands.

The track ran next to a drop of several hundred feet. When it got dark we felt dwarfed by the black cliffs and prolific constellations, and we didn't speak for a long time, listening to the engine, willing it to keep going. Matthew produced a Talking Heads tape, and the first song was 'We're on a Road to Nowhere'. It was very, very black. At about ten o'clock a light flickered in the foothills. Matthew punched the air. It was Camiña.

The guesthouse really did exist, but two men stirring a tureen in its open-air kitchen explained indifferently that the owner was away and all the rooms were locked. We sought assistance at the mayor's house (an old trick), and the incumbent, a well-fed man of Pickwickian geniality, listened to our story, took a key from a hook next to his front door and led us to an unoccupied adobe cottage on the other side of the street. 'Have you got candles?', he asked, scratching his crotch. We had, and we fetched them from the jeep and followed him inside, seeing off several dozen mice. Matthew lit the candles, and we sat on two camp beds positioned in the middle of the front room.

The mayor eyed a mouse in the corner. 'I hope you'll be comfortable here,' he said, his expression indicating that he thought this was unlikely. 'When you leave, pay me whatever you like. If you want food, ask for Violeta at the top of the street. Er, I'll be off now.'

In the absence of a single bar, café or restaurant in Camiña, Violeta, whom we visited later, cooked for anyone 'passing through'. (This must have constituted an extremely erratic

31

income, as I shouldn't imagine more than a dozen people passed through in any one decade.) She ushered us into a room built of unpainted concrete blocks and furnished only with three high-backed chairs and a table covered with a plastic cloth. As we waited, five or six men came in, shook our hands and exclaimed loudly and unintelligibly, whether to each other or to us, we did not know.

Violeta brought the meal in. It consisted of boiled rice with a crusty fried egg on it, stale bread and coffee substitute made out of barley (the latter produced by Nestlé, like so many products which enter the Chilean mouth). It was at this stage that Matthew revealed that he had forgotten to buy the wine. We had divided the labour preparations for the trip between us, and the purchase of water, salt tablets and wine had fallen to Matthew. He casually remembered this omission when I asked for the jeep keys so I could fetch the first bottle. He seemed to think it was some small matter. I saw him in a different light after that.

We breakfasted in the bare room, now throbbing with sunlight, on condensed milk, still moulded in the shape of the tin and served in a blue plastic dish with two teaspoons, and the same bread, eight hours staler, though eight hours constituted such a small percentage of its life that the difference in taste was negligible. Afterwards we settled our account in the shared courtyard at the back of the house, where we found our hostess turning a mangle in the middle of a scene of Brueghelian vigour, fires smoking and dented kettles steaming, small children playing with empty tins, babies crawling on dried mud, women kneading, men drinking beer and a policeman fiddling with a gun in a corner.

Before leaving the village we visited the church on the square, replete with the obligatory garlanded statues and plastic accoutrements beloved of South American popular religion. The building had been under more or less permanent restoration since 1935. Two men working on the flagged floor told us that there was a shortage of sand for the cement to lay the stone tiles. We thought it was a queer thing to be short of in a desert. Next to a Pentecostal chapel around the corner we found a shop resembling a large wardrobe, and stocked up on provisions: tins of salmon, suspiciously familiar hard bread and a kilo of wrinkled apples.

Next to the track we followed into the mountains villagers were clearing garlic fields while their alpacas, tied to adjacent tree trunks, stared impassively into the middle distance. We began a long, slow ascent up a serpentine and precipitous dirt road in candent tropical heat, both glancing regularly at the temperature gauge of the jeep, a snappy Japanese model called Rocky which didn't seem to mind the conditions as much as we did.

The road degenerated. The land we wanted to reach, around the Isluga National Park, was still many hours ahead of us, and Rocky got a puncture; the sun seemed particularly malevolent while we were fixing it. After a side track down to a place called Nama which didn't feature on any of the maps the road deteriorated exponentially until it resembled a casually discarded trail of large and sharp stones. A sign for drivers coming the other way warned of the perils of illegally importing fruit from Bolivia. Anyone who had made it along that road from Bolivia deserved an endurance medal. We had already used our spare tyre, and we didn't fancy the axle's chances. I was instinctively in favour of continuing, but Matthew, always the pragmatist, persuaded me that we should turn back and try to reach the park from another angle. In a spirit of appeasement he suggested that we visit Nama, on the valley floor three miles below us. I was bitterly disappointed, and we drove in silence.

A casual remark which eventually broke this silence led to

an argument over the future tense of an irregular Spanish verb. Matthew stopped the jeep in order to get the dictionary out of the back, but I had left it under my camp bed. When he got back in, he shut his foot in the door.

At Nama we parked outside a small, newish bungalow. A young woman wearing jeans came out. 'Hi', she said. I was afraid Matthew was going to ask her about the verb. The woman told us that she was the village teacher, and showed us the school, which was in the bungalow. She had twelve pupils, and there was a framed photograph of Pinochet on the wall next to their crayon drawings of themselves. Matthew and I glanced at each other furtively as we stood in front of this sinister juxtaposition; the teacher said she wasn't allowed to take the photograph down, but didn't elaborate, and the moment passed.

A sign on a decrepit building next to the school said 'MUSEO'. The teacher told a loitering child to run and fetch the man in charge of it, who duly arrived, followed by two associates, and this triumvirate shook our hands and observed us closely as we perused the two small rooms of the museum. Someone had handwritten a catalogue in an exercise book. A mummified woman was propped up against a small adobe house, fleshless fingers clutching a zampoña, a musical instrument like panpipes. One of the old men took it from her, and gave us a tune.

We ate our salmon sandwiches on the wall of a small church on a knoll, and a middle-aged woman joined us from the fertile plots of land below. 'You mustn't drink,' she said peremptorily, 'or fornicate. The bible says so.' I took the opportunity of remarking airily to Matthew that she would approve of his attitude to drinking. The woman informed us, in parentheses, that she was a Seventh Day Adventist, and concluded a list of other biblically prohibited activities with 'watching television'.

Before we left the teacher asked us if we would take a box back to Camiña for her. I was often entrusted with errands like this in rural Chile. The villages were so remote that each vehicle was obliged to operate as a kind of public freight facility. I donated three pens to the schoolroom and we drove off under the large 'Nama' written on the hillside in white stones. Chilean villagers often proclaim themselves in mosaic writing, just as they lovingly tend their diminutive museums; they cherish a sense of community.

We delivered our consignment to the municipal offices in Camiña, as instructed. As in any good office the week before Christmas, the staff had been drinking for some time, and the parcel's addressee propelled us inside for a glass of *cola de mono*, a seasonal beverage made of milk, clear brandy, coffee and cinnamon. After a few minutes a nun entered the room, and our hosts pointed at us and jabbered. A man began to play the national anthem on a pair of teaspoons. The wide-eyed nun turned to us and said in a Yorkshire accent, 'Is it true then? Are you really English?'

Matthew and I choked on our cocktails and introduced ourselves. The nun, flapping her hands and beaming, invited us home for dinner. The villagers clucked approvingly at this happy gringo reunion.

We reclaimed the camp beds we had relinquished in the morning from the mayor, who had spilt *cola de mono* down his crisply pressed shirt, and spent the evening with two Sisters serving in the County Wicklow-based missionary order of St Columban. Matthew, keen to establish our moral credentials with the nuns, was anxious to advertise the innocent nature of our relationship. He said we had decided to make an Andean trip together 'for mutual support', and I could see the nuns' eyes glaze over as he extrapolated about this support, none of which sounded very familiar to me. I'm sure they didn't believe a word of it; he was protesting too much.

35

The nun with the Yorkshire accent, whose many years on the continent had taught her not to expect much, told us that the valley had been priestless for over a hundred years. Besides the fact that it didn't have any money, the Chilean Church had experienced a chronic inability to recruit priests throughout the century. In 1968, the worst year, only two had been ordained in the entire country. No wonder the Adventists had enjoyed so much success: they had moved into a vacuum.

'The Pentecostals,' she went on, 'have caused a lot of friction, especially in the altiplano. There are masses of them.' Like many fundamentalists before them, the Pentecostals' vision of the world did not extend to religious tolerance. 'They set up a stage outside a church in a large village on the coast once during a Catholic mass and outblasted us with their music! You have to hand it to them, though – they achieve great things among the people. They can reform the hardest of drinkers, once they get their hands on them.'

Catholic men – many of them, at least – continued to put it away.

'But the Pentecostals want to jettison the entire culture of the villages', the nun continued. 'They even forbid fiestas, and you can imagine what a psychological necessity they are in a poor rural community.'

Religious observance throughout the continent was, in general, weak; it had always been weak. The indigenous population had never been properly Christianized: they were 'Churchized'. The *conquistadores* turned their pagan shrines into churches and told them they were Catholics. Naturally, pagan practices were swiftly grafted on to Christian stock, and they took hold. On 1 November each year, we were told, the people of Camiña still proceed to the cemetery to deposit food, drink and cigarettes on the tombs of their dead.

However lukewarm many Chilean Catholics were about the

faith, everyone I met, up and down the country, seemed to have a strong sense of the importance of the Church as a national institution, both historically and in their own time. It was different from faith. It was a sense, or an awareness, which had been bred into their ancestors. It had survived the arrival of the secular age, which by the mid-nineteenth century had dislodged the Church from the privileged position it had inherited from medieval Europe, and it had outlived the 1925 constitution, which officially separated Church and State after almost fifty years of political controversy on the subject. (Disestablishment was characteristic of a trend in Europe as well as South America, and in Chile the transition was a particularly smooth one.) Despite the fact that over the next decades the Chilean Catholic Church moved towards the centre, it remained close to the ruling and landowning élite until the 1960s – and then it was overtaken by a small revolution.

Before we reached their front door we could smell bacon cooking; it was a smell which took me very far from the Andes. The Sisters had invited us for breakfast, despite our early start, and they had managed to prepare an English one. Up there, this was something of a feat. Given my profound attachment to real coffee I never thought that I would be glad to see Nescafé, but the barley substitute had put it into a different perspective.

We made the Panamerican again before eleven, grateful for the comfort of tarmac, got the tyre fixed at a garage and tried to reach our Andean destination by a more southerly route. Turning off at a truckstop called Huara, the kind of place where nothing has ever happened and you expect to run into a serial killer, we followed a wide and deserted road painted with troubling white lines. Neither of us spoke for a while, then Matthew said, 'I don't want to be alarmist, but I can't help wondering why this road is marked out as a runway.' The tarmac petered out soon afterwards, and this bizarre piece of Chilean highway design remained an enigma.

A track careered off to a hill on the pampa, and we took it: on the southern side we found the Giant of the Atacama, 350 feet long and the largest human geoglyph in the world. It had a head like a box, with twelve rays coming out of it, and struck an angular pose, with a creature like a monkey at its side. Nobody knows what these geoglyphs were for, or if they had a function at all. Matthew, a utilitarian at heart, was adamant that the drawings in the soil once had a purpose. It seemed to me perfectly plausible that they were simply aesthetic, and that the hills were a kind of early art gallery. It didn't strike me as an odd concept, having grown up in the English west country where there are plenty of images carved in the chalk. Those white horses galloping through my childhood seemed as appropriate to the benign English hills as this sinister alien-man did to the harsh and spooky desert.

The hot wind which had been blowing through the jeep all day picked up speed in the late afternoon as we took a loop of road to a high village called Chusmiza where, our Chilean guidebook told us with a descriptive flourish, we would find a delightful hotel near a warm mineral spring. This seemed as likely as finding a French restaurant, but we had learnt to keep an open mind. At a small water-bottling plant a man jogged across a yard and flagged us down.

'Hello', he said.

'Hello', we answered.

There was a pause. The three of us smiled inanely.

'Is this the right way to the hotel?' Matthew eventually asked.

The man pulled a key out of his pocket with the figure seven carved on it.

'Yes', he said, holding out the key. 'One thousand pesos.

Just follow the road and you'll come to it.' He smiled again. 'It's a very quiet hotel. There aren't any staff. Haven't had any guests for quite a while now, either.'

We drove on, each constructing this Marie Céleste in our imagination. The track ended at a long thin building on a spur of land above a shallow valley. We left the jeep on a small forecourt and let ourselves into the hotel through the door painted with a red seven. It led into a high-ceilinged room with three single beds, and in the *en suite* bathroom we found a five-foot deep white-tiled bath fed by hot sulphur springs and occupied by a wooden stopper and a family of salamanders. The toilet flushed with hot water too, and it ran from the single tap in the basin. We had discovered a hotel without cold water.

The village was so poor that the roofs of the shacks were made of orange crates. We met a priest called Father Miguel outside the water-bottling plant later, and he took us to a truckers' café. A man disappeared into the back and returned suggesting roast llama and rice. Father Miguel enthusiastically explained that llama is cholesterol-free.

We made another attempt to reach the Isluga National Park. It was a hard three-hour drive to 12,000 feet, the tracks so corrugated and pitted by Bolivian juggernauts that we were frequently obliged to slow down to ten miles an hour. We had bought some packets of strawberry wafers for breakfast from the roast llama man. They were a scientific triumph, as they had absolutely no taste at all. We were thirsty all the time. The jarring discomfort and the heat made us both irritable. Matthew made his hundredth joke about women drivers, and I snapped at him. Underneath a cosmopolitan and right-on exterior he was deeply conservative. He freely admitted to what he referred to as a 'fundamentally right-wing perspective on life'; he thought having a liberated attitude towards women meant feeling okay if I poured the petrol while he held the funnel. While we were driving along one day he asked me what impression I had got, in general, of Australian men when I was down there for a couple of months earlier that year. After I told him he didn't speak to me for two hours.

In Isluga itself, a typical altiplano village and the eastern gateway to the park, narrow streets of thatched adobe cottages formed a semi-circle around a church painted white with marsh lime. At the top of the uneven stairway of the belltower I rang the angelus on two copper-green bells. Next to the church they had built a bandstand in a green meadow. There was nobody in the bandstand, or the meadow; in fact there was nobody anywhere. The shepherds of the altiplano used to build their villages for festivals and funerals, living ordinarily near their llamas and alpacas and returning only on special occasions. It was a tradition which had been eroded in most places, as the villages had acquired schools, and other institutions, and the populations had stabilized.

After an argument about whether a distant camelid was a llama or an alpaca we picnicked by a fast stream, both remarking how different the park was from the landscape around Chungará only sixty or so miles to the north (but requiring hours and hours of hard travel). There was hardly any snow, to start with, more animals, more water, an abundance of short green grass and an irritating profusion of flies. It was less harsh, and not quite so other-worldly.

At one village we were closely observed by a small gang of Aymára children who had been playing in the potato fields. Their parents, said a small fourteen-year-old wearing a black hat with a narrow brim, were at the market at Colchane. Other children clutched their younger siblings protectively. One girl took us into a shack, hoping to sell a meagre bundle of woven goods. Her mother was crouched in a corner, suckling a baby with a shock of shiny black hair. I bought a bright strip of thick woollen ribbon, and when the girl gave it to me I saw that the skin on her hands was dry and scaley, like a reptile. The children stared at us, unsmiling, as we drove off and whipped up the dust.

We approached the Salar de Surire, a great salt flat, and walked for a while, short of breath. The cone of the Isluga volcano was smeared with snow. When we turned back, later, we travelled up to the border village of Colchane, a dusty, straggling place cluttered with trucks and decaying cars piled with Bolivians, their possessions bulging out of cardboard boxes. The road from Bolivia to Chile through Colchane is a well-known cocaine route, or at least a route for cocaine base or paste. People walk across with a pound or two in their pocket, or else drive shipments through in lorries. Peru and Bolivia – both on Chile's doorstep – supply a very high percentage of the world's coca-leaf crop. While Chile doesn't produce cocaine in any quantity, it does supply precursor chemicals, and both use and trafficking of the final product are common. Local dealers sell it in units called *empanadas*, the name of the pastry envelopes stuffed with meat, vegetables or shell-fish which are ubiquitous (and delicious) throughout the continent.

On the long drive back down to our hotel we passed open trucks with large families huddled in the back, shivering as the evening set in, their alpaca earflaps pulled under their chins while they bounced along. The sun slipped behind the most westerly ridge of the Andes, straight ahead, and conferred a halo upon the mountains while the sky turned itself into an excited configuration of pinks, reds and purples.

At a truckstop we ate a bowl of *cazuela* perfumed with a mound of coriander, but it was not a good one; it was tepid and greasy. There were two posters next to each other on the adobe wall, one showing Christ in close-up, wearing the crown of thorns, and the other, equally close-up, the glamour

41

model Samantha Fox, wearing a pair of yellow knickers. This was less of a surprise than the Adventists: I had been expecting to find religion comfortably coexisting with trash culture. Both functioned at the centre of public life; religion – as a concept, if not a living faith – had not yet been pushed out to the margins. I thought then that perhaps I had underestimated the reality of their faith. It was easy to see the failings of Catholicism, and more difficult to appreciate the bedrock it was for many Chileans. Going to mass wasn't everything.

The dust, when we reached the hotel, had coated us and our possessions like fur. Besides that, we were burnt by the sun, chilled to the bone marrow by the cold night air and battered by the tortuous roads. It had been a hard day.

'Well done,' said Matthew. 'You didn't flag.'

Patronising bastard, I thought. He applied himself to the task of clipping his nails, and I removed a new branch of the salamander family from the soap dish, filled the bath and got in, the steam-filled room lit by a single candle. A bottle of chilled Krug would have gone down nicely. I would have settled, in fact, for a pint of warm Chilean Sauvignon blanc, but I had nothing, not even a cigarette, as I had given my last packet to an old Aymára in the back of a broken-down truck. Even coffee would have provided a token stimulant. I considered inviting Matthew into the bath, *faute de mieux*, to make an occasion of it, but decided against it and ate half a packet of the flavour-free strawberry wafers.

Chapter Three

The Walrus and the Carpenter
 Were walking close at hand;
They wept like anything to see
 Such quantities of sand

Lewis Carroll, *Through the Looking-Glass*

As we lurched down to the Panamerican I began to glean one of Chile's less visible but most salient characteristics: the geographical differences between north and south – the feature that had brought me half way across the world – were only part of the story. It was the contrast between the interior and the coastal plain that struck me then – a contrast which manifested itself in the landscape, economy, infrastructure, social organization and even racial mix, as – generally – the higher you go the purer the indigenous blood. People seemed very conscious of the division between mountain-dwellers and plain-dwellers: I had heard several men in Arica referring to themselves as *costeños*, coastal people. Christopher Isherwood came across this distinction in other South American republics, and in his excellent travel book *The Condor and the Cows* he calls the two groups of people the Ups and the Downs.

You end up driving around a lot in the desert. You have to.

Distances between anything except sand are long, and when you do get somewhere, nothing happens. It was curiously agreeable, as if our minds had flattened out like the baked plain. The sun blanched our anxieties, and life began to seem less complex. There was a tension out there on the sand, but it was a subtle, faintly delicious one, hinting at the possibility of creative eruptions.

We stopped at a semi-derelict complex of buildings, a 'Keep Out' sign dangling vertically from one nail on a wall next to the entrance. Once the flourishing nitrate community of Humberstone, since the people had disappeared the buildings had dried out into sturdy husks, potent symbols of the transience of the Chilean nitrate age. Inside an exercise book lay open on a classroom floor, its pages bleached, and on the basketball pitch the indentations of feet that had scuffled round the posts were filled, emptied and refilled with fluid sand. The tricks of the sun coloured in the gaps, and if you turned your head too quickly you caught a child running through the streets or a couple kissing a first kiss under the moulded iron streetlamps.

The resources of the desert have bestowed upon the northern provinces (about a third of the country's landmass) a significance out of all proportion to their meagre population (less than 15 per cent of the total). The nitrate industry was a nineteenth-century development; it was Chilean acquisition of the land after the War of the Pacific that marked its beginning. In 1883, Chile's industrial working class was born up there in the north.

Small metal plates nailed to rusted engines were engraved with the words 'Made in Lancashire', or 'Cobb & Son, 1897'. Señor Keith had shown me a curling photograph of his great uncle attending a meeting at Humberstone. He was standing next to six handlebar-moustached Victorians sweating in their worsted shirts.

'Fertilizer', said Señor Keith emphatically. 'He told me they were arguing at that meeting about how best to refine their nitrate ore to make it into fertilizer and export it.'

The government quickly learnt to depend on the fiscal revenue the burgeoning industry brought it – though it also had to get used to the socio-economic volatility engendered by dependence on a world market over which it had no control.

The population of the north doubled in twenty years as the nitrate plants sucked in manpower. The workers were exploited relentlessly in the usual horrific ways, but for the first time they used a collective voice in protest, and Chile had its first general strike in 1890. The labour movement spread south and into the new manufacturing businesses, and the country was soon experiencing the problems of urbanization faced by most of the nations of the developed world as they ushered in the industrial age. The rapid transformation led to more or less permanent economic conflict.

During the First World War German scientists started trying to make synthetic nitrates, and when they succeeded the Chilean industry went into long-term decline. The Depression of the 1930s hit the country harder than any other, according to League of Nations statistics, and many of the British left; Señor Keith's great uncle had been virtually abandoned. Chile was to look to the United States from then on, in almost every area.

Humberstone was shut down completely in 1960, and its shell had been designated a national monument. I had already learnt that if the authorities didn't know what to do with something they turned it into a national monument in the belief that the gesture absolved them of responsibility towards it.

We got back into Rocky and kept driving, mesmerized by the hot, empty space, and later we left the highway to penetrate the interior. The style of the churches had altered dramatically during this short journey southwards, and the simplicity of the white thatched altiplano chapels was gone. We stopped for Matthew to photograph gaudy iron buildings with large dented domes and chipped plaster columns. Then the trees faded away and we entered a textbook desert landscape consisting of nothing except undulating smooth sand and throbbing air. We sweated, even with the wind rushing through the windows, and spent a lot of time refilling our water containers: however much we drank, it was never enough. A village appeared in the distance, a dark green, abruptly circumscribed oasis, and we stopped to drink juice freshly pressed from its citrus groves.

We took a different route out, though it was almost identical to the one we had taken in, and saw nothing for twenty-three miles except sand. Later, on the edge of the Pintados salt lake, a collection of geoglyphs – almost four hundred different images – broke up the sandy surfaces of the hills. To get to them we had to cross a long-disused and once nitrate-bearing railway. The railway came to Chile in the middle of the nineteenth century to facilitate the copper industry, and by the early 1880s the nitrate lands had railways too, most of them built by the British – the railway engineers of Conrad's Sulaco. A hundred years later a family had installed themselves in two broken-down carriages rusting next to the weedy track, and their washing was drying over the long axles.

Rocky the jeep had to go back to Hertz in Iquique, where I had arranged to leave him. He was no longer white. Matthew, also considerably darker than he had been at the outset, was to be deposited in Iquique too. I was going to catch a night bus to Calama, a town further south in the Atacama, as I had made arrangements to meet my friend James Lloyd, who was flying from London to visit me for his Christmas holiday. It was Sunday 22 December, and honking trucks cruised the streets

46

of Iquique playing 'Jingle Bells' over their tannoys and bearing black-haired Father Christmases and beribboned acolytes who tossed sweets to children on the pavements.

I bought a ticket for a bus leaving at midnight, and before settling into a bar with Matthew admired some of the grand old residences of the nitrate barons and the opera house built by Eiffel. Iquique was a town of Parisian elegance after the parched and cracked utilitarian style of Arica. The well-stocked shops were full of customers, and the tarmac streets were thronged with cars; I would have liked to know if this prosperity extended to the kind of behaviour referred to darkly in an article in the *Chilean Times* in 1878 which described Iquique as 'the Sodom and Gomorrah of the Pacific coast'. The town had survived the collapse of nitrates, emerging in the 1960s as the centre of a major fishing and fish processing zone (the waters were as rich as the arable land was barren) and by the 1980s the government was claiming that measured in volume handled it had become the largest fishing port in the world.

At eleven-thirty Matthew kissed me goodbye and pushed me into a taxi to the bus station. I was sorry to leave him; we had got on well – most of the time – despite his unrecon-structed attitude towards women and especially considering that we hadn't been out of each other's company for five days and had barely met each other before that. He was a good travelling companion, really, and the difficulties and isolation of the trip had forged a bond between us whether we liked it or not.

The station was jammed with people; I couldn't imagine where they all came from, although they had apparently all been shopping, as most of them were labouring with huge boxes of electrical goods from the tax-free commercial zone just outside Iquique (which in Aymára means 'rest and tranquillity').

47

I fell asleep almost as soon as we left, but at three o'clock in the morning we had to get off at a customs post. All the luggage was lifted onto a long bench and an official walked along inspecting it, mechanically inserting both hands inside each bag while he looked at a girl in a miniskirt at the other end of the station. The passengers stood around like the living dead, pale-lipped and flesh tinged blue by neon signs offering them draught beer, *empanadas* and cigarettes.

I had known James since university, and we had met up in various spots around the world over the years in spite of our foolishly blasé attitude towards *rendez-vous*. 'It's always better,' we used to say, 'to have a very vague arrangement, because anything more precise is always thwarted.' A plain case of hubris. This time I had told him to get on a bus from Santiago as soon as his plane landed, and that I'd meet him twenty-four hours later in Calama.

Seventeen buses a day arrived in Calama from Santiago at five different terminals, each located in a different part of town. I met all seventeen, and James wasn't on any of them. I knew he would call at the tourist office if I didn't appear, and as it was permanently shut I pushed a note halfway under the door with his name visible in big letters and anchored it with a stone. The note told him to go to my hotel. I spent the day shuttling between bus stations. In one of them I made friends with a small girl who told me her name was Laydee. When her mother appeared she told me that she had named her child after Lady Di.

I filled in the time between buses buying Christmas presents for James. I found him a pink woven duffel bag – suitable for a barrister, I thought – and matching pink plastic sunglasses, a bottle of clear brandy and a loaf of special Christmas bread. As I walked past the post office I suddenly remembered that back at home I had given my December address as Poste

Restante, Calama. Inside they had pinned up neat lists of recipients' names, but as mine did not appear, I queued up and enquired if there was any possibility of an oversight. The functionary clearly thought there was a very strong possibility, and after several minutes of fossicking around under her desk produced two bundles of letters held together with elastic bands. When she had gone through these and found nothing, she admitted that a big box of unsorted letters was languishing in the basement. I asked if I could look through it myself. After some hesitation and in order, I suspected, to get me out of the way, she ushered me into the bowels of the post office, pointing at an orange crate overstuffed with an assortment of envelopes. At the bottom of this crate I found an orange and a letter for me from my vicar. I waved the letter around in triumph; the staff evidently thought it hilarious that someone had found something they wanted in that crate. They probably still talk about it now at office parties. Reading the missive as I left the building, I collided with a back-to-front tricycle carrying an uncovered tray of rum babas. Father Tom said they missed me at St Mark's, and wished me a Happy Christmas.

At half-past ten that night I was drinking James' Christmas present out of a toothmug alone in my room. The brand name on the bottle, I noticed, was 'Control'. I had repeatedly checked that my message remained in place at the tourist office; I had left notes in the gents' toilets at the bus stations; I had given careful instructions to officials about tall, red-haired gringos; and I had telephoned James' mother in Kenilworth to check that he had left. In the furthest station, at midnight and with Puccini playing over the tannoy, I met the last bus, and he wasn't on it.

The shops were just closing on Christmas Eve when an unshaven James ran out of a bar as I walked past.

'I got your message! I told you the wrong arrival date. Sorry.'

We were out of Calama within ten minutes. Several weeks previously I had booked us a room in one of the only decent hotels in the Atacama desert, planning Christmas in an oasis as a treat. The relief which followed the anxiety of the previous twenty-four hours imbued the project with a real sense of celebration.

I procured another jeep from Hertz and we travelled for two hours through the sand to reach this oasis.

Twenty-six political prisoners were shot somewhere along that route in October 1973. They were journalists, lawyers, union officials – the usual kind of people – and they had been held at a military installation nearby. It happened during General Sergio Arellano Stark's now famous helicopter tour of six such installations in the north. He had ordered a tribunal for the twenty-six the next day, but while he was having his dinner in Calama they were murdered. Did he know it was going to happen? He says he didn't. He was called 'the Wolf'. When the junta came to power Pinochet had been head of the army for only three weeks, so he had to purge it quickly. Arellano took off on this tour, making it clear that army personnel were going to have to be tough to survive.

The time came, of course, when the Wolf too was surplus to requirements. Pinochet didn't have him killed; he just brought his career to an end.

Daliesque configurations of rock led into San Pedro de Atacama, an old and fertile oasis village with a thousand inhabitants. Arriving in an oasis is like waking up from a dream: everything is different, and you feel momentarily disorientated, then relieved. The hotel I had booked us into was quite famous, but it was characterless, with nothing much to recommend it, and the food was poor. Poor food didn't matter too much when it cost tuppence, but when it was expensive – well, that was galling. On that first night we had dinner in the village square instead. It was lined with pimento trees, and at eleven o'clock we watched young villagers dance around the church to a military drumbeat. Another group, in possession of an amplification system, acted out the nativity scene, and a crowd of small shepherds brought a recalcitrant llama to the crib.

Just before midnight we followed clusters of people into the church, built in the eighteenth century of big, bulbous lumps of rock and painted white. The dancing troupe fidgeted in the aisle during the service (led by a woman, as there weren't any priests available); towards the end the dancers began gyrating energetically, changing tempo when an MC blew a whistle. More flamboyant than the girls in every way, the boys were wearing black satin waistcoats sequinned with a cross.

We both forgot that it was Christmas Day at first. After breakfast we packed up Rocky II with the few Christmas presents we had, a spartan picnic, a six-inch inflatable Christmas tree, two crackers which James had brought (he had wondered if they constituted firearms) and ten bottles of water. We set off south, alongside the greyish-brown Atacama salt flats, frayed white at their curling edges, a vista of emptiness extending to every horizon. The sun was already punishing. We were waved through a police control post (the policeman had threaded tinsel through the belt loops of his shorts) and stopped in the square of another oasis to climb up the exiguous eighteenth-century belltower, built of volcanic rock and cactus wood, and after that we watched a woman working llama-wool on an open-air loom, cactus wood needles slung around her neck.

Every day was hotter than the last, or so it seemed to our European physiologies. To the east of the village we took off our boots and walked along a shallow river in a ravine. The

51

still air, closed in by steep cliffs, was perfumed by citrus groves.

There was a lake called Laguna Lejía up in the mountains near Argentina, and we had settled on it as the venue for our Christmas dinner. The roads were terrible. Someone had marked the Tropic of Capricorn with a pile of volcanic breeze blocks, cemented together at odd angles. It was on a mountain pass which scalloped ahead for miles, the kind of mountain pass on which you might imagine spotting a caravan of yaks in the far distance. At about 12,500 feet the lake appeared, and in its shallows stood many hundreds of flamingos. They took off, when they felt like it, great sprays of pink foam crossing the volcanic backdrop and coming down on another part of the fluorescent water.

'Beats the Queen's Speech,' said James.

The wind was gusting between the mountains and the party hats from our crackers were soon whipped off, brushing over the heads of horned coots and geese in the shallows. We read the cracker jokes to each other. (*Man on telephone*: 'Is that four four four, four four four four?' *Voice at other end*: 'Yes it is.' *Man*: 'Would you mind coming over? My finger's stuck in the dial.') Then we opened our gifts and sat on the sand next to the lake to eat a Christmas lunch of stale cheese rolls, a small, raw plum pudding my mother had insinuated into my bag before I left, apparently assuming that a four-hour steaming facility would always be near at hand, and *chirimoyas*. This fruit, as yet not exported, had become one of my greatest pleasures. It has a warty olive-green rind, a pulpy white flesh, and glossy black pips; it is a member of the custard apple family and I believe is properly called a Jamaica apple in English. Its technical name is *anona cherimolia*, and it tastes like pears and honey.

James was happy, because he claimed to have seen, on the far shore, a group of James' flamingos, the rarest species in the world. He had brought a field guide with him just to identify this bird. I was never convinced that he really had seen any.

On the return journey, beyond the miles of salt and borax the mountains were phosphorescent and flushed with burnished copper. Whilst we were enjoying the view, we bogged Rocky in deep sand at Zapar, a small oasis in a concealed valley. The tinsel policeman had led us across the sand to this place, driving his jeep as if he were competing in a grand prix. He had disappeared, and we were stuck four hours' walk away from the nearest inhabited shack. 'Happy Christmas,' said James. By some seasonal miracle two small boys emerged from a derelict cottage and fetched branches which we wedged under the back wheels. Hearts beating with relief when we finally drove the vehicle out, we gave the boys a huge tip, forgot about the prehispanic ruins we had gone to Zapar to see, and headed home to San Pedro as quickly as possible for a large Christmas drink.

James and I were used to each other's company. We could sit up till three with a bottle and our books, not saying much. That evening we were lounging at a table on the grass outside our room, the air still enough to read by candlelight. Suddenly Colin appeared, the Canadian engineer from Arica.

'Happy Christmas,' he said. 'I thought you might be here.'

I was delighted to see him. He had a German man with him, and quickly told me that Paul from Tucson was about to join us. He hadn't been able to shake him off. Paul was the traveller none of the gringos in Arica had liked. He was in his early forties, quite a loudmouth, and he had given up a well-paid job designing industrial air conditioning units in order to see the world for a year or two. One day he had told us in some detail about a recent sexual encounter with a Chilean woman. He wasn't boasting; quite the reverse, actually, as he said he hadn't made a very good job of it (those weren't his exact words). It is a universally acknowledged truth that there

53

is no more popular topic than other people's sexual pecca-
dilloes. But Paul achieved the impossible. He made his sound
boring.

Six or seven other gringos turned up, bearing cartons of
wine and diluting Paul's company.

'We won't swap addresses', said Colin when he lurched off
into the darkness many hours later, 'as I know I'll see you
again down the track.'

But he never did.

Compared with most indigenous cultures in Chile, Atacaman
civilization, much of which has been preserved in the desert
sand, is reasonably well documented. In the museum at San
Pedro they had a mummy, labelled Miss Chile; even her long
dark hair was intact. The museum made me feel I could walk
out into the desert, dig my fingers a few inches into the warm
sand and pull out a broken cup or a human bone. The arid
sands struck an odd contrast with the rich treasures they
yielded. There was a statue outside the museum of the grand
master of Atacaman archaeology, the Belgian Jesuit Gustav Le
Paige (he was a dead ringer for Gordon Jackson from the
television series *Upstairs, Downstairs*), and alongside a paean
to his life's work I read that the Atacameño were agriculturalists and herders, oppressed by other tribes prior to the
Conquest. Their little-studied language, *Kunza*, was spoken
up until the end of the last century.

North of the village the landscape transformed itself into a
still and rocky valley where sapphire dragonflies pitched on
the marshy riverbanks. We climbed to the top of the ruined
Pukará de Quitor, a fort built in about 1200. A Spaniard
attacked it three hundred and forty years later, and with just
forty men on horseback he took it.

Pre-Columbian peoples had no concept of geographically
defined nationality. Tribespeople in what has become Peru

referred vaguely to the land to the south as Chilli or Chile, and a *conquistador* appeared there on his horse in 1535, forty-three years after Columbus first crossed the Atlantic. Diego de Almagro, an illiterate peasant like many of the Spanish conquerors, had been granted a slice of territory south of Peru called Nueva Toledo by the Spaniards. His expedition to this unknown land, where there were no glittering piles of gold and silver as there had been in Peru and Mexico, was such a disaster, and he spoke so bitterly of Chile, that the tribes there were left in peace for five more years. (Almagro was subsequently strangled in Peru by a rival army of *conquistadores*.) But in 1540 Pedro de Valdivia – in whose honour the love hotel in Santiago had been named, four hundred years later – set out from Cuzco in Peru with between five and twenty Spaniards, hundreds of indigenous people, and his mistress, Inés. The boy in the café where we drank our morning Nescafé in the square in San Pedro said that the house opposite was Valdivia's, and perhaps he was right; the social status of the Spaniards and their workers diminished in line with the distance they lived from the *plaza*.

Valdivia called the country Nuevo Extremo or Nueva Extremadura after his homelands in Spain, the harsh Extremadura which bred many of the hungriest *conquistadores*, and in 1541 he founded the first colonial settlement, which he named Santiago. It was destroyed within six months by the locals, but Valdivia was not a man who gave up easily. He waited two years for reinforcements, refounded the city and soon made himself governor. During the next decade his territory was confirmed as the Kingdom of Chile, extending from Copiapó down to Osorno. Settlers began to arrive, almost all in the central valley. The heart of the Spanish empire remained in Peru, however, and Chile, controlled at least partially by the viceroy in Peru and the king in Spain in a kind of double slavery, was perceived as the poor relation of that great empire – though Valdivia did find some gold. In 1553 he was killed by a group of indigenous people; the apocryphal history of the country has it that they poured molten gold down his throat.

At dusk we drove out to the Valley of the Moon, where the hot wind had sculpted the soft rock and banked the sand to create a desertscape unique even in the Atacama. There was a ridge of sand so high and so straight that it looked as if Julie Andrews might appear over it singing 'The Hills are Alive'.

There was no question of finding the Tatío geysers in the dark, so we hired a guide for the day to come with us in the jeep. He called at our hotel at quarter past four in the morning, as we had arranged, in order to reach the geysers by seven and see them at their best.

It was very cold as well as very early, and James refused to get out of bed. Ruben the guide, who was wearing a black headband, offered to drive, and immediately pushed a salsa tape into the deck. I thought it was a bit early for salsa. He was rather a diffident type, and the music meant that he didn't have to talk. When he did speak, he did it quietly. I guessed he was about my age. He was tall, and strong, and walked with a limp; I got the impression that he suffered a good deal because of that limp. After an hour the sky began to lighten. You couldn't sleep through the colours of an Andean dawn. A volcano was smoking, silhouetted against a silver blue sky, its mouth edged with a fine yellow line.

The fumaroles around the El Tatío geyser field, at 14,500 feet the highest in the world, were gurgling, croaking and exuding sails of vapour, and mineral deposits had solidified like anaglyptic contour maps on the hard ground. A sculpture of rusted desalination apparatus stood nearby, the relic of a failed project to convert geyser energy into electricity. Ruben produced two eggs, lowered them into the shallows of a geyser and walked off to smoke, leaning against the bonnet of the jeep. Fifteen minutes later he handed me a peeled hardboiled egg which tasted of sulphur.

As the morning went on we discarded layers of clothing; at seven we were wearing woolly hats pulled down over our ears and by ten-thirty we were sweating in T-shirts. We followed ridged tracks for a couple of hours through mountain pastureland until we reached a cemetery just before the altiplano village of Caspana. It looked more like a fairground than a cemetery, bedecked with lurid wreaths and other garish accoutrements of death. The village itself didn't appear to have changed much since the first settlement in about 800 BC. The uneven houses were thatched, with hive-shaped ovens built among ancient cypress trees, and the hillsides were cultivated in traditional Andean terraces (the word 'Andes' comes from the name of the terraces created by early agriculturalists). A boy crouched in the pampas grass next to the stream and flicked a llama-hair whip at three grazing donkeys.

A woman was suckling a child in the thatched bandstand, and beyond it and her we climbed up to the crooked houses of the old village and a church with a tottering cactus wood choir. The dwellings in these lumpily flagged streets had no plumbing, and three dry-stone toilet cubicles balanced over the edge of the cliff, cunningly built around indentations in the rock face. The toilets themselves were wooden boxes, and when you lifted the lids you looked down the valley.

I had brought a picnic lunch for us both, and we ate it on the bank of the stream, fending off noisy llamas who were being shepherded home. Ruben told me that the five hundred inhabitants of Caspana possessed four surnames between them. The sun seemed to thaw him out, and he began to talk about himself. He was from Santiago, a canapé chef by trade, and had come to San Pedro on holiday five years previously and immediately decided to abandon the big smoke. As there was little call for canapés in the desert he worked as a driver.

On the long journey home we watched llamas and ducks on the salty edges of the Putana river, tracked a rhea (properly Darwin's or lesser rhea, a South American ostrich), and frightened a troop of nine baby partridges following their emerald mother in small circles. At the old sulphur works we prodded hillocks of lime-green powder, and at the end of the day Ruben smoked while I sat in the thermal pools of Puritama on the floor of a deep and deserted valley half an hour north of San Pedro.

James decided that he wanted to see Chuquicamata, the site of the biggest open-pit coppermine in the world, so we packed our things and drove there before taking Rocky back to Hertz in Calama. We saw Chuqui in the distance, like an eruption in the desert. It was as if we were approaching a pollution factory. When we got there, the streets were empty, their identical houses built in close rows and numbered like prisoners. We walked around for a while. Besides the plant and the houses there wasn't much, except a Seventh Day Adventist church designed to resemble one sail of the Sydney Opera House, some semi-detached managerial houses and, in the middle, an army barracks guarded by soldiers who looked at us as if we had just murdered their children. Chuqui's colourless, austere buildings and joyless streets where the odd dog pursued a plastic wrapper caught by the breeze reminded me of the outskirts of Warsaw. A man passed us on a bicycle, pedalling in the direction of the obese chimneys which cast a yellow pall over the houses.

The town was built and is maintained by copper, and the size of the operation was out of all proportion to everything else I had seen in northern Chile. Salvador Allende, President from 1970 until he died in office in 1973, referred to copper as 'the salary of Chile'. Large-scale exploitation began in the nineteenth century, mainly funded by foreign capital, and although it was temporarily overshadowed by nitrates, later it regained its pre-eminence as the country's main export: up until the mid-1970s it accounted for between 70 and 80 per cent of the value of Chilean exports and by 1991 had settled to about 40 per cent. Dependence on the international copper price has been an almost permanent cause of national pain.

More importantly, years of US ownership (mainly through subsidiaries of two powerful companies) has meant that this vital national resource has been subordinated to the interests of another country. In the context of this complex dependency culture, copper has always been a controversial issue, even during boom periods, and serious trouble began between the wars as a result of the US government's obeisance to the interests of international capital.

It was clear that Chile was not making as much money from its copper as it should or could, and Chilean politicians recognized the urgent need for a shift in the balance of power. In 1964 President Frei, a Christian Democrat, launched a Chileanization programme, but it was ultimately perceived as a botched job as it failed to place copper under Chilean control, and the US parent companies continued to reap plentiful profits. The next government – Allende's – nationalized the large companies. It was one of the few proposals the leftist coalition got through Congress with a large majority. Most of the North American ex-owners were promised compensation payable over the next thirty years, but Allende announced that the two big ones weren't going to get anything: they had made enough already, and should really pay some of it back. It wasn't the end of the industry's problems: it might have won its independence, but it still had to operate within a world market.

The US businessmen didn't have long to wait. In 1974 they

began to invest in Chilean copper again. Pinochet did not privatize the industry, however; he needed it. In his 1980 constitution he stipulated that 10 per cent of all copper sales (not profits) were to be handed over to the military to finance, specifically, the procurement of weapons.

A large sign at the police post on the way out of Chuquicamata wished us a very merry Christmas from the police force of Chile. James wanted to photograph it, but was too frightened to get out of the jeep in case a policeman shot him.

We took the back roads to Chiu Chiu, past salt lakes, slag heaps and outposts of the mining empire. Chiu Chiu was an oasis with cobbled streets, and at the end of one of them we ate our lunch outside San Francisco's church, built in the early seventeenth century and allegedly the oldest in the country. Further into the interior we climbed up a twelfth-century Atacaman fort at Lasana and watched figures working in the cornfields on the valley floor below. A football match was in progress nearby; I had been impressed to see that every two-bit village in northern Chile not only had a pitch but a mini-grandstand too. How such tiny, remote villages managed to raise both teams and a crowd to fill the stands, however, remained baffling.

The only things we saw, for the first twelve hours of the bus journey to La Serena, were sand and a water pipeline. The bus made one short detour to the ocean at Antofagasta, the largest port in northern Chile, dipping through several miles of urban squalor which had seeped up from the central basin of the town. Antofagasta was a grubby, lustreless hole. I read in a guide book that 'city tours' were available, and that they took three hours.

We had given Hertz their jeep back and taken another overnight bus trip, moving south of the desert to spend James' last few days with me in a more temperate climate. It was too big a step for me to take downwards all in one go, but we needed a break from the punishing desert environment, and I planned to sneak back up a little way, after James had gone.

The sound tracks of the US films shown on the bus were so poor that we couldn't tell if they were dubbed or not. The vehicle smelt of turpentine (this turned out to be a woman behind us eating mangoes). I managed to sleep, but James didn't, and he was in a very bad mood when we arrived, shortly after dawn, at La Serena, an affluent colonial town at the mouth of the Elqui valley. We almost immediately caught a *colectivo* up the valley to a village called Vicuña, where we checked in to a 'hotel' with the Tolstoyan name of Yasna. Our room was made entirely of hardboard, the bathroom locked on the outside and we had to unscrew the bulb to turn the light off. In addition, a chalked board of bar prices was propped against the doorframe, and early in the evening a drunk veered in demanding a glass of wine.

'It's green!' said James as we strolled around the outskirts of the village. The cultivated fields were soft on the eye, after the desert. It was like switching a television from black-and-white to colour. The angles of the hills were gentle, and the proliferation of plants, shrubs and trees belonged to familiar species. We felt we were breathing more deeply, as if the desiccation of the north had constricted us, and although it was hot, it was a benign heat. It was only when I arrived in this temperate zone that I realized the implicit threat of the desert, a threat constantly hovering just below the surface. Like an intense relationship, I had loved it passionately but I felt the relief of getting away.

The Elqui valley was burgeoning with neat and healthy moscatel vines. The grapes are eventually crushed and distilled to produce pisco, a clear brandy which is widely drunk throughout the country (and other South American countries) and probably constitutes the national drink. I

61

myself had drunk it widely too, usually in pisco sours, mixed with egg white, a little sugar and the juice of tiny lemons.

On the third day we took a bus up to Monte Grande through more of these vineyards and made a pilgrimage to the grave of Gabriela Mistral, among Chile's finest poets and the first Latin American to win the Nobel Prize for Literature (only four others – Asturias, Neruda, Márquez and Paz – have won it since). She was born in Vicuña and went to school in Monte Grande, where they had restored her classroom, a polished wood abacus in the corner and a six-foot long relief map of the country on the wall, the tips of the Andes worn away by children's fingers. In the back garden the branches of the pimento trees were sagging, and the papery covering of the dusky pink fruit came off in our fingers.

'La Gabriela', as they call her, asked to be buried 'in her beloved Monte Grande', and her tomb, in a leafy grove, was diligently polished and swept by the reverential villagers. (Monte Grande hadn't been quite beloved enough, as she moved to New York as soon as she became famous.) A man with a wooden leg was watering the iridescent blue convolvulus. 'I knew her, you know. When we were children, she used to play at the river with us. She left here when she was eleven, but she was always one of us.'

She would have been pleased with that; she felt closer to ordinary rural people than to the literary establishment. Her poems are lyrical and expansive, emanating spiritual passion and a Romantic vision of nature; there was something noble about her. Her real name was Lucila Godoy Alcayaga. She was a teacher (Neruda was one of her pupils in Temuco) and, like many South American literary figures, later a consul in the foreign service. When she was twenty she fell deeply in love with a man who later committed suicide, and she never married; she always carried that within her. People thought she was eccentric. Her work has never found its translator:

perhaps it will, but I had a feeling that the US critic Margaret J. Bates was right when she wrote of her, 'She has created a plant that does not grow on English soil.'

The next village, Pisco Elqui, used to be called Unión, but they changed the name in 1939 to counter what they refer to soberly as a Peruvian initiative to claim international exclusivity on the name Pisco, which comes from the Quechua *pisku*, flying bird. Tired out by the walk, we sat under a trellis of vines in the courtyard of an inn painted tangerine orange and green. It had a large wooden balcony, and below it a man kept winding up an old gramophone and playing scratchy French 78s.

We discovered a boarding-house straight out of a Gothic horror novel. It had a high pointed roof, an overgrown garden, arched and cracked windows and a sign painted with the flaking words 'Don Juan' which was obligingly swinging in the wind and creaking when we arrived. We stayed one night there, fussed over by an old woman who had lived in the house for forty years. The staircases and panelling were solid mahogany, the walls of our bedroom, at the top, were made entirely of glass, and in many of the velvet-curtained rooms downstairs thick layers of dust had settled on heavily tinted photographic portraits.

We returned to Vicuña on New Year's Eve on an overburdened bus which stopped every few minutes to disgorge passengers and pick up replacements, most of them clinging to battered cardboard boxes tied up with string. Children were sitting at the side of the road making floppy monkeys out of rags and cardboard; these were to be burnt as the old year passed. We were ineluctably drawn back to the Yasna, and drank a bottle of cold Chilean champagne in the courtyard. I was glad to be sharing the New Year with an old friend.

At dinner later we got friendly with a lively young waiter.

His family were throwing a party at home, and he invited us to go along with him when he finished work at midnight. We killed time very agreeably.

The waiter lived with his mother in a small, modern house in which a variety of aunts, uncles, cousins and nieces had convened. James and I were obliged to dance with everyone, and they even made us do the *cueca*, the national dance (now rather hackneyed), despite our total ignorance of its steps. The general idea was evidently to imitate a cockerel and wave a hanky. Much later, most of us adjourned to the community hall, where a six-piece band was playing an exuberant blend of rock and folk music and there was a bottle of pisco on each table. The only tense moment in an otherwise delightful evening came a couple of hours later when our waiter friend told James that he was a very bad dancer; but we got over that. Almost the whole village had turned out for this occasion, and they were still making the most of it when we crept off at four-thirty and knocked up the crusty proprietor of the Yasna, who emerged in his pyjamas to unlock the door, unmoved by our New Year's greetings.

Chapter Four

Chile is at least a place where one can find oneself and find other people with a compass which is that of real life.

Victor Jara, folk singer, 1970

There can be no better land to live in than this one.

Pedro de Valdivia, letter from Chile to Charles V of Spain, 1545

It was unfortunate that we had planned such an early start the next morning that we had to wake the old man up again to let us out. I was to set off on a quest to discover one of the communes reputedly concealed at the top of the valley. I had heard about them from Chileans I had met in London when I was organizing the trip; everyone seemed to know about these communes, but nobody had been to one, and I had failed to obtain any reliable information on the subject when I made enquiries in Santiago – though everyone there had heard about them, too. I just had to go. James was off to spend a week in the south, so we said goodbye in the square, too numbed by the after-effects of the previous night to feel sad. 'I must take a photograph of you,' he said, 'in case you're never seen again.'

The location of these communes (if they existed) was not arbitrary; not at all. The upper reaches of the Elqui valley have become a kind of mystic spiritual centre, attracting a range of disparate tranquillity seekers from Vedic sects to devotees of the extra-terrestrial. We had come across various hippy types in the valley playing plangent guitar music and chanting in incense shops run by women in kaftans. A combination of geographical and atmospheric factors, notably the Humboldt current offshore, the vast cloudless Atacama desert to the north, and the laminar air flow over the Andes (whatever that is) creates the clearest sky on the planet right over the Elqui valley, and it has consequently been labelled 'a window to the heavens' and 'the magnetic centre of the earth' – hence its concentration of 'spiritual' disciples. Naturally the valley has attracted the scientific community too, and three of the most important astronomy centres in the southern hemisphere have been built, with foreign capital, in the region.

Thus the Elqui valley is a kind of astronomical and spiritual Mecca.

By some small miracle a bus arrived in the square and took me up to Monte Grande. From there I walked a mile or two; I had a hunch that if I moved upwards and away from the villages, I might find a commune – or find something, anyway. I felt so ill that I thought I might actually die, and I made the usual New Year's resolution about never drinking again. By another, larger miracle (1992 was performing well) a shiny new car pulled up next to me. A spruce, balding man in his forties got out, skipped towards me and shook my hand enthusiastically, revealing himself to be a farmer from the south (a wealthy one, judging by the car and his appearance). Pedro was alone, wanting a few days of mental space to take stock of his life, and as such he was as anomalous as me. Neither of us knew where the communes were, or if they really existed, but we both wanted to get to one, so we naturally started looking together. This was one of my great slices of luck, as I never would have found a commune if I hadn't met Pedro. His most salient characteristic was a tendency to talk all the time. He often wanted to discuss history. In the stifling car on a deeply rutted track half-way up a mountain near Argentina he asked my opinion on the fall of the Roman Empire.

We came to dead ends, reversed out of them, and at midday stopped at the end of a long avenue of raspberry bushes. An old woman appeared, and we found out that her son ran a commune beyond the house. She had thirty grandchildren, and two of their offspring were persecuting chickens among the raspberries. Pedro kept talking as we picked our way on foot along a path above a river. At the end of it, in front of half a dozen huts, two children up an apricot tree were shaking branches, and the fruit was bouncing over the mud courtyard. A handsome, youngish man with white hair came out of a hut, smiled, and signalled for us to sit down in some old cane chairs in the shade.

Pedro explained for both of us. The white-haired man said, 'You are welcome to stay with us. We are Chilean practitioners of Agnihotra, an ancient Vedic science of healing. Only my family and I are here at the moment. Our ceremony takes place at sunrise and sunset. You can join in, or not, as you like.'

A modest daily rate was quickly agreed, and Pedro and I were installed in two small wooden cabins on the riverbank. One side overlooked the green, fruit-filled valley and the other a path heading towards the high pass to Argentina, along which miniature straw-hatted shepherds occasionally appeared on horseback, threading their way behind a flock of ragged sheep to their pastureland in the cordillera. We ate with the white-haired Leo and his wife in their hut; the food consisted mainly of vegetable and herb stews, apricot tea and bread cooked in a hole in an outside wall. It was very good. The wall of the hut was decorated with two pictures of Hindu holymen who looked terminally ill and a lifesize poster of Christ.

'The ceremony' (correctly called homa) took place in a bare room further up the slope. We sat cross-legged on purple cushions while Leo prepared a fire in a copper pyramid using sun-dried cowdung coated with ghee, and at the exact moment of sunset he began chanting the first mantra. Precision, apparently, is crucial, and a computer printout is dispatched from Agnihotra headquarters in the United States with daily timings – down to seconds – calculated according to latitude and longitude. During this mantra he sprinkled grains of ghee-moistened brown rice onto the fire. This was repeated with another mantra, and meditation. The principle behind Agnihotra is that fire purifies the atmosphere, releasing healing energies: 'Heal the atmosphere, and the atmosphere heals you.' Some people eat the ash of the cowdung as a sifted powder after the ceremony, but we were spared this.

Leo didn't care what we did during homa, as long as we kept quiet. There is no hierarchy among Agnihotra practitioners, and no sacerdotal status; anyone can attend the ceremony, and anyone can perform it. Pedro told me afterwards that he felt perfectly relaxed sitting in the homa room (though when I asked him what he had thought about during the first ceremony, he said he had been worrying about whether anyone was feeding his cows).

Late one night Pedro announced soberly that he was trying to decide whether to marry his girlfriend. That was why he had come to the commune: to think things over. He wanted to know what I thought.

'Are you in love with her?' I asked, casting around rather desperately.

'I think so. But I'm frightened about giving up my independence.'

He came from a small village of farmers; in that environment a single man of his age must have constituted something of a social aberration. I thought I was probably the wrong person to consult about relinquishing independence; I was still constitutionally unable to 'undertake joint trips to the supermarket.

We were sitting on the riverbank, and it was rustling with its night noises. The stars were like a fine layer of icing sugar. Pedro talked about his village. He had grown up there. It wasn't long before he got onto 1973.

'They came to interrogate a man from Allende's Popular Unity, but took another one whose name was the same, by mistake. They made him walk across the square – it's a very old one, in our village, with beech trees round three sides – and shot him first in one knee, then the other. Then he had to drag himself forward in order to be shot in the head.'

During the day I often sat under the willow tree next to the river, and sometimes Leo came down to catch trout. He was a calm, charismatic figure, dedicated to 'self-realization' and a lifestyle which in the city would be pigeonholed as 'alternative'. I wasn't very keen on the idea of burning cowdung, but I admired his commitment to the transcendental within himself. He could never have been a proselytizer, and that appealed to me too; he thought there were many different spiritual paths to choose from, and that they led to the same place. He drove me down the mountain after three days at the commune and dropped me at Monte Grande, and as I watched his trailer disappear, four small children waving from the back, I felt unexpectedly regretful.

It took me a whole day, after he had left me there, to fail to hitch a lift to Vicuña, take recourse in a bus two hours later, locate my other bag at the Yasna, pick up a *colectivo* to La

Serena, unite myself with the press pass I had arranged to get me into the observatory the following day, collected Rocky III from Hertz, and check into a hotel in town. The Regional Director of Tourism had arranged the pass for me. The observatory was famous; it had the biggest telescope in the southern hemisphere. It was famously difficult to get into, as well, and it was that, of course, which made me want to go there.

Visiting regulations at the Tololo observatory, shrouded in a conspiratorial veil of formality, stipulated arrival at the lodge on the valley floor at nine o'clock in the morning sharp. This entrance turned out to be a forty-five-minute drive from the observatory itself, and when I drew up in front of the barrier a uniformed official appeared to check me off on his clipboard. He returned to his office, made a phone call, came back and told me that the road was extremely dangerous and that in the event of breakdown I was forbidden to leave my vehicle. The man at the tourist office, the man at Hertz and the man at the hotel had already explained, patiently and with relish, how dangerous this road was. They had clearly never driven on the Andean passes to the north. The road was a hundred times better than those the Rockies and I were used to.

Nine vehicles had been granted permission to enter that morning and we crawled up to 6600 feet in convoy, emerging above the clouds moving briskly along the Elqui valley. At the top of the mountain three white domes rested on stainless white stumps, like futuristic mosques, and a row of equally immaculate white VW Beetles glinted in the sunshine. The neat white gravel paths were roped off. The driver of one of the cars, standing between two domes, coughed to confound the silence, and when I looked over the uninterrupted view of mountains below us, I felt a visceral thrill.

A man in a white coat came through a door concealed in a stump and introduced himself: he was an astronomer, he was called Gonzalo and he was going to show us round. We filed into the middle stump. I had assumed that I was going to be looking through large black telescopes and seeing things. But it wasn't like that. It was like looking round a nuclear power station. The biggest telescope had a lens measuring twelve feet in diameter which could capture light as far back as fourteen thousand million years. Its movable portion weighed around 300 tons and looked like a Cyclopean blue doughnut, yet it was so finely balanced that with the brakes off Gonzalo could move it with two fingers.

I had also assumed that I was going to be seeing stars. It hadn't occurred to me that it was daytime.

Scientists at Tololo reckon on between a hundred and fifty and two hundred nights a year with perfect visibility into infinity. The big telescope had taken pictures of the birth of a star. 'We,' said Gonzalo, 'are those who look into the past. Astronomy is anthropology – we see the birth or death of a star, and we learn to know ourselves better.' This last part sounded like something Leo might have said.

Tololo is financed by the US Association of Universities for Research in Astronomy (Aura), and Chilean scientists are granted 10 per cent of the night. Astronomers visit from all over the world, and have to book a year in advance. Gonzalo told the story of a Japanese scientist who had come recently for one night, but clouds prevented him from seeing anything, and he had to go home again. Everyone laughed, and Gonzalo looked pleased.

As I was well into the valley already, I decided to travel further inland when I left the grounds of the observatory; I had no plans for the afternoon. It was a perfect day which even a puncture couldn't spoil. I was lying under Rocky, grappling

71

with a hydraulic jack, when a pair of blue boating shoes appeared. A face came down to meet them, and it offered to help.

This person was about my age, he had black hair which curled over his shoulders, and he looked like a youthful Salvador Dali. His name was Pepe, and his smile was dangerously beguiling. When we had fixed the tyre we went to his sister's cottage to clean up. He asked me where I was going, and when I told him I planned to head straight up the valley he said,

'No, don't go there. The river's dead up there. Polluted by the gold mine. I'll show you a better place.'

He was an agricultural scientist recently turned freelance, and although he lived in Santiago, he spent as much time as he could in the Elqui valley. Pepe hated Santiago. He was an ardent ecologist, and became quietly passionate on the subject of the many scandalous depredations of nature for which he held his country responsible. He knew a lot about these things, and was making it his business to learn more; the idea of illuminating me, a foreigner, who might go off and tell others, appealed to him a good deal. He was gloomy about the possibility of whipping up any concern among his countrymen.

We walked along the bank of a clean river to a deserted grove of stiff green fronds, the ground covered with a thin layer of sweet apricots and the white fruit of the first fig crop. Further upstream we visited a friend of Pepe's, an actor from Santiago. He had put his tent up on the riverbank for a month, and was lying in it. When we arrived he gave us a pot of warm apricot jam he had just made on a primus stove, and two spoons.

'Are you North American?'

'No, English'.

'*Es mejor, por lo menos*' (That's better, at least). I was always chastened to remember that 'at least'.

Pepe took me to a cave on the hillside with a sign outside which said, 'We villagers pay homage to our ancestors, who gave us their name.' Inside they had made lifesize models of these ancestors. The cave overlooked a hamlet called Diaguitas, the name of the people who once occupied the valley. Most of the Diaguita, who spoke *Kakan*, farmed territory which is now in north-west Argentina; some of them came over the Andes, but their culture was probably eradicated by the Inca even before the Conquest.

The villagers were working in a large shed, packing bunches of table grapes, and a long row of young women wearing hairnets sat on stools snipping off bad fruit. The men were spraying, and puffs of sulphur rose very slowly into the still air.

We visited friends living on mountains in half-built houses, drinking herbal infusions and generally chilling out in the great Elqui valley tradition. Pepe was a hippy at heart. He didn't own anything, he didn't eat any refined foods, he rejected politics on the grounds that all its practitioners were corrupt, and he rejected too the values he had grown up with. His parents, who had been semi-skilled manual workers, were dead; he had two sisters, both married with kids in the city. They complained at him for not having a house or a wife or a full-time job.

At one hippy house in the valley there was a very small slug at the bottom of my tea mug. I didn't like to say anything; I thought perhaps it was supposed to be there. Our hosts were listening to Pink Floyd on a battery cassette player. (People often mentioned Pink Floyd as soon as they met me. Eventually I realized it was because they wanted to demonstrate the only two English words they knew.)

Before I drove back down to my hotel in La Serena we went to watch the sunset over a glass of wine at the Peralillo social club. Peralillo is a ratty little village, but its *club social* was spectacular. We sat on a Raj-style raffia sofa with blue silk cushions on a balcony overlooking the whole valley, as well as the mountains beyond, and a man with unzipped flies brought a wicker flask of local wine.

Pepe and his sister, a feisty woman living in the valley who had told her husband that he was looking after the baby for once, called for me in La Serena early the next morning and we set off on a day trip. It was a plan conceived at the Peralillo social club. Pepe had the idea that we should visit Enchantment Valley (Valle del Encanto) a couple of hours away in the semi-desert.

When we got there a man with no front teeth emerged from a hut. Pepe went in to pay the entrance fee, and when they both came out of the hut the man looked suspiciously at me.

'Is she foreign?' he snapped.

He's going to say only Chileans are allowed in, I thought. Then I realized that being foreign meant I had to sign the visitors' book. I had already signed getting on for forty visitors' books, and I wondered if this enthusiastically pursued national obsession reflected their sense of geographical isolation.

The valley was as still as a mausoleum and spread with a deep layer of smooth boulders. Between them spherical fruit blistered from the tips of cacti. Pepe took a great interest in the San Pedro cactus, still used for its hallucinogenic seeds – it was an ideal landscape for hallucinating, too.

As the unusual climatic conditions of the region create the astronomical near-perfection of Tololo, so on the coast to the south they enable a small rainforest to flourish in the semi-desert. We drove on towards the ocean through familiar dry and cactus-spiked terrain, past hopeful vendors waving prawns and fat discs of goat's cheese, and arriving at the Fray

74

Jorge forest was like walking through the looking-glass into another world – a lush and verdant one, blossoming with tiny purple and yellow flowers and clammy creepers which clung around our ankles. Fray Jorge is a rainforest in a zone where annual rainfall may be as low as three inches. Sea-mist, produced by warm river water discharging nearby into a cold ocean, provides the equivalent of between twenty-four and thirty-six inches of rain a year, sustaining its own private tropical forest.

All three of us were hungry, so we stopped at Tongoy, a popular resort village impressively devoid of character. Past the densely peopled beaches and rows of Coca-Cola and burger shops Pepe found a quieter beach at the poor end of town. Even the sand was inferior. But there was a shellfish market, and a restaurant where we ate *paila marina*, a crabby bouillabaisse which was to become my favourite Chilean food, with a mound of tiny lemons and a bottle of cold white wine. Shifty individuals sidled in to sell wet handkerchiefs' full of illegally caught *locos*, a Chilean mollusc with no common name in English but usually referred to as abalone, which it resembles. *Locos* are so sought after that capture is illegal during the breeding season, and confiscated catches are reported in the papers as if they were cocaine hauls.

The road back to La Serena was clogged with refugees from the beach. It was one of the most developed strips in the country, burgeoning with holiday apartments, villas, pizzerias and beach bars. At a place called Peñueles a particularly disfiguring welter of construction was occupied mainly by holidaying Argentinians (we could tell by the number plates of the cars parked outside). Pepe had it in for Argentinian drivers. He had it in for Argentinians in general, in fact, an attitude shared, as far as I could see, by the entire Chilean nation.

*

75

Pepe and I decided to go north for a week or two; this constituted my sneak back up in that direction, a one-off deviation from my steady progress southwards. He was good company, exceptionally well-informed on anything to do with the countryside, and his well-developed and dry sense of humour made him a very congenial companion. He enjoyed travelling as much as I did, so it seemed natural that we should do it together.

We borrowed a tent and a gas cooker, bought supplies, found a cool-box in his sister's shed, procured foam mats, checked Rocky's tyres, stocked up on *chirimoyas* (the pears-and-honey fruit, which an old woman in Peralillo sold from a box in a windowless room at the end of a passage) and went over route maps at the social club. I was sure that I wouldn't regret the decision to travel with Pepe.

Besides papayas, the stalls on the highway out of La Serena were touting papaya honey, syrup, juice, sweets, cakes, bars and peeled papayas suspended in jars of sugar syrup. There was clearly nothing which could not be made out of a papaya. We bought some juice and travelled north until Pepe spotted a sandy track to a village called Choros, where everyone sat on their front step and stared at us. We stopped for directions to the headland at a 'soda fountain' where a man with braces holding up trousers several sizes too big served us a soft drink – warm, as usual – in a small dance hall with immaculately clean floorboards, bunting across the corrugated roof, nude calendars from the 1970s and pennants advertising the Choros football team.

We followed a set of tyre tracks in the sand to a small, windblown memorial fenced off in the scrubby semi-desert. There was a large cross behind it, and in front someone had put a bunch of fresh flowers in a tarnished silver vase. A fisherman told me later that the memorial had been erected to honour the dead of the *Itata*, which sank in the bay in 1922. Seventy crewmen made it to shore, but they died later, of dehydration. Nothing grew on that arid peninsula. At the windy coast skull-and-crossbone flags flapped from one or two antediluvian shacks. When I asked a crone sitting on the sand sewing up a net what these flags meant she said they were from the time when pirates were frequent visitors, adding darkly that many of them had been British.

We found a beach, and parked Rocky on the white sand. I should have guessed that a tent borrowed from a resident of the Elqui valley would be a pre-war model with most of the zips long-since broken and attached to the fabric with rusted wire. It was a huge, thick brown canvas tent like the ones you see in films shot in the Western Desert, and it had no guy ropes. The floor had bits of marijuana stuck to it. We improvized guy ropes with lengths of plastic cord Pepe had brought (he must have known), lashing each around a rock. The tent began to sag immediately, and then the deadly combination of hot sun and cold beer conspired to cause the afternoon to evaporate.

The beach was a perfect semi-circle, framed by dunes and wrinkled grey rocks. As we were walking over these rocks in the early evening another walker greeted us. He was in his forties, tall and rangey with a deeply lined face, and he immediately introduced himself. After chatting for a few minutes he invited us for a drink at his tent. He had two women friends with him, and when we arrived they kissed us on both cheeks. Chileans are keen cheek-kissers. It seemed the perfect paradigm of the Latin temperament, especially when compared with the British handshake. I suddenly thought of a moment during the preparations for my trip, when I had gone down to Dorset to visit a half-Chilean, half-British man called Tony who was a descendant of José Miguel Carrera, one of the most influential figures in the Independence movement and a member of a distinguished aristocratic family. We were feeding Tony's pheasants in a field when he was struck by a reflection. 'You know, it's awfully difficult, this business of being both Chilean and British. I feel split in two, with no point of contact between the two halves.' He had been smoking a pipe when I arrived, like the perfect English gent. After an hour the conversation turned to Chilean history and Bernardo O'Higgins, another Independence hero, whose relationship with Carrera developed into a public feud. In 1821, amid the bitter rivalries generated by the struggle for self-government, Carrera was executed, as his two brothers had been before him. Tony leapt from his chair and strode about the kitchen, waving his arms and telling me that his family used to go to the abattoir on O'Higgins' birthday and buy a bucket of blood to throw over his statue. 'And of course,' he said, pouring himself a straight Scotch, 'we would never dream of sticking the O'Higgins postage stamp the right way up on our letters.'

We sat on the sand watching a pair of pelicans while Rafo squeezed lemons and made jugs of pisco sour. He had caught some *locos*, which one of the women boiled in seawater and handed round, shells gaping. I had eaten abalone in Asia, but it hadn't prepared me for the sweet, nutty taste of *locos*; I could understand why they were such valuable contraband. As the pile vanished Rafo told us he was a novelist, and that he had been in exile for most of the dictatorship. Although not a member of any party, he had publicly supported Allende for many years, and had protested during the first months of military rule. It was difficult for writers to be apolitical in Chile. José (known as Pepe) Donoso, a major contemporary novelist and a member of the group which emerged during the 1960s and 1970s when the Latin American novel was 'internationalized,' said that 'justified political passion relegated literary passions to a secondary position'. There was a sense that those who left voluntarily had betrayed Chile; Donoso said that South American literary critics 'seldom forgive exile'. I asked Rafo if he felt that intellectuals were polarized into those who had stayed and those who had gone.

'Definitely. Each group resents the other: they think we whimped out by leaving, we think we suffered more by being away. That was one of the regime's most potent poisons, you know – it set us against each other. Not just in a straightforward, left or right way. In more insidious ways, too. When it did that, it weakened our collective spirit.'

'Can't you strengthen yourselves again, now?'

'It takes a long time. It's like healing the body after deep trauma. Anyway, some of us – like me – feel those were our most creative years – I mean potentially – and now they're lost.

'The problem is,' he went on, 'that you don't stop being an exile when you get home. It becomes a state of mind. You can be an exile inside your head. Perpetual travellers are often like that.'

He poured me another drink.

'Mind you, you don't necessarily have to go anywhere to feel that kind of permanent alienation. Perhaps the worst kind of exile is mental.'

The next morning a fisherman gave us a lift over to an uninhabited islet we had spotted from the tent flaps. We slung the tent, gas cooker, bread, wine and five gallons of water into the boat, and the other fishermen left off mending their nets and scraping their hulls to push us off. It took twenty minutes to get over there, and the boatman, who left us standing on a long white beach, agreed to pick us up on the way back from the following day's trip. 'I hope he remembers,' said Pepe as we waved him off.

It didn't take long to become acquainted with our island. It was full of cactus fruit, black lizards, whales' skulls and boobies nesting in the cliffs. We put the tent up again, and caught some fish with a length of nylon and bits of bread. The boobies eyed us suspiciously.

There was sand in the wine; there was always sand in the wine. There was sand in all our pockets, in our ears, and in most things that we ate. Sand was always with us; we had stopped noticing it. We ate the fish as the sky turned opal before the sun set, feeling lordly, on our private island.

It was warm enough to lie out after supper. The sea was touched by a light breeze, like a wheat field. It was un-utterably peaceful. At that moment the past held no regrets and the future no fears; I could have given up everything worldly to live the rest of my life on that island – except, perhaps, the plastic tumbler of wine in my hand.

When I put this thought into Spanish and told Pepe, he said, 'Do it then. Change.'

His vision of life was straightforward not because he was incapable of sophistication, but because the purity of his vision meant he was not troubled by conflicting values. We got talking about his adolescence. He grew up during the dictatorship. He said that he remembered the early years with 'frigidity', and told me long stories about his uncle, whom he loved very much, and who had 'disappeared'.

'I always thought he was going to walk through the door. It wore us all down to the bone, not knowing, like acid dripping on our flesh.'

Listening to him speak of the pain caused by a dis-appearance, perhaps the acutest pain of all, was like flossing with barbed wire.

'Absence has a shape, you know. It exists.' The whole family had lived on the far edge of anxiety for eight years, and then they received confirmation of his death. Each one had emerged from that peculiar South American darkness pro-foundly altered.

'I sort of feel that I haven't seen straight since,' he said.

*

The boatman did come back for us, and asked if we had seen any vampires. I laughed blandly at this joke, then listened in appalled amazement as it became clear that it wasn't a joke at all.

'Up there, in those caves,' the boatman said when I asked where these vampire bats live.

'They're all up and down this desert coast. They live off animal blood – only sealions here. But don't worry – hardly any of them are rabid.'

On the way back we made a circuit of Isla Choros, the largest of three islands opposite the headland. There was a small colony of Humboldt penguins living there, and they were standing in a row like clergymen queuing to vote at Synod. I had never seen a penguin outside of a zoo before. Around a corner, among a configuration of caves and rocky outcrops, a hundred southern sealions raised their fat necks and blunt faces. They hooted and grunted, and they smelt very strong. On land they were chestnut brown and suedey, and when they got wet they went slippery black, like rubber rings. The younger bulls sat together, apart from the others on a high ledge, and on one side of a choppy channel the patriarch lounged, inscrutable and alone. He was the size of a small elephant, and he had extra-long whiskers and wrinkles around his eyes like spectacles.

Rafo was waiting on the beach when we got back. The fishing boats were coming in. Pepe bought armfuls of clams, but I was too afraid of cholera to eat raw shellfish. Rafo tried to persuade me.

'Look, the ocean's pure here. The shellfish are only contaminated near conurbations. You can eat anything from this water.'

The fishermen, surrounded by cats, began gutting large fish like fat rainbows. Rafo, his two friends, Pepe and a small boy

81

started prising clams open on an upturned boat, loosening their bodies from the viscous muscles, squeezing a lemon on the pearly flesh and tipping them down their throats, chased with cans of cold beer. It was, of course, too much for my constitutionally low reserves of restraint.

The next day, walking through miles of red flowers which mottled the dunes, we came across the much-publicized new project for obtaining water from the *camanchaca* sea mist. This mist is caused by cold, upswelling water landward of the Humboldt current which cools the stable air and produces condensation. In order to trap it they had hung something similar to thick black net curtains between poles along the top of a hill, with halved drainpipes below them to collect the water.

We had planned to move on that day, and we did, but we set off too late, and had to pitch the tent a few hundred yards from the Panamerican, in the savannah. At sunset the temperature dropped so fast you could have watched the mercury moving on a thermometer. We couldn't see what we were doing, and the tent blew down in the night. I fell onto a cactus in the rescue operation, and a jab in the arm from a needle later went septic.

When we drove past a sign indicating that we were leaving the Fourth Region Pepe registered his disgust at the colourless numerical toponyms invented by bureaucrats when Chile was divided into fourteen regions in 1977. I remember that in Bristol we were similarly outraged when Avon was invented. We scorned it as a construction of civil servants, devoid of character, meaning and history. But it was better than Region Four.

Travelling north, I felt like a salmon going the wrong way up a river. There were mountains joining the Andes and the coastal cordillera there, like rungs on a ladder. It was just as well, as we were almost out of petrol, and had to cruise the downhill parts. We filled up at Copiapó, a town on the edge of the transition zone before the desert gets serious, built with mining money and still flourishing. Pepe told me it was rich, violent and full of cocaine. The first mass ever held in Chile was said in the Copiapó valley, when Diego de Almagro rode down in 1535.

The Panamerican touched the coast at Caldera, an ugly village where they had just finished building a fruit-loading bay. They were funnelling iron-ore into a hopper: there were pockets of minerals everywhere in the interior. The village had a wooden church with a Gothic spire. It looked familiar, and I found out later that it was built by English carpenters working on the railway.

We camped that night in the Pan de Azúcar National Park, obliged to pitch the tent in a regulation red brick bay. This bay was only twenty steps from the ocean, and ours was the only tent. In the morning we went out with a fisherman from the small community living in the park. The original occupants of the zone, the Chango (probably our man's great-grandparents), who were nomadic fishermen, had built their shelters on the rocky slopes of the sugarloaf – the *pan de azúcar* – island in the bay. On this island, its promontories spread with South American fur seals, Conaf was monitoring the breeding habits of the largest colony of Humboldt penguins in the country.

The next day we collected razor clams and washed our clothes in the ocean. I had special eco-detergent for ocean laundry, and I washed myself with it too. The worst part was not the cold or the salt, but the cormorants and grey gulls swirling purposefully above me. That day a Pacific marine otter paddled nearby with a baby clinging to its neck, portions of its long back appearing above the water like the curves of the Loch Ness monster.

I very much wanted to explore the interior of the park, but Pepe was unusually hesitant about planning a long trip as the terrain was hostile, even with four-wheel drive. At dusk I climbed up to the Conaf offices on the top of the cliff and persuaded the amiable head ranger to lend us a guide the following day.

We set off early with a ranger who had been working in the park for ten years. The hard ground was exploding with cacti. There were hundreds of different types of cacti, taller than us and smaller than our little fingers, unwieldy and delicate, smooth and warty. The most prolific were cacti of the *copiapoa* genus, and there were tens of thousands of these, short and tumescent with wrinkly folds of flesh and flaccid spherical fruits, and out of a tiny hole in the rounded tip leapt a yellow waxy flower.

We travelled from plain to gully to volcanic escarpment, through dried mudflats and on top of cliffs. Guanacos lowered their ears and slid away. Guanacos can live in totally rainless zones. They eat plants which absorb the sea mist, and cactus fruits, which lay on the ground with a fluffy white coating, like a certain type of tennis ball. The Conaf rangers have their water brought in by truck.

Pale mauve and yellow long-stemmed desert flowers bent in the wind, fragile against the harsh landscape, and suddenly a mass of the brightest tangerine stretched into the distance. But the *camanchaca* crawled in from the sea as we drove, obliterating everything with opaque whiteness.

We had decided not to push further north, as we wanted to stop over on the return journey. A cluster of wetsuited shellfish divers engaged in conversation at the edge of the water waved us off. We travelled south as far as Bahía Inglesa (English Bay), a village whose name harked back to the landing of the English pirate Edward Davis in the *Bachelor* in 1687. According to the guide books, there was an 'English pub' in the village, and I had been away from home long enough to think of such a thing fondly. It turned out to be something of a mystery, as it didn't appear to have ever existed – though it was marked on two of my maps, and the *South American Handbook* went as far as detailing its attractions ('darts, dominoes, pints . . .') and gave the name and address of its English owners.

I knocked on the door of the house where the pub should have been. No response. We drove out of the village, beyond a group of campers, and put our tent up on a beach the size of a small national park. Pepe went off to find fishermen and shellfish, returning an hour later with bucketfuls of *locos* and crabs. I was drawn back to the non-existent British pub. This time a tall, attractive woman appeared at the door of the blue wooden house, and I asked if she was the owner of the chimeric pub.

'Yes, that's us,' she said in an accent that wasn't English. 'I'll get my husband.'

Before she had time to turn around a person resembling a caveman shot out of the house and skidded to a halt in front of me.

'Yes?' emerged a voice from the long beard.

'Um, I'm looking for the English Pub and I wondered if . . .'

'My God, you're English!'

He said it as if it implied I was extra-terrestrial.

'*But how did you get here?*'

He was expecting his lawyer to arrive at any minute, so we arranged that I would pick them up later; they said they would prefer to come to the tent than meet anywhere in the village. I returned triumphantly to Pepe, who was grappling with a scrubbing brush and *locos* in the heavy waves.

The caveman's name was Tom Clough, and he used to be a trombonist in London. When I arrived at his house later to collect him, he carried out a large brown box.

'Have I got a surprise for you,' he said.

It was a case of Bateman's Triple X which he had imported,

together with crown-and-seal glasses and a Tetley bottle opener. It was a rhapsodic moment on a hot, windy beach in what Tom later described as 'the black hole of the Third Region'.

'Is it beer?' asked Pepe as we drank a toast in front of the tent.

Tom had achieved notoriety in Britain several years previously during a live radio broadcast of a new Edward Cowie piece by the BBC Symphony Orchestra. He was the lead trombone. He was also pissed, and when a reverential BBC presenter finished the announcement at the end with the words, 'This was the first performance,' a voice from the pit shouted, 'and the last!' I had read about this in the *Guardian* (it was a music critic's dream). When summoned, Tom had denied it, until they played his voice on the tapes. But he kept his job.

A strong wind off the ocean meant that the gas cooker had to be lit in the tent, but Pepe was not easily deflected and he produced a supply of shellfish while Tom told the story of the 'English Pub'.

'We researched the project really carefully, bought the house and imported all the important stuff from the UK – we had a great pub sign painted with Mrs Thatcher on it, got some umbrellas for the beer garden and all that and worked out an arrangement with Bateman's to import their Triple X on an exclusive basis. [He was a founder member of CAMRA.] It was all small-scale; we were aiming at the locals.'

He poured four more bottles of Bateman's.

'When we first arrived there was tremendous goodwill – everyone invited us over, dropped round. We had a contract drawn up with a builder from two doors down for the conversion, and for the two-bedroom b & b we planned out the back. We paid him quite a lot in upfront instalments – it was written into the contract. We gradually began to worry about his work. On the day we made another big payment – we would have been breaking the contract if we hadn't – the municipality stopped the work because it was illegal. Two neighbours are taking us to court because the builder infringed upon walls that were theirs. We can't recover any money – we're waiting for a court case, of course, but it could take five years, and we're not allowed to rectify the damage until the case is heard. So we can't go forward or back, we have an open sewer in the yard, and our business is ruined. We've been told lies from start to finish. What really hurts is that the villagers have closed ranks. Nobody talks to us anymore. We're totally isolated – you can't imagine.'

Even the architect had allegedly displayed gross professional incompetence. The story went on to include anonymous phone calls and all the symptoms of a personal vendetta. Tom and Teresa (she was Bolivian) said they had never experienced such cruel people.

'We've had so many revolutions in Bolivia that nobody is affected by them anymore. But here – I've never seen such paranoia.'

We were invited for breakfast on our way out the next morning and were offered real coffee, one of my more conspicuous addictions and something which I never got used to living without. I failed to understand why Chileans had not developed a taste for it, especially with such great coffee-producers on the continent. Even the best restaurants in Santiago served Nescafé, distinguishing themselves from lower-grade establishments by proffering the powder in a small silver dish and inviting customers to help themselves.

It was Sunday and the village was still quiet when we left except for the voices of two or three workmen painting a holiday complex purple in the main street. In Santiago the word 'yuppie' is often used to describe the clientele of Bahía Inglesa. They only overrun the village in February, however. The Chilean concept of summer is remarkably short; it is a state of mind rather than a season. Often, in December and January, people had said, 'When summer comes ...', whereas I in my gringo ignorance had been under the illusion that it was already summer.

Tom and Teresa waved us goodbye as we drove down the straight road, still waving when it eventually veered south and they disappeared.

'Some days,' Teresa had said, 'it's just too hard to get out of bed.'

On a detour from Copiapó, up a fertile valley, we passed hundreds of vineyards where millions of the earliest grapes were already spread out on swathes of cloth, turning themselves into raisins. We drove into one vineyard, and after a few minutes a man appeared. When Pepe asked if we could buy some grapes, the man passed amiably under the trellises, clipping off purple bunches, and we paid in shellfish we had brought from the beach. Next to the vineyard there was a house with broken windows, a veranda and a wooden lookout platform with small doric columns around it. It overlooked one of the finest churches I saw in Chile. It had a pediment, fluted columns and a hexagonal wooden tower, but everything had collapsed behind the façade, which stood on its own, like a film set. A woman appeared from behind a jacaranda tree, and when Pepe said we were admiring the house, she took us inside. It was built around a courtyard full of aloe vera, and was originally the *casa patronale*, or landowner's home, expropriated in 1942 in one of Chile's many attempts at land reform, and the estate had been parcelled out in small lots. In the hall they had an olivewood telephone which still rang a bell.

The woman asked my name.

'Ah! Sarah Ferguson!'

I had already noted the Chilean fascination with the British royal family. I had experienced the same phenomenon in lots of places around the world. On the day of the Royal Wedding in 1981 I was hitching from the Sea of Galilee to the Lebanese border (I thought that was far enough away) and an Israeli army officer picked me up. When he found out where I was from he told me immediately that I looked like Lady Diana. It would take considerable effort to find a Caucasian woman who looked less like Princess Diana than I, but it made me realize how closely Britain is associated with the royals.

Much further up the valley, among the vestiges of an Inca foundry, we stood on the chiefs' platform, the sun burning like stage lights. The platform looked towards miles of hills tinged green with copper deposit. Nothing much had happened in the hills since the Inca arrived, led by Topa Inca, in the second half of the fifteenth century. They got about half way down the country, and conquered the Aymára, and probably other groups, but although they exacted tribute and influenced most of the northern and central tribes, their power was limited, and their impact on the subsequent development of the land and people minimal.

It was the last stop before a long journey home to the Elqui valley and so we lingered, just to prolong the trip. After depositing Rocky the next day I had to get to Santiago, my midway point. I would be seeing Pepe later, when he too was back in Santiago. It was hard to believe that I was half-way down already.

Pepe's sister and her family had gone to Santiago, and the Elqui valley cottage was empty. I was very tired, and after we had unloaded Rocky we ate the last two crabs and I went to bed. I had just blown out the candle when ten hippies crashed into the house whistling the Mr Men theme tune. They were friends of Pepe's from Santiago, and had been staying in the house all weekend. It was the Elqui valley, after all.

Chapter Five

A book read on a journey usually sticks to the ribcage of memory. Such associations are closely formed. I got on a bus back to Santiago having just finished three novels by the Chilean writer Isabel Allende, each more overblown than the last, and I turned in gratitude to a copy of *Heart of Darkness* which was becoming dog-eared in the carpetbag.

In Santiago I was again looked after by Simon and Rowena, who behaved as if it were perfectly normal for strange British women to pitch up from the bush. Beatriz, their amiable maid, took Rowena aside.

Beatriz (conspiratorially): 'I've put Miss Sara's clothes in the machine on a pre-wash. They smelt.'

Rowena (breezily): 'Well, I'm not surprised. She's been living in the mountains and camping on the beach for almost two months.'

Beatriz (shocked): 'She didn't camp alone, did she?'

Rowena: 'No, she met a Chilean man and camped with him.'

Beatriz (appalled): 'I see.'

Decently dressed for the first time in two months, I made an appointment to visit La Chascona, once a residence of Pablo Neruda, the colossus of modern Chilean literature and the best-known poet ever to emerge from South America. He was also a Communist, a diplomat and a committed bon viveur with roots in the green and fecund south; he said that he didn't understand the language of the desert. When he died, shortly after the coup, his disciples liked to say it was of a broken heart, but he did have cancer of the prostate at the time. The house was closely associated with his great love and last wife Matilde Urrutia and named 'The Tangled-haired One' after her. She became an icon in her own right to the generation of left-wing writers to whom Neruda was a god; Pepe Donoso's novel *Toque de queda* (Curfew) is written around her funeral.

La Chascona was at the end of a quiet cul-de-sac at the foot of San Cristóbal hill in the centre of the city. A disciple from the Pablo Neruda Foundation showed me round; he was a passionate man with strong opinions, and he was very knowledgeable about the master. Neruda picked the spot for the house in 1953, and everyone told him he was mad, as it was on the slope of the hill – very bad for his phlebitis. It was not so much a house as a collection of small buildings around an irregularly shaped courtyard spread over several levels. More than anything else it was a testament to Neruda's obsessive desire to collect things. He used to press requests for particular pieces upon friends in a position to acquire them for him – and he didn't forget if they failed him. His many collections included glasses (he said that even water tasted better out of coloured glass), ships' furniture, *belle époque* postcards, paperweights – and books, of course. On the library wall he had put up four portraits of his literary idols: two of Whitman and one each of Rimbaud and Baudelaire. Despite the proliferation of *objets d'art* from around the world, if the house did have a unifying theme, it was Neruda's love for what he called the thin country.

He was an extremely sociable man. There were bars everywhere, and a long dining table. The walls were hung with affectionately inscribed works by distinguished Chilean artists. The paintings included two large and very wonderful images by Neruda's second wife, Delia del Carril, an Argentinian twenty years his senior. He met her in 1934, and left her twenty-one years later for a much younger woman.

Three dolls were propped up in the living room. Neruda used to carry them into the bathroom every time he had a bath.When asked about this, he always said that he liked to bathe surrounded by beautiful women. The guide thought this was hilarious.

The soldiers broke into La Chascona several days after the coup and ransacked the house. Shortly afterwards the poet died in hospital, and they brought his body to the broken glass of his home for the wake. When I left, I thought of the street during the wake, full of distraught and shell-shocked mourners and Pinochet's hit squads.

I was so near the San Cristóbal funicular that I decided to go up it. It was a big tourist attraction of the capital. At the top there was a massive statue of the virgin, erected in 1908. It was ghastly. Everything up there was ghastly, from the tack stalls – it wasn't even particularly Chilean tack, it was the usual

international toxic waste of famous shrines – to the smog-
ridden view of the urban sprawl. The outline of the Andes was
barely visible, as if the city had almost succeeded in obliterating them too.

As I got to know Santiago I found a home at the *marisquerías*
(seafood cafés or bars) of the central market, where I could
linger anonymously at a gingham tablecloth after a bowl of
shellfish and a glass of cloudy white wine, looking out onto
wet fish counters piled with gleaming fish, exotically nameless
in English, and heaps of prawn tails and bristly sea urchins.
Men in black caps slammed machetes onto outsize chopping
boards, and others pushed trolleys between the aisles, white
boots meeting white rubber aprons. Itinerant guitarists played
Violeta Parra folksongs to diners, and the waitress called me
the South American equivalent of 'pet'. A handful of suited
executives came in and out, but the *mercado* was largely the
territory of the old school, slicked-back hair, cardigans and
string shopping bags. I even got used to spooning shellfish
juice into my wine.

One evening Rowena and Simon took me to an ex-pat party,
and I met an English mining engineer. We stood on the neat
lawn, attended by discreet waiters bearing trays of delicious
morsels, and the engineer told me that he'd casually been
asked to play cricket for Chile, as there weren't enough
Chileans to raise a team. Four Australians had agreed to make
up the numbers. The team had been assembled only because
Brazil had invited the non-existent Chilean squad over for an
international; the engineer was leaving the next day for São
Paulo.

I spent several enjoyable evenings with Germán Claro, the
quixotic aristocrat who ran a hacienda hotel and whom I had

met at the end of my first week in Chile. He was determined to get me to the places I wasn't officially allowed to go, and through his machinations I was offered a private tour of La Moneda, the presidential palace in the heart of the city.

'I like the way they usher in any foreigner whom they like the look of but don't let us see it,' said Pepe, who had also returned to Santiago. 'Some of the most important pieces of our cultural heritage are in there – I'd like to have a look at them, for one.'

This was a fair point, and I looked away in embarrassment. Then it occurred to me that I could just take him with me.

'We could give you a bogus role,' I said.

'Photographer!' he suggested enthusiastically.

'Do you have a camera?' I asked doubtfully.

'Of course.'

The camera, it emerged, was an East German instamatic, *circa* 1975. I tactfully wondered aloud if this was the kind of equipment to convince the authorities of his status as a professional photographer.

'What about interpreter then?'

'But you can't speak English. What if they ask you to interpret?'

We settled on the idea of a nebulous role as guide, and I was sure I could bluff it out.

At the entrance to La Moneda I was met by a pack of khaki-suited, rifle-wielding officers in knee-high black patent boots and white gloves with razor creases, all well over six feet tall. After questions, a frisk and a bomb-detection test, a man in a suit appeared asking for Mrs Wheeler. He shook my hand with typical Chilean vigour, crushing a couple of unimportant bones, and I introduced Pepe as my guide. The man looked puzzled.

'Are you her interpreter?' he asked.

'Yes!' panicked Pepe, and my courage faltered.

The palace was built in the eighteenth century as a mint, designed by an Italian architect called Joaquín Toesca who had worked on the royal palace in Spain. He was dispatched to the New World (new to the Spaniards, that is) by the king, first of all to build a cathedral in Santiago. This mint became the seat of the Chilean presidency in 1850, under Manuel Bulnes. From the outside it was austere; if it were in Paris it would be a military library on one of Haussmann's boulevards. The colour didn't help: it was dark, steely grey. The façade said, 'Don't come in here'.

Inside it lost its harsh edges – it was pure, beautiful neo-classicism. George Vancouver called it 'the best building in all the Spanish colonies', and Maria Graham, a lively English-woman who lived in Chile in the 1820s, wondered in her journal (later published) if it weren't 'too magnificent for Chile'. Two layers of high-ceilinged rooms concealed behind arches, columns and external staircases were arranged around large courtyards stalked by presidential staff, from snappily dressed civil servants to three men in blue hats carrying a basket of watermelons. Off the first courtyard we visited the frugally decorated presidential chapel.

The guide pointed to an oyster-coloured velvet seat, and said something unintelligible about the Pope. (Despite John Paul's attempts to make one or two anti-regime gestures during his last visit, Pinochet had the forthcoming plebiscite in mind, and he had engineered a propaganda coup by getting photographed kneeling with the First Lady while the Pope blessed the chapel.) When he saw that I didn't understand, the guide tried out his English.

'The Pope,' he said, 'naked here when he wisit Chile in 1987.'

'Naked?' I questioned.

'Naked?' the guide looked at interpreter Pepe for confirmation.

95

'Naked,' repeated Pepe authoritatively.

'I see,' I said gravely. I never found out what they meant.

In the salons, echoing with our footsteps like a museum after closing-time, the guide told us about Chilean oils, French chandeliers and Napoleon III bronze clocks, and from the famous Yellow Room, properly called the Salon Carrera, where the President receives heads of state, we entered the Cabinet Room. It was long, green and stygian, the style dislocated by unwieldy and old-fashioned Philips microphone boxes and thick net curtains redolent of Eastern Europe.

In the Orange Tree Courtyard the guide waved his arms around enthusiastically, demonstrating the position of the canopies when the President entertains guests under the trees. Pepe inspected the fruit trees. 'Those trees,' he told me later, looking serious, 'were diseased. They have an aphid. The oranges of the Republic are rotten.'

Until 11 September 1973, when Salvador Allende died in office in the Moneda, the presidential headquarters were off this Orange Courtyard. The orchestrators of the military coup ordered an aerial bombardment of the palace. Allende almost certainly shot himself with a sub-machine gun Castro had presented to him when he visited Chile, though the far left still insist that he was gunned down, a story promulgated, ironically, by Castro himself. There will always be a doubt, and Allende's death has acquired the status of modern myth. In the troubled weeks before the coup he had said this to an opposition leader: 'You are looking for a military dictatorship. I do not believe there is anything after death, but still, if there is, I shall look down on you all when you have your dictatorship and find you all together, casting about for ways to get out of power the military man you replace me with ... Because it won't cost you much to get him in. But by heaven, it will cost you something to get him out.'

We loitered in the first courtyard. 'Take a picture of me in front of the arch,' hissed Pepe. I tried to do it while the guide wasn't looking. He was talking to a stocky man in a dark suit. I recognized this man from newspaper pictures as a controversial and unpopular minister – and rather a stupid one. During the next few seconds I realized that the guide was going to introduce me to this man. Yes, he was turning now . . .

'Señor, can I introduce our distinguished British guest?'

I caught the contempt on Pepe's face as he stared at the politician.

'Señora, are there are questions you would like to ask the minister?'

I grasped for suitably anodyne topics. I thought of John Cleese pretending to faint in Fawlty Towers when he was introducing an important guest and forgot the man's name. But it was all right. An aide rushed up and absorbed the minister, and the moment passed.

We strolled on. I asked where the bombs fell. The guide looked shifty.

'Well, the first rocket struck over there, on the left of the entrance to the first courtyard.' He paused. 'There was a lot of damage. We restored it exactly as it was. We hope now that we can restore its . . . symbolic associations too. For many people, and I must say this is unfortunate, the Moneda represents 1973.'

Twentieth-century Chilean history reveals a traditional electoral model referred to as the *tres tercios* (three thirds): one-third of the electorate on the left, one-third on the right and the rest in the middle. During the 1960s, a period of increasing social unrest, the reformist legislation of Eduardo Frei's Christian Democrat government managed to alienate both right and left, ultimately and crucially leading to a collapse of support for the political middle ground. Salvador Allende, a Marxist and leader of the Socialist Party and of the leftist Popular Unity coalition, was elected in 1970 within the context of this polarization.

Popular Unity had emerged out of the Popular Action Front, another left-wing coalition, and it was committed to a 'peaceful road to socialism', christened *'la vía chilena'* (the Chilean way) by some theorists. The country it inherited was experiencing severe economic and social disorder. Allende didn't win a majority, he won a plurality, and he only took office after the Christian Democrats voted for him in Congress. They soon decided they had made a mistake, and began to undermine him. The Christian Democrats constituted the largest single party in the two houses throughout Allende's term of office, and he was consistently hamstrung by the legislature.

Chile was at that time – and for many years – perceived as an important Cold War battlefield, and the CIA had it exceptionally well covered. Washington reacted hysterically to the prospect and then the reality of a Marxist President in the Moneda: just as after Cuba it had been Chile, so after Chile it would be the whole of Latin America. The journalist Seymour M. Hersh, in his book *Kissinger: the Price of Power*, quotes Roger Morris, a member of National Security Council staff at the time who said, 'I don't think anybody in the government understood how ideological Kissinger was about Chile. I don't think anybody ever fully grasped that Henry saw Allende as being a far more serious threat than Castro.'

A leftist government was seen to be a danger to US commercial interests. The powerful International Telegraph and Telephone Corporation owned 70 per cent of the Chilean Telephone Company, and even before Allende had been sworn in it had set out an elaborate strategy to ensure that he failed. This included the following advice and instruction: '1. Banks should not renew credits or should delay in doing so. 2. Companies should drag their feet in sending money, making deliveries, in shipping spare parts, etc ... 4. We should withdraw all technical help ...'

Washington's policy was to take advantage of the existing polarization and push the disenchanted politicians and voters of the 'middle third' – the Christian Democrats – away from Allende. It was a successful strategy. Many Christian Democrats supported the coup in 1973 and believed that Pinochet would clean out the left and return the country to them.

Congressional hearings in Washington later revealed that Nixon, Kissinger and numerous others were directly involved in manipulation of the Chilean economy and political machinery, largely through the CIA. Kissinger made his now famous remark, 'I don't see why we need to stand idly by and watch a country go communist due to the irresponsibility of its own people,' and Nixon informed CIA Director Richard Helms that an Allende regime in Chile 'would not be acceptable to the US'.

The White House and the CIA were so conspiratorial that they didn't tell their ambassador to Chile about their plans to ensure Allende didn't take his seat. Hersh compares White House behaviour regarding Chile with its conduct during Watergate: cover-up payments for CIA crimes, the destruction of records and the distortion of documents, perjured evidence to Congressional investigating committees and liaisons with violent, unscrupulous men. Was Washington so afraid because of its two top-secret National Security Agency facilities operating on offshore Chilean territory and monitoring Soviet submarines, among other things? Both sites were evacuated overnight when Allende came to power. No, it wasn't under-cover security facilities which set White House passions alight. The reaction was more visceral – a white-hot scream of hatred. Nixon had developed a pathological antipathy towards Chile; David Frost records in his memoirs that it was the subject Nixon's aides warned him off before he interviewed the President. This high-level animosity was duly translated into policy and cultural indoctrination and funded by millions of dollars, right down to the distribution of comics on the streets of Chilean towns and villages reinforcing the 'good' US image over the 'evil' of Communism.

By the middle of 1973 the Allende regime was tottering, though the various factions of the opposition also had their difficulties. A June coup orchestrated by the right-wing *Patria y Libertad* and officers of the Second Armoured Regiment was cancelled when plans were leaked, but three combat groups, including tanks, went ahead and converged on the centre of the city. The US ambassador at the time, Nathaniel Davis, reported that the vehicles all stopped obediently at red traffic lights and that at least one tank called into a regular garage to fill up with petrol.

Many of Popular Unity's policies – those to reform land ownership, for example – were developments of policies pursued by the previous regime. But they were often radical developments nonetheless, and some of them attempted the impossible. In addition, a collapse in world copper prices handicapped Allende's already massively challenging undertaking. More has been written about the three years of his government than about any other period in Chilean history, and the reasons for its failure are still bitterly disputed. There is little disagreement that it did fail. Hyperinflation and escalating economic, political and social chaos had paralyzed the country by 1973, although the government still won an increased majority of 43.4 per cent in the March 1973 elections at an extremely difficult moment in the socialist experiment. (In the British general election in 1992 41.85 per cent of the electorate voted for, and returned, a Conservative government.) Some of the ideas spewed out by the Popular Unity cabinet were too theoretical to stand any chance of being converted into successful practice. The ultra-leftists weakened the socialist movement. The coalition itself was fragmented, yet it faced a press virtually united in opposition, much of it funded by foreign dollars. Allende ignored constant warnings from within his party that he should slow down the pace of his reforms to prevent a right-wing backlash. Agrarian reform incensed the élite. US manipulation of class conflict was highly successful. By September 1973 Washington didn't have to worry about directly funding a coup: it had destabilized the country so effectively that it could leave the mechanics to the Chileans.

When Jimmy Carter was elected in 1977, four years after the junta entered the Moneda, he tried to make the United States confront its shame over Chile. He had said, in a campaign debate in October of the previous year, that the Nixon–Ford administration 'had destroyed elected governments like Chile'. Unpalatable truths were dished up in the US over the years to discredit the network of people involved, provoking fraught public debate and interminable press coverage.

Allende had tried to redistribute Chilean wealth and owner-ship to benefit the poor; he had aimed at the creation of a more equitable society, and for this there were many who never abandoned him. His government represented hope for the economically disenfranchised and the exploited, and for that reason those likely to see a reduction in their own slice of the cake hated what he stood for. But he never gave up his hope for the people. On the day he died he said in Churchillian tones over the last radio station loyal to him which had not been disabled, 'I say to you that I am assured that the seed we have planted in the dignified consciousness of thousands and thousands of Chileans cannot forever be kept down.' His voice, he said, would soon be silenced (the Hawker Hunters had already taken off); 'You shall continue to hear it. I shall always be with you.'

101

It was an ironic detail that in his last public utterance the world's first democratically elected Marxist President used the same words as Christ did when he left the eleven disciples for the last time on a mountain in Galilee.

Germán, who was able to sort out so many of my logistical problems with a telephone call to a cousin or an old schoolfriend that I had taken to thinking of him as Mr Fixit, also arranged a personal wine tour for me. I had merely asked him to recommend two or three wineries offering public visits – but if Germán did anything, he did it in style. He had fixed up my tour like most people book a dentist's appointment, apparently by dint of being related to most of the vineyard owners. The forty or so 'old' Chilean families were like that; it made the country seem very small.

I spent a week being shown round baked vineyards and mildewed cellars, dispatched first to the Maipo valley on the outskirts of Santiago, an area which has become synonymous with fine Chilean wine. There I visited Cousiño Macul, a family-owned company with the best vineyards in the country and a hundred and twenty-acre private park to boot. Like many Chilean wineries, the business was founded with capital amassed from minerals, in this case silver and coal. Arturo Cousiño, export director of the company and the son of the current owner, came to the reception area to greet me, impeccably turned out in a tweed jacket and polished brogues like a model for a *Country Life* shoot. He was in his thirties, one of a generation of wine producers to have increased the quantity of Chilean wine drunk abroad almost fifteenfold in a decade, pushing the country to third place among exporters to the massive North American market, led only by France and Italy. The wine critic of the *New York Times* recently described Chile as 'probably the most exciting wine region in the world right now,' and the walls of Arturo's office were hung with framed certificates printed with medals and rosettes and inscribed in various foreign languages.

'The only reason the industry is taken seriously inside Chile is because of our export success,' he said as we strolled out among muddy rows of vines. 'Domestic consumption is not only relatively indiscriminating, but it has also dropped off dramatically over the past two or three decades from about sixty litres [eighty regular-size bottles] per capita per annum to about twenty-eight [thirty-seven bottles].'

I thought, That's nothing.

'Beer has become more popular, and sugary fizzy drinks have appeared from abroad. Besides, the standard of education is far higher than it used to be, and that's created a heightened social consciousness. In other words, a number of factors have contributed to vastly reduced wine consumption. I might add that between 1938 and 1974 certain laws virtually prohibited the planting of vineyards – that was the government's way of controlling alcoholism!'

Every vintner I spoke to complained about the absence of a wine culture in the country. 'No one in Chile knows anything about wine,' one said. 'They think it can't cost more than a thousand pesos [less than £1.50] a bottle.'

Later I found that I couldn't buy the fine wines I tasted on my tour in the supermarkets. It was all being sent abroad.

Traditionally, they were great wine drinkers, consuming prodigious quantities made from the *país* grapes brought over by the *conquistadores*. Much of the wine drunk is still produced from these grapes, cultivated largely on unirrigated land; quality wines, including almost all exports, are made from pre-phylloxera grapes shipped from Europe in the nineteenth century.

Arturo told a story which showed that the authorities and the winemakers take the industry seriously, even if the punters don't. When a freak frost struck the Maipo valley in

October 1991, the army offered their helicopters for hire, and they duly took off over the vineyards, creating a wind to thaw the frost. It was one of Pinochet's more heartwarming acts (he was still commander-in-chief of the army).

The thin branches were already bending under the weight of a heavy crop.

'Yes,' said Arturo, when I remarked on it. 'And although our average yield here is extremely low for Chile, it's still far higher than a Bordeaux yield. If we can make wine like we do with our abundant crops, just imagine what we could produce with a low yield like they get over there!'

We arrived at a row of brand new stainless steel vats outside the brick cellars. The country won its reputation with red wines, largely because no one had enough money to purchase the technology required for fine whites, but most top producers went on, in time, to acquire state-of-the-art equipment, and their subsequent success has occasioned a rush of foreign investment and joint ventures. Cousiño Macul, which claims to be the only winery in the Maipo valley not to buy grapes to supplement its own crop, was wooed by Moët & Chandon, but having been independent since 1856 the family were anxious to remain so. As Arturo put it to me, 'We can make a good wine alone.'

Germán came with me when I visited Errazuriz Panquehue, the only quality winery in the Aconcagua valley north of Santiago. The oenologist took us to lunch at a local restaurant owned by an old gaffer who used to sell pigs door-to-door in Santiago. He had started the restaurant with one table in his front room, and now turned over about four million pesos a month. The food was famous, and it all came from the fields at the back. He was particularly proud of his *arrollado*, a boneless roll of pork served with raw onions in wine vinegar. When we thought we had finished he lurched out of the kitchen carrying a dish of *alcayota* with chestnut puree and walnuts. *Alcayota*, which looks like a melon, is a dark green squash-type vegetable with white crunchy flesh. We ate it with jugs of *chicha*, partially fermented grape juice, which was dark orange and very sweet.

When I went down to Concha y Toro, by far the biggest wine producer in the country, the staff were in a panic, as it had been raining hard for two days and the vines were beginning to spoil. I panicked myself later that day when I was driving back (Hertz had again obliged, though with a car, not one of my Rockies) and discovered that the streets of Santiago have no drainage. The speed with which the whole of the south of the city virtually stopped functioning was astonishing: roads turned into torrents and cars were abandoned, up to their doorhandles in water. A black economy loves a crisis, however, and out of nowhere sprang an army of men riding tricycles with high platforms attached to convey people across the streets.

It took me hours to get home, and even in the heavy rain people on crutches limped to the car window asking for money. I sat in the darkness in a stationary line of traffic in a rough and anonymous part of the town, the reflections of streetlights distorting into oily rainbows on the surface of the water swirling around outside. Cold and totally unable to move the car, I was shocked that this could happen to me only a few miles from the city centre, and for the first time in months I was afraid.

In the days following the wine tour the Chilean newspapers, which I read nursing cups of Nescafé at noisy pavement tables, were full of stories about a new development in the long-running drama of the political prisoners. Out of almost four hundred *presos políticos* in jail when Patricio Aylwin's government took over from the military in 1990, approximately three hundred and fifty had already been released. As most of those who remained had been charged with or convicted of blood crimes (they were called political prisoners nonetheless), the government – who would have been delighted to get shot of this emotive issue once and for all – was compelled to keep them locked up. Some were awaiting trial, some had been convicted, some were up for multiple charges, and all their cases were complex.

It was clear from the newspaper stories, and from a number of conversations I had at the pavement tables, that the question of what to do with the political prisoners was tremendously important; it had become a symbol of the national healing process. The jail most of them were held in was in central Santiago, and it occurred to me that I should visit it, and meet some of these famous prisoners. I had a feeling that this was not something on which I should consult Mr Fixit.

One unusually cold summer morning I stood outside the monolithic old jail itself, more Victorian in appearance than anything built under the auspices of Queen Victoria, and when I knocked two dark-eyed men opened a hatch in the door and pressed their noses to a grille. A queue of women stood in a line by this door, waiting in silence for visiting time. They weren't allowed to take anything in with them, so a crippled woman with an eye for the main chance had set herself up in business, squatting on the pavement guarding handbags, baskets and pushchairs for a small fee. Wielding my press card like a weapon and repeating faceless names culled from numerous telephone calls and frustrating visits to offices within the Department of the Interior I got in, and was shunted from one room to the next by 'prison guards' who looked suspiciously like soldiers. After a lot of doorclanking I was dispatched for a final administrative check to the *Dirección Nacional*, a kind of state department, in order to obtain one of the *papels* (pieces of paper) so beloved of

Chilean bureaucracy. After sufficient authority had been exercised on the various floors of this building I was sent back to the prison with a message that the governor had been telephoned: I was in.

The governor was a short, balding man with a squint and an eggstain on his tie, and he seemed to be under the illusion that I wanted to talk to him. I fidgeted on the dralon sofa in his office for half an hour until I was delivered to a member of staff, frisked and escorted across a high-walled courtyard reminiscent of Colditz. A hatchet-faced guard held open a grey metal door, and I stepped into a room with cracked plaster walls and a high ceiling, bare except for a formica table and three chairs. Sunlight from a single, high window gilded the opposite wall, and in an arc of this light stood two men.

They were wearing jeans and sweaters, and they walked towards me, cold hands outstretched, and kissed me on both cheeks, introducing themselves as representatives of the National Coordinating Committee for Political Prisoners. We sat down.

'Thank you,' said the younger one, 'for coming to us.' He had shoulder-length frizzy hair and large, deep brown eyes, and he was a *mirista* – a member of the Movement of the Revolutionary Left – in his late twenties. The other man, about forty, was larger set with short black hair plastered to his head. He told me that he was a Communist, and I later learnt that he was a member of the Manuel Rodríguez Patriotic Front, the armed wing of the Communist Party, formed in 1983 and named after an Independence hero. (This man was subsequently offered voluntary exile in Belgium in exchange for a life sentence, and left Chile later in 1992.) They had both been inside for six years.

'Our organization,' said the *mirista* in a soft voice, 'is made up of Communists, Socialists, *miristas* and independent leftists. It campaigns for fair punishment for everyone tried and found guilty of torture and oppression during the dictatorship, recognition of human rights – to be more specific in this last field, action against poverty – and liberty for all political prisoners.'

They thought the Rettig Commission, set up to document human rights abuses during the dictatorship, was a joke; they said the government wasn't prepared to confront the right, because it was frightened. They were both unimpressed by the Aylwin regime, and said repression was as bad as it had been under Pinochet. This sounded like an absurd statement – people weren't disappearing anymore, after all – but what I think they meant was firstly repression of justice, as exemplified by the difficulties involved in bringing prosecutions against the torturers, and secondly the lack of basic human rights within certain sectors of the population, for example stigmatized ex-prisoners of conscience or simply Chileans caught in the poverty spiral. They talked at some length about despair in the slums.

'Many of the people who once protested for democracy while others were silent,' said the Communist, 'are the dispossessed of today's democratic Chile, and although it is often proudly stated that human rights abuse no longer exists, in the wider interpretation of that concept it's difficult to maintain that these people have any rights at all.'

The *mirista* had been tortured in 1989; they had put currents through his head. He was still on medication. The Communist had a perforated kidney from beatings in the early 1980s and needed microsurgery. His wife had died in a detention centre. I never found out exactly what they were in for, but I knew that in both cases they had been found guilty of a serious crime.

Purity of vision is often seductive. I made myself think about the terrorist murders committed by both the FMRP and Mir – for all I knew, by these two sitting in front of me. That was where absolute commitment had led their groups – to the intellectual arrogance and political suicide of terrorism. But I couldn't help feeling that everyone else, who wasn't passionate about the poor, and about justice, was leading a compromised existence.

They had no complaints about the conditions they were held in; they were treated well in prison. When I asked if I could bring them anything they said they didn't need personal stuff; I asked again, and they said blank cassettes, which they record on and send to supporting organizations abroad. I lived with their faces inside my head for days, and all the anguished novels I had read, written during the Pinochet years, came into focus in my imagination.

The Chilean government has no policy on female incarceration; over a century ago it handed over responsibility to the Church, presumably with a deep sigh of relief, and there it has resided ever since. The flank of the Church in question was the Order of the Good Shepherd, founded in Angers. Sheila Cassidy was placed under the care of Good Shepherd nuns when she was imprisoned in Santiago in 1979. She was a British doctor, and she had been arrested in a house belonging to the Columban Fathers for treating a wounded revolutionary. The housekeeper was murdered and Sheila Cassidy was taken away and repeatedly tortured. Later, after three weeks in solitary confinement, she was moved to Tres Alamos prison. There were eighty other women there with her, and on Christmas Day they stood on tables at the appointed hour of ten in the evening and sang songs like 'Take Heart, Joe, My Love' to prisoners in the men's jail over the spiked concrete wall. The men were waiting, and shortly their song of reply drifted across, faint on the wind. The British ambassador took Sheila Cassidy a Harrods' Christmas cake.

The women's prison I visited was the largest in Chile. The

Mother Superior and prison governor, grey-haired and benign of face, explained that the objective of the prison was to reconcile women with God. It would be interesting to put that forward as government policy in the West. Many of the prisoners were in for armed robbery, and many for trafficking and possession; these were the areas *Madre* had seen explode in her many years in the service. This prison was not austere, or even institutional; it was a small, modern community. We strolled between the buildings chatting politely and taking in impromptu and embarrassing visits to sewing and pottery groups, and as we crossed a garden in the sharp sunlight I asked *Madre* if she thought the government should exercise more responsibility towards the penal system.

'I have no opinion on that,' she said, as if I had asked her whether one should put limes or lemons in a pisco sour. Shortly after this she stopped, placed her hand on my wrist and looked serious.

'There's something I want to ask you,' she said conspiratorially. 'Is it true that Andreas and *La Fergus* are separating?'

Before I could answer we were interrupted by a sunny young woman in a red striped dress who, I later learnt, was a *lautarista* (member of another terrorist group) and had already done eight years for murdering an old woman.

Chapter Six

Yet all these things had no effect upon me, or at least not enough to resist the strong inclination I had to go abroad again, which hung about me like a chronic distemper.

Daniel Defoe, *The Life and Adventures of Robinson Crusoe*

It was one of those days ... when I forgot all my cares, all my failures, all my anxieties about writing. I was exactly where I wanted to be, doing what I liked most. I was far enough offshore ...

Paul Theroux, *The Happy Isles of Oceania*

A contact of a contact at a travel agency called me one morning at Simon and Rowena's flat.

'There's one seat left in an air taxi leaving for Juan Fernández tomorrow. You have to decide immediately.'

Deciding immediately wasn't a problem. I had been trying to fix up a trip to those notoriously inaccessible Chilean islands since I first arrived in the country. They were located between three hundred and fifty and four hundred miles out in the Pacific, and they were occupied by five hundred and fifty people and two cars. The largest of the three islands, and the only one which was inhabited, was called Robinson

Crusoe, as for four years it was the home of the man Defoe based his character on, the mercurial Scottish mariner Alexander Selkirk.

Early the next morning, therefore, I arrived at a small airport on the outskirts of Santiago thronged with air force personnel. It didn't take my pilot long to locate me; I was one of the only people not wearing a light blue uniform. He was a middle-aged man with an affable face and hair the colour of cornflakes.

'Hi,' he said, taking the carpetbag. The weather had broken, and a gold-coloured six-seater was waiting in the sun on the tarmac. The pilot put me up in the cockpit, in the passenger seat, as it were; four islanders were already strapped in behind us.

Once the plane had lifted out of the Santiago basin and over the coastal mountains it cruised over the melted blue candlewax of the Pacific, set in gleaming folds with a light dusting of white ash. Figueroa, the pilot, had been flying the same route for twenty-five years. Before they blasted an airstrip in 1977 he used to do it in a sea-plane. When he lowered us through a bank of dense cloud later a spectral outline appeared ahead. It was a small mountain range sticking out of the ocean.

'Robinson Crusoe!', shouted Figueroa over the noise of the engine.

I could see why it had been so difficult to find a site for an airstrip. The land-mass consisted of high cliffs, peaks like spikes and almost perpendicular slopes, and as we approached the uniform brownness transmogrified into a myriad delicate hues in stripes, blocks and pools. It must have come as a shock to Juan Fernández himself when he spotted it from the mast of his ship. He was a Spanish priest and navigator, and he arrived some time between 1563 and 1574, though Spain didn't take legal possession of his islands for almost two hundred years.

112

Figueroa landed us on a reddish brown strip of earth next to a wooden hut, and chickens scarpered from the runway. Two men in woolly hats came out of the hut. Cold, damp winds whipped around the plane as we jumped down and piled luggage onto a rusty pickup, and there was a frosty bite to the air. As the only ground flat enough for this airstrip was at the western tip of the island and it was out of the question to get to the only settlement in a vehicle and took five hours on foot, anyone arriving by air was obliged to travel round to the north coast by boat. Figueroa, also the pickup driver, drove the cargo down to the shore, and we followed on foot.

In the brilliant indigo bay Juan Fernández fur seals were swimming around a rotting jetty.

'Your countrymen,' said Figueroa, 'hunted them almost to extinction.'

I was quite used to being held responsible for the actions of the entire British nation. It was part of the job description. He was referring to the sailors who skulked in and out of the Pacific in the eighteenth and nineteenth centuries and killed the double-coated Juan Fernández seals for their thick under-fur and their blubber. The pelts were dispatched to China to be turned into felt, and the blubber was boiled down for oil. Entrepreneurs from North America couldn't resist it, either, and within a five-year period at the turn of those two centuries three million fur seals were killed off Juan Fernández.

The boatman, waiting next to his small blue boat, lifted the lid of a box Figueroa had unloaded from the plane.

'Tomatoes!'

It was a highly dependent community: almost everything had to be flown in or sent on an infrequent sea cargo service. We even had a gross of eggs with us.

It rained. Wind and rain are as much a feature of life in the archipelago as they are in the Shetlands. As we pulled round the bay and out into the ocean the cliffs and rocks, spotted

113

with seals and striped ochre, veiled themselves in a fine mist. It was a cold, wet ninety-minute trip. About half way, the first wooden boats appeared, fishing for *langostas Juan Fernández*, large red crustaceans like pincerless lobsters which dominate the island economy and fetch a hefty price in the wealthy districts of Santiago.

Cumberland Bay and the wooden buildings of the settlement were circumscribed by forest. It was not an inhospitable sight, and it presumably gave Selkirk some measure of courage when he was rowed ashore in 1704. He was the sailing master (like a first mate) of the *Cinque Ports*, a British privateering vessel circumnavigating the globe. It had not been a happy journey, and at Juan Fernández Selkirk had a row with the unpopular captain over the ship's seaworthiness. When the captain insisted on continuing, leaks or no leaks, Selkirk demanded to be set ashore. (Defoe decided that a shipwrecked but innocent Crusoe was a better idea.) The story goes that Selkirk's courage failed him as his colleagues rowed back to the *Cinque Ports*, and he shouted that he had changed his mind. The captain had not. Selkirk was not a man of phlegmatic disposition, and when he realized what he had done it nearly killed his spirit.

Later, the island was named Más a Tierra (Nearer Land), and the second island over a hundred miles away became – obviously – Más Afuera (Further Out). It was Crusoe, not Selkirk, who became an international star, and Más a Tierra was renamed after him in the 1970s. Further Out was simultaneously transformed into Alejandro Selkirk.

The first person I met on the island was an old salt called Robinson Green. For no reason except to welcome me as I stepped ashore he shook my hand enthusiastically, so I took the opportunity of asking his advice on where to stay; I wanted to rent a room in a cottage. Robinson thought for a few moments, then spoke to Manolo the boatman, who, it turned out, had built a cabin in his garden. A workman from the electricity board was staying in this cabin until the next day.

'But you can rent it after that,' said Manolo, wiping grease onto his trousers. 'Come and stay at our house tonight.'

Robinson was delighted, which I later found out was particularly generous-spirited of him as his family owned a 'hotel' on the island. After Manolo had dealt with the boat we walked along a wide mud street which turned into a coastal path, and at a small house next to an even smaller pine cabin Manolo said, 'Welcome'.

Inside we sat on chairs covered with penguin pelts and drank pisco while Mrs Manolo made six loaves of bread. I learnt that I was to share a bed with a twenty-two-year-old daughter. Manolo told island stories. Even isolation wasn't what it once was.

'Now the government pays for schooling on the mainland for all children over eight – didn't when I was young. They're brought back by the navy in December, and leave again in March. Mind you, we still don't have a doctor.'

They did have a nurse, and she was one of the most important people on the island as it was she who decided who was sick enough to require a free flight to the continent.

'We still don't have telephones, but we have access to a radio phone sometimes. There's no crime here, you know – none at all. We can leave our doors open.'

In the evening I went to a café on the waterfront and ate a fried fish under a naked bulb, rain and wind pounding on the cracked windowpanes. People came in and out, and chatted over congealed sauce bottles. When I got back, Manolo and his wife were studying their accounts on the kitchen table, the Sony system between them pumping out the music of the Smurfs.

The next morning was bright and clear, and after moving

the carpetbag into the vacated cabin I set off for Selkirk's lookout, in a saddle in the mountains where he climbed each day to search the horizon for rescue vessels. The vegetation translated itself from eucalyptus groves to rare indigenous ferns and creepers, and then to pungent rainforest, and the smell of the rainforest hit the back of my throat like nitroglycerine. At the top I stood among red hummingbirds looking out at tiny *langosta* boats crawling around the rich sapphire of the bay.

I had long cherished the idea of visiting that spot, as it was what William Cowper had in mind when he wrote 'The Solitude of Alexander Selkirk', which begins famously, 'I am monarch of all I survey'. Cowper knew a good deal about isolation and incapacity, though he had learnt it while surrounded by people. Selkirk and the island were Cowper's perfect symbols of the terrifying solitude of mental anguish. The poem goes on,

> O Solitude! where are the charms
> That sages have seen in thy face? . . .
> How fleet is a glance of the mind!
> Compared with the speed of its flight,
> The tempest itself lags behind,
> And the swift-winged arrows of light.
> When I think of my own native land
> In a moment I seem to be there;
> But alas! recollection at hand
> Soon hurries me back to despair!

The cabin was sandwiched between the mountain, which always wore a turban of cloud, and the bay, and it had its own balcony, with a treetrunk table. It even had a tiny kitchen, though buying anything to cook in it was barely possible. There were half-a-dozen shops on the island, all with five shelves lined with widely spaced tins of spam and tinned peas and numerous packets of a product called fairy whip which I supposed to be a food substance rather than a sex aid. There were no fresh goods. I enquired if anyone made their own goat's cheese which I might buy. They did not. Was there no fruit in season? There was not. On my third day, with a small flush of triumph, I located a tin of olives.

One night I ate at the Daniel Defoe Hotel with two Danish chemical scientists on an adventure holiday. They were the only guests there. The salt and pepper on the table were kept in old Jean Patou perfume bottles, which didn't go down very well with the Danes. We were served mussel soup and *langosta* cooked in wine and cream, and it was very good. I guessed what the dessert would be before it arrived and, yes, it was fairy whip, as pink as nail varnish and I imagine fairly similar in flavour. After dinner I looked through the visitors' book. In 1989 HMS *Newcastle* had docked. A marine signing himself Phil 'I can't whistle' Renton had written, 'This place very similar to Berwick-on-Tweed,' and his colleague below him, 'Had a few, got pissed, then did duty watch.' I had to explain this to the Danes, and they spent the next hour suggesting Danish equivalents to Berwick-on-Tweed to each other. Exactly ten years before my visit (a decade only took about twenty pages of the book) I found Gavin Young's entry. He had described himself as 'another Robinson Crusoe and a dipsomaniac to boot'. Pinochet, on his page, had been less self-deprecatory.

The days went by, and I followed paths that tipped over mountains and rubbed themselves out or sat on walls talking aimlessly with anyone who stopped (it was starting again they had trouble with, not stopping). I made friends with one of the three policemen. How the island justified three, I couldn't imagine. I watched people making jewellery out of black coral wood. They carried branches of it from their boats, and the wood looked as if it came from a regular tree, but inside the flaky bark it was black and nacreous and had to be cut with a hacksaw. I was initiated into island lore. One of the more recent additions to its tomes concerned a collision between the only two vehicles on the island. It was hard to believe that this impressive victory over the laws of probability had actually occurred; but they all swore it had.

Another popular story involved a plane that crash-landed in the bay on its way back to the mainland, and it illustrated the importance of *langostas* in their lives. This tale was recounted to me half a dozen times, always embroidered with the same details about how it was the pilot's birthday, how he radioed a distress signal to the village and they all came out of their houses to look for the plane, and what a great crack it made when it hit the water (they all remembered that). The story always ended with the same dramatic climax. 'And do you know what? There were three hundred *langostas* on board.'

At the back of a cemetery on the western edge of the village someone had put up a monument with an inscription in German. It was in memory of the dead of the cruiser *Dresden*, which sank in Cumberland Bay on 14 March 1914 when the captain blew up the magazine. It had been cornered by the British warships *Kent* and *Glasgow* while it was trying to get repaired, and shells from the battle were still embedded in the cliffs past the lighthouse. This was my first encounter with the *Dresden*. In southern Chile I was often to hear stories of its almost miraculous passage up the coast.

I went to mass. The thirty islanders in the diminutive church shouted choruses in a very un-Catholic fashion. When I spoke with the Argentinian priest afterwards he was rather apologetic about the size of the congregation, as if it were his fault; perhaps it was. Four hundred miles of Pacific and a meagre five hundred and fifty potential converts hadn't deterred the Pentecostals, or the Mormons, or the Jehovah's Witnesses, all of whom had established a base in the village. The growth of other Churches and sects is a Latin American phenomenon, not a Chilean one; in many countries – Guatemala, for example – the influx of 'new' denominations is even more visible. It has been likened to a new Reformation.

The Pentecostal movement, which claims most Chilean Protestants, rooted itself in the continent in about 1910 and grew swiftly in the 1930s and 1940s in the expanding urban centres. As traditional social structures collapsed, notably the feudal haciendas, Pentecostalism offered an alternative to a Church which the migrant poor identified with the Establishment. Everyone participates in a Pentecostal service; it doesn't replicate the rigid, hierarchical nature of society like traditional Catholicism. It's no wonder that they went for it, or that they still do go for it.

Protestantism has come a long way in Chile. An Englishman travelling through in the 1790s found that everyone was convinced Protestants had a reptilian, Satanic tail. One old woman lifted up his coat tails to find it – or that was her story.

The Mormons sustained an impressive growth-rate in Chile throughout the 1980s, and in 1992 they were claiming over 314,000 Chilean members. According to Mormon teachings, two prophetic utterances have conferred special status upon the country. The nice man I met at the vast and gleaming headquarters of the Church of the Latterday Saints in Santiago a couple of months later told me that more than half their missionaries were still North American. The close identification between the Mormons and the United States, and specifically US money and foreign policy, was presumably one reason why their chapels were subject to terrorist bomb attacks whenever a US politician visited the country.

Two Frenchmen in their fifties came to the cabin. They were on holiday on the island for six weeks, and didn't like it much.

119

'We heard you were here. Come and have dinner with us.'

They had read an article in a French magazine describing Juan Fernández as paradise on earth, like a Bounty ad. It had led them to expect sun all the time, warm seas, delectable food, comfortable accommodation for several francs a day and lots of people who spoke French. It wasn't like that, and the pair of them spent a good deal of time plotting revenge on the journalist who had so cruelly deceived them.

One was a Vietnam veteran. He had fought in the Algerian War in the late 1950s, too, and later it came out that he had been a mercenary in Africa for fifteen years. His card was embossed with the words '*Légion d'honneur*' in a heavy Gothic script. He was entirely bald, and had halitosis and the most extraordinary piercing pale blue eyes. His companion, also a retired military man, was much quieter. His wife had died of cancer a year before, and he seemed to be only half present. The bald man insisted on two large rounds of sweet martini, and found a bottle of champagne to go with the rabbit, the only dish on offer at the restaurant. It wasn't champagne actually, it was sweet foamy liquid, like Asti Spumante. In his cups the bald man began to rave.

'I never sleep, you know. Hardly at all. Can't be bothered with tablets. I go over things in my mind, you can't imagine. If I could draw, I could draw my memories for you in the finest detail, though most of the people in them have been dead for years. You don't forget, you know. Africa, Indochina, Algeria ... I always see one face, Bernard Groutier, he was twenty-two, and he was going to marry my sister. He was one of the best – we were never apart. He would have been my brother-in-law. Smashed in the forehead at point-blank range.'

The pale blue eyes had filled with tears.

I had asked if it would be possible to go out with a *langosta* fisherman.

120

'Of course,' said a boy who often stopped on the wall. 'You can go out with my dad. You don't get seasick, do you?'

'No,' I laughed.

He came back later and told me to meet his father, who was called Alejandro, at seven-thirty the next morning, by the jetty.

There would only be one thing more difficult than finding the right Alejandro in Juan Fernández, and that would be picking out the Robinson you wanted. The entire male population of the archipelago were eddying around the little harbour in their woolly hats, preparing their boats, filling water containers and pulling on yellow oilskins.

When I found him, he was a wiry little man with a deeply creased face, like a tortoise.

He said, 'You don't get seasick, do you?'

'No,' I said confidently.

'Are you sure?', he said doubtfully.

'Yes,' I said loudly.

Alejandro shouted across to another fisherman that he'd be back around seven. This meant that we'd be out for almost twelve hours. The other man replied that he was going to Santa Clara island for three days, and I thought, You've got off lightly.

Alejandro's first mate rowed the twenty-five-foot *Norma Hortensia* to the jetty. The mate was in his early twenties and had a startling exuberance of hair and a sour expression which turned sourer as he watched me climb in. He muttered to Alejandro, 'I bet she gets seasick.'

We rowed out, switched on the motor and puttered to the edge of the bay, where I was handed a spool of line and told to catch small fish (as if I had any say over what size of fish might bite). I did catch some fish, and they were small, fortunately. Most of them were used to bait large ones, which in turn were going to attract the *langostas*, and Alejandro fried

121

the last six over a fire he made in a tin drum. They were sweet and delicious, but I only ate one, as my stomach was on my mind.

Langostas are caught cooperatively. Wooden cages are suspended from floats and drift permanently about a hundred and twenty feet under, whereupon hungry crustaceans crawl through the large-holed rope netting on one side to take a bite out of the juicy fish in the cage. The fishermen simply take it in turns to service the cages, and they pull them up by hand. Some of ours contained as many as thirty *langostas*. The first mate measured the body of each scrabbling red creature with an object resembling a bristle-less metal scrubbing brush, and if it didn't meet the standard requirement (about nine inches body length) it was tossed back. The others were stored in a wooden compartment; on shore they are kept alive in seawater until they leave for the plane. They must arrive in Santiago live, for if they are cooked dead they lose their flavour.

I believe the scientific name for the *langosta Juan Fernández* is *Palinurus Frontalis*, a species which has no common name in English but which is referred to, along with several other species within its group, as the spiny lobster, rock lobster or marine crayfish. Why the genus was named after Aeneas' helmsman I do not know – except perhaps because Palinurus fell into the sea when he dozed off on the job.

The pair mainly worked in silence. They regularly spent several days alone together, and seemed not to feel the need for verbal communication. They were either concentrating on catching things or far away on their own private oceans; the first mate didn't address a single word to me during the long day we spent in the small boat.

When we moved out into the ocean a violent swell tossed the *Norma Hortensia* into the air. I clamped my jaws together. Several waves broke over us. I turned my head away from

Alejandro and swallowed hard. We were trying to spot the floats of a missing cage, and twisted around fruitlessly. My stomach contracted urgently.

When we headed back to calmer water, Alejandro started talking about lunch. Even the word made my throat go into spasm. I lay down in a snug hole under the prow and watched two rosy *langostas* vibrating in the pot. Twenty minutes later Alejandro split one in half with a chopper which looked like a murder weapon and placed it in front of me, bright white flesh and gooey brown entrails gleaming in the pink case. The men licked out their shells and set about a flat black fish they had fried on a griddle. I lay back on my bed, where I remained for the next few hours, snoozing (this was not respite, as I suffered two-second dreams in which I was suspended by my feet from the top of a tall building) and occasionally calling out questions in an attempt to allay suspicion. I was not sick.

Another problem defined itself. I was desperate to go to the loo. I considered various strategies, but they all risked capsizing the vessel. Although I tried to focus on desert landscapes, the desert seemed a very long way away; it's not easy to think of dry things when you are surrounded by thousands of miles of water.

It was eight o'clock when we got back. We had been out for thirteen hours. I quickly paid for a *langosta* to take to Rowena and Simon and ran off.

At dinner that evening the patrons of the café were gripped by consternation over the fate of my gift. They weren't used to selling their crustaceans to real consumers – usually they sent them off in boxes to anonymous wholesalers. The entire village mobilized in its anxiety about what the foreigner was going to do with her *langosta*. They were afraid it would die in the carpetbag on its way to the continent. Eventually, exhausted by the toll this was exacting upon my Spanish, I agreed to cook it straightaway in my cabin. A green nylon net sock was immediately produced for the purpose. I considered burying the *langosta* in a deep hole when they were all asleep. But I did not do this. I cooked it, and I was very grateful to it for not squealing as it died.

I woke with burnt and swollen eyelids, presumably the result of falling asleep in the boat. I looked like a *langosta*. It had rained in the night, and my newly washed clothes were damp even though I had left them under the roof of my balcony. I had no others, so after making a pot of tea I tried to dry a pair of knickers over the gas flame. They soon caught fire, inevitably, and Manolo appeared at the window to see me brandishing a pair of flaming pants. Another man on another, larger island might have interpreted this as a gesture of feminist solidarity; but not Manolo.

The Frenchmen arrived at the window next. I had them in to share the tea. The grief-stricken one asked me if I had plans for other expeditions, after Chile. At the time I was plotting a sojourn in the South Seas, and when I told him he said, 'Would you mind if I came with you?'

I thought about Selkirk as I prepared to leave. He had been roughly my age when he arrived on his island, and he lived alone there, mainly eating goat flesh, for four years and four months. When the *Duke* and *Duchess* – both Bristolian ships – dropped anchor in February 1709 there was a famous seaman aboard called William Dampier who knew Selkirk and could vouchsafe for his skills as a sailor. So Selkirk went home.

He had taken a Bible onto Más a Tierra, and on his return was often quoted as saying that he 'believed himself a better Christian while in this solitude than ever he was before, or than, he was afraid, he should ever be again'. This realization didn't stop him drinking and whoring his way around Bristol and London for quite some time. (He also said, 'I am now worth 800 pounds, but shall never be so happy, as when I was not worth a farthing.') When he went home to Scotland he built a kind of cave in his parents' back garden, and down in Bristol he was taken to court for assault. In the end he had to go to sea again; there was a kind of unappeasable unrest within him. On that voyage, he died.

There had been others before him. A reputable account exists of a man called Will from the Mosquito Coast who was abandoned on Juan Fernández by privateers in 1681 and picked up three years later by the *Bachelor's Delight*. William Dampier was there on that occasion too, and he wrote a touching memoir of Will's reunion with another Mosquito man who rowed ashore from the ship to greet him. Similarly, a story was handed down about a survivor of a shipwreck, many years before Will, who lived on the island for five years before he too was rescued. It isn't surprising that they were all rescued: the archipelago was sometimes used as a refitting station after the trip around the Horn.

Defoe, writing machine *par excellence*, transformed Selkirk's story; it was even relocated thousands of miles away, to a more exotic island somewhere east of Trinidad. He extended Selkirk's stay to twenty-eight years, and gave him Man Friday. But one sentence he wrote for Crusoe could have been Selkirk's epitaph: 'I, that was born to be my own destroyer ...'

On my second day on the island I had lost my watch; it had fallen off on the way up a mountain, and I was sorry, as it had a sentimental association. It was valuable, too, and would have raised more cash in Santiago than several hundred *langostas*. As I picked up the carpetbag to board the boat to the airstrip a woman came running up, breathing heavily and holding something out to me.

'I found this in the forest. It must be yours.'

*

Besides two hundred *langostas*, four islanders were flying to Santiago with me. Watching the plane land, they said,

'Good, it's Figueroa.'

'What,' I said, 'can you tell who the pilot is just by looking at the plane coming in?'

'Of course,' they replied, as if I were foolish.

One of them was a Jehovah's Witness. Two-and-three quarter hours of enforced company suited her purpose nicely. I noticed that the other three soon feigned sleep, and the pilot kept his earphones clamped on. Shortly after boarding he had indicated the in-flight facilities with a wave of his hand: a bottle of Johnny Walker wedged behind his seat. I availed myself of this service, and the Jehovah's Witness fell silent, realizing that she was looking at a lost cause.

Chapter Seven

I believe in Chile and in her destiny. Other men will survive this bitter and grey moment ... sooner than you think avenues shall again be opened down which free man shall march towards a better society ... These are my last words. I am convinced that my sacrifice shall not be in vain. I am convinced that at least it shall serve as a moral judgment on the felony, cowardice and treason that lay waste our land.

Salvador Allende, 11 September 1973

I went to visit another Nerudian house while I was still in Santiago, my mid-journey base, and Rowena came with me. It was the most famous one, in Isla Negra, a coastal village a couple of hours' drive away. The population of Santiago shifts westwards during February and colonizes the coast, which we met at Algarrobo where men were gutting fish on trestle tables on the beach in front of the summer houses and the yacht club, eyed by a large statue of Jesus proclaiming optimistically that he would make them fishers of men.

At Isla Negra we drank coffee at a *hostería* festooned with bougainvillea. A poster in the bar displayed a big photograph of the poet Vicente Huidobro. Neruda would have hated that

– they were terrible enemies. I wondered if that was the tavern immortalized by Antonio Skármeta in his novel and film *Ardiente paciencia* (Burning Patience), which is about a postman in Isla Negra with only one client (Neruda), poetry, and the events of 1973, when the postman was taken away and the poet died; and it is about the power of ordinary people to survive, to overcome and to hope.

The house was built on a high outcrop of rock, overlooking the Pacific. Neruda had a collection there of golden-haired figureheads culled from shipyards. He loved to surround himself with beautiful things, and carried it off with such style; he had a fine aesthetic sensibility which I couldn't help reflecting is often absent from his poems. The guide, referring reverentially to Don Pablo, waved his hand at numerous framed photographs around the house, and in all of them Neruda bore a striking resemblance to Nabokov. As if he were aware of it he had framed a small collection of butterflies.

To the south one resort village melted into the next, and in Cartagena I forced Rowena to climb with me high above the plethora of shabby boarding-houses and cheap cafés to find Vicente Huidobro's tomb. He died in 1948, and had chosen for his grave a solitary spot overlooking the dusty green hills and the ocean and surrounded by iridescent violet thistles. It also overlooked the Isla Negra peninsula, on which Nerudian pilgrims converged in their hundreds every day. I hoped he couldn't see it from wherever he was.

That evening it was warm and clear in Santiago with a light breeze and a brilliantly blue sky even at eight o'clock at night. I met Pepe. A small group of his friends had planned a special dinner in my honour, and we got on a crowded bus and headed south, towards the *poblaciones* where hundreds of thousands of poor Chileans cling to the urban conglomeration.

The friends lived in a five-storey tenement block, and in front of it a pile of plastic rubbish sacks had been ripped open, spilling their glistening innards onto the street. A smiling man in shorts opened the door, and he kissed me on both cheeks. I saw his wife behind him, picking children's toys off the floor. When we went in, a tray of long pisco sours appeared, and we drank them wedged into the kitchen while Enrique, the man in shorts, prepared three large fish. I could see through an open door that the couple shared a single bed, and that their child slept in the same room. Two more people arrived, arms full of pale orange melons, and the fish were dispatched to the oven.

Conversation turned, as it often did, to the international status of Chile. Everyone always wanted to know what we of the West thought of the country, and it was hard to tell them that the majority of the West never thought of it at all. I often thought that I noticed a kind of national insecurity and identity crisis. Relentless foreign influence in almost all sectors of society presumably contributed to it. Victor Jara, a leftist folk singer murdered in the National Stadium a few days after the coup, said this: 'The cultural invasion is like a leafy tree which prevents us from seeing our own sun, sky and stars.' After a newspaper ran a small piece about Jara's death, the authorities banned his name from the media. But they couldn't obliterate his spirit. A day or two later, an unknown employee at the television studios inserted a few bars of Jara's '*La Plegaria*' (The Prayer) over the soundtrack of a US film.

After dinner pisco was supplanted by wine and tobacco by marijuana (most Chileans I met seemed to have a little bag of the latter about their person). They took off Pink Floyd and put on Chilean blues, and two people danced. Later Pepe began reciting a Neruda poem, and the others joined in. They knew it by heart. I couldn't think of a poem which all the guests at a dinner party in London would know. Pepe and Enrique and their friends were all leftists, and Neruda had given them hope; he was able to raise their souls above their suffering. He affirmed their identity, too, and made them feel their dreams were valid, dreamt through long years of austerity and exploitation, a rosary of broken promises. Neruda had been an inspiration to many people, not only in Chile. He spoke for the continent. When he was awarded the Nobel Prize he was cited by the Swedish Academy for 'a poetry that with the action of an elemental force brings alive a continent's destiny and dreams'. Che Guevara always carried two books in his duffel bag, and one was Neruda's *Canto general*. He used to read it to his guerillas at night in the Sierra Maestra. Neruda gave them something to cherish, in the Bolivian mountains, and in their tenement blocks.

I liked the idea of him so much that it took me a long time to admit to myself that I didn't think he was a very good poet. Once I'd read more of his prose I decided I didn't like him much, either. He was tremendously keen on himself, and had a dubious attitude towards women. He could be amusing (in mid-sentence, in his *Memoirs*, he slips in, '. . . Hitler, the Nixon of that era . . .') and, on isolated occasions, painfully moving. He wrote about his grief at the death of his friend Alberto Rojas Giménez, another Chilean poet. It was a particularly searing grief, as Neruda was away in Spain at the time. He describes taking a tall candle to an empty church and sitting watching the flame, drinking a bottle of white wine and feeling that although he didn't believe, the 'silent ceremony' brought him closer to his friend.

Neruda was committed to the idea that a writer should be interested in truth, and that it was more important than style. His poems are not lean; they are fat. He paints word pictures, sometimes with great charm, of things you and I recognize, both from the inner world and the outer, but he does not compress the meaning of language until it vibrates, or take you where you have never been. But a great poet – a Hopkins, say – wouldn't have been much good to them, night after grim slum night.

This is what the exiled Argentinian newspaper editor and writer Jacobo Timerman wrote:

> The common destiny of lovers in Latin America is to return again and again to Pablo Neruda. He accompanied us from our first kisses; he helped us to get through, with sensuality, our early adolescence; he was with us during our first major political upheaval – the civil war, the fall of the Spanish Republic, and the fascist inferno that followed. With Neruda we were able to grasp and understand the earthy romance and magic of Latin America ... Not even the bad poems ... could diminish in any way the presence of Neruda in our dreams and our romances. No particle of our sensibility could be separated from the poet. His words and his rhythms will forever be the only expression that we Latin Americans have when our heart overflows with love for another human or with love of the universe.

Timerman was an exceptionally cultured man.

'This is what you need to know of our country,' said Enrique, sliding another cassette into the machine and passing me the case. The label said Violeta Parra, and showed a bad drawing of a woman with large eyes and long black hair.

'Now our culture is to consume,' he said. 'But this is what we were, and we still know it. She sings our north, our south, our centre.'

What she was singing about was pain and betrayal.

Although he was by now quite drunk, I was struck by the words 'our north,' 'our south' and 'our centre' from a man who had barely left the central valley. I had, in my ignorance, looked at the shape of the country, considered the massive social, economic and climatic differences between the north and the south and concluded that there couldn't be much of a national consciousness. But the reality was that their sense of nationality bound them together as closely as if the country were a perfect circle.

'Violeta, Neruda and *La Gabriela*, these are the ones who express what we are,' said Enrique's wife, swaying slightly. 'Their work is an expression of our culture – our real culture.'

When I left, Enrique stood at the door.

'This country, it has many problems. We want to be more like you. But underneath there is pride. Sometimes it's difficult for us to find it now, that's all, because there's so much junk on top.'

I had been invited to stay in the country for a weekend, and I was pleased to get out of the city again, as Santiago was oppressively hot, and the choking smog had thickened. It was also an opportunity to experience a very different side of Chilean life from everything I had seen up until then.

The bus south west to Peñaflor was too hot. I got off at the red bridge, as I had been instructed, and left the tarmac behind, following a track into a green and sun-flooded valley. An empty corn truck picked me up, and I stood up in the back as it lumbered up a steep dirt road, great bowers of eucalyptus hanging over my head. The flat, squared floor of the central valley shone out, and the Andean foothills beyond it quivered.

The Mallarauco valley was transformed during the last quarter of the nineteenth century by an innovative and energetic landowner called Patricio Larrain Gandarillas. By tunnelling through a hill he built a canal which fed off the Mapocho river, and it irrigated the land for miles. This feat of engineering took him twenty years. He brought over expertise from the European Alps, and the workers dug from both sides of the hill. The locals still tell the story that the two teams were only a few inches out when they met. It was polluted water now, as it ran down from Santiago, but it still watered the land all right.

I stayed with the canal-builder's grand-daughter-in-law, a stately Englishwoman from Kent who married a Chilean fifty years ago and shocked his parents by wearing trousers. When I arrived she was sitting under the front porch, reading the *Guardian Weekly* with a large red dog asleep under her chair. She had invited me to stay whenever I liked, but I hadn't told her what day I was coming, and as she didn't have a phone she wasn't really expecting me. Pepe, who had introduced me to her a week before in a café in Bellavista, Santiago's bohemian quarter, had laughed when I had told him I was worried about just turning up.

'Don't be so English!' he said.

The ancestral farmhouse had adobe walls a foot thick, spongy high beds, heavy, creaky wooden furniture and an abundance of assorted books, paintings and pieces of tarnished old silver. It was roughly a hundred years old, typical of a period when there were huge fortunes in Chile. The flaky turquoise swimming pool was decorated with a child's white handprints, and around it the estate flourished with bending trees of fruit and avocados, bushes of berries, thick stalks of corn, a citrus grove and tall red hot pokers.

The châtelaine was exceptionally hospitable; she ignored her guests most of the time, which was actually quite refreshing. She was a widow, and had embraced Chile, for better or worse, like a marriage vow. On the first evening she interrogated me about Britain, as exiles usually do. Talking about the state of it made both of us depressed.

Grandchildren and dogs roamed around unchecked and unmatched cane chairs with stained cushions, open books and crumpled articles of clothing idled in lush long grass. Houseguests appeared, and others vanished. We ate corn and potato stews, tomato and basil salads and slabs of dark pink watermelon at wooden tables on the banks of the river, shaded by willows. Conversations broke out spontaneously in the cool kitchen or the hushed library. I thought of novels set in the 1930s peopled by the British upper classes. This was what life had been like for the old landowning families of the central valley. No wonder they didn't want it to change. It was very agreeable.

When I went back to the city it was on the daily bus out of the valley, an old boneshaker which had been rattling up and down the steep Mallarauco roads for years. Next to the sign displaying fares there was a yellowing list of prices for other items passengers might wish to bring with them. These included a bed (450 pesos), a gas cooker (350), a television (250) and a sack of flour (150).

Up in the north I had met a woman who was organizing local branches of the *Alianza*, an up-and-coming alliance of Greens and Humanists, both fashionable words in the Chilean political vocabulary. She had urged me to call a colleague of hers when I was in Santiago who was one of four vice presidents of the *Alianza*, a candidate in the forthcoming municipal elections and a feminist to boot. The colleague's name was Sara, too, and I met her in a crowded coffee bar near the party office opposite Santa Lucía hill.

She was exactly my age, and I liked her at once. She had in her hand the proofs of an article she had written about the background to the Chilean women's movement. This latter had been nourished during the fight for suffrage in national elections, but when that was granted in 1949 the victory failed to lead to wider reforms or even to begin to challenge male ideas about the role and value of women in public life, and the women's movement disintegrated. I wondered where it had got to after another forty years.

134

'Still very fragmented,' she said after a long pause, during which she stirred her empty coffee cup. 'And to a certain extent the movement has withdrawn into itself since the dictatorship fell. Its role for all those years was to promote the notion of non-violence, and now it has to reconsider its position. But there is a good network, yes, with a strong working-class constituency.'

(Most organizations with any kind of social concerns were grappling with the question of what to do now they had achieved what they had campaigned for over so many years.)

She had hope for a better future for Chilean women.

'Though not for our generation. The men still had a very *machista* upbringing. But younger ones can see the flexibility of roles. Yes, I am hopeful.'

I wasn't sure I could have been, in her position. There were three women senators and seven *diputadas* (members of the lower house), and although Chilean politicians had recognized that it was fashionable to show themselves to be pro-women and almost all the parties of the centre and left had instituted women's sections, the trend had translated itself into reforms that were purely cosmetic. Pinochet had appointed numerous women mayors, but Sara dismissed them as 'honorary men'; that, in the political context, was at least a concept I was familiar with. A recent public opinion poll among both sexes had revealed considerable resistance to women in power at parliamentary level (they liked them being on municipal councils, though; that was a projection of the domestic role, running the local scene like the house, no really big decisions involved). During my visit a drama was being played out involving the eventually aborted presidential campaign of Evelyn Matthei, an eminently capable politician. I heard many sexist comments about Matthei, even from leaders of her own National Renewal party. Although some male politicians would deny it, the whole complex business of

135

her failed campaign demonstrated to many liberals that the country simply wasn't ready to allow women into the upper reaches of power.

I was supposed to be leaving the luxuries of the metropolis for the southern half of the country, but there was always a reason to stay another day, and then another. It wasn't that I didn't want to go – I felt a leap of excitement whenever I thought of the glaciers and the fjords of the far south – but Santiago was a cornucopia, and I was very happy.

Pepe and I went to Valparaíso, Chile's second city and first port, only two hours from the capital. The first building I saw there was an old hat shop with elderly assistants in white coats serving at vast polished wood cabinets and counters, round hat boxes piled on shelves behind them twenty-five feet up to the ceiling. We took a tram past the magnificent pink customs house on the quay and rococo houses built in the nineteenth century during Valparaíso's glory days as one of the leading ports on the Pacific rim (though most of these houses were reconstructed after an earthquake in 1906). The former government house, a grand and elegant confection, had been turned into naval offices and in the square in front of it Arturo Prat, most revered naval hero, was buried under an elaborate monument.

I had heard the port called Pancho (the familiar version of Francisco). A sailor in a café where we stopped for a late breakfast told us that the spire of San Francisco's church was the first thing seamen saw when their ships sailed into the bay. Pepe, however, thought it was a reference to Sir Francis Drake, 'your pirate'.

'He wasn't a pirate,' I said. Pepe opened his eyes very wide and laughed. He was laughing at me.

I had absorbed all my history in Britain; I had the idea that Drake was a hero. In reality, his conduct up and down the

Chilean and Peruvian coasts was so barbarous that his name entered the language as a synonym for terror and destruction. A nineteenth-century traveller records, 'The mothers on the coast, when trying to hush their babes, cry, "*aquí viene Draake*"' [sic] – Here comes Drake. It wasn't just him. The British had recently transformed themselves into an ocean-going nation, and the close relationship that existed between trade and violent theft failed to dampen the admiration in which the heroic expansion was held at home. By the 1560s, before Drake, routine plunder of places the Elizabethans had never heard of was apparently *de rigueur* – especially if they were Spanish. Some history books call the privateers armed, privately owned vessels commissioned for 'war service' by a government; in fact they frequently operated as officially sanctioned looters. Three centuries after Drake, Darwin travelled extensively within Chile during his expedition on HMS *Beagle*, and he tells a story which illustrates how profoundly English pirates had impinged upon the Chileans. He heard of an old woman who, at a dinner in Coquimbo in the north, remarked how wonderfully strange it was that she should have lived to dine in the same room as an Englishman, because she remembered very well that on two separate occasions when she was a girl at the mere cry '*Los Ingleses!*' everyone hastily packed what they could and fled to the mountains.

There were so many British in Valparaíso during the nineteenth century that it was often referred to as a British colony. The city's importance in the establishment of the Chilean Jewish community is a lesser known aspect of its past. There are probably not many more than half a million Jews on the whole continent (and over half of those are in Argentina) but, in Chile at least, they played a vital part in the modernization of the country.

Despite the Valparaíso settlement in the nineteenth century

and an influx of Jews after the Californian gold rush, by about 1910 there were still fewer than 500 in Chile. During the inter-war period, however, approximately 15,000 Jews settled in the country, mostly from Eastern Europe and Germany. Few Chileans appreciate the role these immigrants and their descendants played and continue to play. Not only were most people, in my experience, anti-Semitic, but they were openly so; even otherwise liberal types paraded a distinctly un-raised consciousness regarding Jews with equanimity. This was a facet of a broadly Catholic society within which cultural pluralism was only a shade more visible than in Iran. Later in the trip I asked a well-known Jewish MP about this.

'You can be a Jew here,' he said candidly, 'but you can't be Jewish. The culture is so powerful that it occupies the entire space. Society doesn't see diversity – it doesn't see anything except itself. There's no such thing as multi-culturalism in Chile.'

Above the flat strip of land occupied by offices, venerable buildings, old-fashioned shops and the straggling port, a series of steep hills revealed an entirely different Valparaíso. We took an odd single-carriage funicular, and afterwards walked up uneven steps through quiet cat-filled streets where washing was drying outside multi-coloured houses jammed together in aleatory confusion.

Neruda called Valparaíso 'a filthy rose', and bought a house there. He was fascinated by the sea. Disliking him and his poetry didn't mean that I disliked his houses. On the contrary – and furthermore I had a strong feeling that I would be leaving the picture unfinished if I didn't find his third home. It was concealed at the end of a narrow passage up in the peaceful hinterland, next to a narrow pink 1930s theatre. The façade of this theatre was pure art deco, 'Teatro Mauri' written at the top in angular black and silver letters, and as the old stage door was ajar, I tiptoed in, hoping to spy on a rehearsal.

It had been turned into a dog biscuit factory.

He had persuaded two friends to buy half of the house – called La Sebastiana – and one of them was a ceramicist who used uncut pebbles like a mosaic. Neruda had examples of her work in all his homes, and in La Sebastiana he had got her to copy an old map of Patagonia and Chilean Antarctica. The house was tall and thin, and Neruda had made his part of it a jumble of cluttered and brightly coloured nooks, bulges and unorthodox shapes, as if he were trying to copy Valparaíso itself.

The numerous Argentinians strolling in the streets vexed Pepe. All over Chile, people regularly launched into the Argentinian-bashing routine for my education, and it was always backed up by confused historical data centring on 1878, when Argentina 'stole' most of Patagonia (in reality a treaty was signed). This episode had burned itself into the national consciousness, and it was trotted out with grossly exaggerated rollings of 'r's to mock the Argentinian accent. The mutual antipathy reached back a long way. I had read about it in nineteenth-century editions of *The Times*. Even then the Argentinians had considered their country pre-eminent on the continent, and I detected more than a trace of an inferiority complex on the part of the Chileans, though I generally kept this opinion to myself. For many years the Argentinian economy had been vastly superior to that of its thin neighbour. That was presumably why the Chileans only looked down on the Bolivians, and didn't hate them: the Bolivian economy was quite a joke even by the demanding standards of South America.

We ate lunch in an old restaurant near the port. It had dark wood panelling and embossed, peeling wallpaper, a high ceiling with two large whirring fans, colossal gilt-framed mirrors, a tiled floor and tables draped in starched white linen

139

with tiny darns. The barrels behind the bar breathed a winy smell over the room, and the waiters wore bow ties and white jackets. It was the kind of place to drink a bottle of heavy red wine and snooze behind newspapers in the lounge after lunch. With unusual restraint we did not do this, but we did eat a bowl of especially pungent shellfish, and afterwards, full and content, we lay down on the grass in a palmy park next to the monstrous new parliament building. An old man in a cream jacket, as old fashioned as everything else in Valparaíso, offered to take a photograph of us with a box camera.

I had intended to visit a museum, but it was hot, and the perfume of the flowers in the park was like a narcotic; the museum was altogether too much trouble.

'Where did parliament sit before this was built, then?' I asked Pepe.

He turned to look at me quizzically.

'Well, there wasn't one for seventeen years.'

He often came out with prosaic remarks which made the horror of the junta more real than any academic analysis I read. Once, I said that I was anxious to get back to London in time for the election. He had looked blank, and screwed up his eyes.

'Well,' I went on, 'don't you feel at election time that you wouldn't want to miss it?'

'For almost all my adult life there haven't been any elections.'

The Vicaría de la Solidaridad was located on the top two floors of an unmarked stone building next to the cathedral in the main square of Santiago, and its doors were always open. When I walked through them, early in the afternoon on a hot Tuesday in January, I found the cloisters hung with appliqué collages incorporating messages about peace and justice, and black-and-white photographs of young men, tiny on the massive walls, captioned, '*Juan Luis, where are you?*' The Vicaría was an institution born in adversity, and it had been David against Pinochet's Goliath; it was a symbol of right against wrong. There wasn't much for the Church to be proud of in modern Chile, but it had the Vicaría. Its work in assisting ordinary Chileans and organizing their legal defence during the dictatorship had been of incalculable value.

The Church had not consistently taken the victims' side. In 1973, the bishops' individual reactions to the coup cast some light on the officially neutral line they had taken during the socialist experiment. On the day of Allende's death, Bishop Francisco Valdés of Osorno wrote a public prayer of thanksgiving, giving God the credit for having freed Chile 'from the worst clutches of lies and evil that have ever plagued poor humanity'. A retired Archbishop of La Serena presented his episcopal ring to the junta. There were others. I wondered how Catholics whose sons and daughters had electrodes clamped to their heads and genitals as their spiritual fathers thanked the Lord reconciled themselves to their religion.

The bishops did explicitly condemn violence, especially as the extent of the horror was revealed; generally, nonetheless, the hierarchy agreed to keep fairly quiet in return for the freedom to do what it wanted.

One official move, however, was of superlative importance. Almost immediately after the coup the Church set up a cooperative venture with the Protestants, Greek Orthodox and Jews. This led to the Committee of Cooperation for Peace in Chile, known by its acronym Copachi, which offered legal help and economic aid to people suffering under the junta. This committee helped well over 10,000 Chileans. Pinochet inevitably asked Cardinal Silva to close Copachi. He did so, in December 1975, but in January 1976 set up the Vicaría de la Solidaridad, which was exclusively Catholic and part of the Church – so Pinochet couldn't touch it, at least openly.

The dictator meanwhile clung to his belief that it was he and God against the Marxists. Like Maradona, he claimed 'the hand of God' was with him, and in his 1988 campaign he used the allegory of Christ and Barabbas to portray the choice before the voters (he was not Barabbas). When a cardinal with a conservative reputation was chosen to replace Silva, Lucía Hirart, the First Lady, said, 'Our prayers have been answered'.

Though formal ties were maintained, during the later years relations between the Church and the junta became increasingly strained. This made the Church more popular with the left, and much less popular with the rich, who once saw it as their own province. It was clear to me as I travelled down the country that this polarization still prevails. Intellectuals of the right used to love to tell me, with some bitterness, how the Vicaría had been infiltrated by Communists. I was talking once to an upper-class banker about an encounter with a priest. Before I had said anything about the priest's views, the banker asked sharply, 'Was he a Communist?'

The director I met at the Vicaría was a gimlet-eyed man in his early forties. He was immediately engaging. When I asked about the Vatican, he said, 'Pablo gave us real help. Juan Pablo, well, the Vatican's priorities are different now. It wants more explicit evangelization, emphasizing individual morality, not so much the world we live in ... The Chilean Church is helping us a lot, though the conservative bishops don't let us work in their dioceses. Luckily there aren't many of them.'

A poster on the peeling office wall said, '*No a l'impunidad*' ('No impunity') in lime green letters. *Impunidad* was an inflammatory word. The Rettig Commission (properly called the National Commission for Truth and Reconciliation) had been set up by the new government to document human rights abuse during the dictatorship, and the Vicaría had provided much of the information. It was one thing, however, to document the crimes, and another to try the accused.

Although several trials were working their way through the courts, the government was moving slowly, and its efforts were frequently stalled or stymied by the military courts, the Supreme Court (the judges of which had been appointed for life by Pinochet) or the 1978 amnesty law. This law, which applied to all 'authors, accomplices or concealers' of politically connected crimes between 1973 and 1978, could not be annulled, as Pinochet appointees still controlled the Senate. I had met someone who lived in the same block of flats as a known torturer. If the two met in the lift, the torturer would travel up to the top floor, where my friend's flat was, and then descend alone, so he wouldn't be obliged to reveal his own floor.

I asked if the government was afraid to confront the powerful right wing.

'*Miedo* [fear] is too strong a word. But the majority of the crimes were committed by military personnel, so the government has to weigh up the cost of annoying them with prosecutions. Political instability is a high cost, very high. The government wants it all behind it.'

Did he have hope? He closed his eyes and pushed his head back in anticipation of a sneeze which never came.

'I have no hope that the torturers will be punished. Our democracy is weak. But punishment was never our principal objective. That was and is to defend the victims. Of course, punishment is one way of making amends, but it is equally, if not more important to ensure that the experience is not repeated, hence our educative role. For this I have hope, yes, I do.'

The question of impunity for the perpetrators of the crimes of the dictatorship was a major issue – perhaps *the* major issue. I asked Jorge Schaulsohn about it when I went to talk to him the next day in his twenty-first floor office in downtown Santiago. He was an MP for Santiago Central, and a leader of the Party for Democracy (PPD), a new progressive party on the centre-left of the governing coalition. As a young radical activist during the dictatorship he had been sent off to the US by his father, also a politician, and he returned the epitome of the exile caught between the two realities of Chile and the United States. He was intelligent, committed, pragmatic and a man of integrity; Schaulsohn was the kind of person who gives you hope for the continent.

'You can't apply the standards of a fully fledged democracy here. We can't annul the amnesty law, and that's that.'

'Doesn't that weigh heavily on your conscience?'

'Not at all. I have to decide what's best: to take the line you are implying, and pursue the guilty, or to maintain a stable society and work for the betterment of the people within it. We can't have both.'

His confidence has been supported by events, at least to a certain extent. In January 1993 Congress impeached a Supreme Court judge, and shortly before that a military court ruled that the amnesty law did not preclude certain kinds of investigation against the torturers. On 3 February 1993 the *Guardian*'s excellent correspondent in Chile, Malcolm Coad, published a story in which he said, 'Chile has won an international reputation as an example of how a nation can come to terms with a legacy of repression and abuse without tearing itself apart.' He quoted José Zalaquett, former deputy general secretary of Amnesty International, who said, 'Chile is now widely seen as the country in transition from dictatorship where social peace has been achieved most completely and most rapidly.'

After I had left Chile, in November 1992, the Vicaría closed itself down. In its official statement, published in several newspapers, it acknowledged that there was still work to be done, but asserted that state institutions and secular organizations must take up the baton. It was a highly symbolic move which marked the end of an era, but – as many who opposed the closure of the Vicaría said – it did not mean that the work or the healing were complete. A quasi-replacement Vicariate for Social Action was established, to work in the field on behalf of the Church.

'We don't want to relinquish the Church's role as a champion of human rights,' said the director I had spoken to when I telephoned him from London to ask about the closure. 'In 1973 the poor didn't know what human rights were; they certainly didn't know that they had any. It's imperative that we continue to educate, so that if it happens again . . .'

Germán Claro, now Mr Fixit, invited me down to his hacienda, suggesting that it was well placed for the first night of my trek southwards, and it was this which finally propelled me into action. He decided to get out of town for a few days and come with me, and I was glad.

He told me we would be leaving at eight in the morning, so I got up early, packed and said a grateful goodbye to Rowena and Simon over breakfast. Our departure was delayed by ten-and-a-half hours – a modest discrepancy, in South American chronology. In the late afternoon I wondered if we were going to leave at all, as one of the main reasons for the delay was a convivial lunch which showed no sign of reaching its natural end. We got away at six when Germán's father telephoned the restaurant to say he was about to drive to the hacienda, and did we want a lift.

'You can do the talking,' said Germán as he got into the back of the car, where he immediately lay down and went to sleep. Germán *père* was a charming, suave and very hand-some man who had enjoyed a career as a captain of industry before devoting himself to his equally handsome hacienda. His family had owned it since the King of Spain bestowed a vast tract of the central valley upon a mayor of Santiago in the sixteenth century. They were distant cousins of the British Queen. I was moderately anxious about what we might find to talk about; whether the shameful quantity of champagne we had drunk at lunch increased my anxiety or decreased it I cannot say, but it was all right, as far as I can remember, and by the time we were out of the inner city I was feeling comfortable. Don Germán had a twinkle in his eye but an otherwise inscrutable manner.

We passed Rancagua, capital of the Sixth Region, at about eighty miles an hour. It was the site of the largest underground copper mine in the world, owned by Don Germán's family until the late nineteenth century. The rest of the landscape resembled an enormous market garden. Several mighty US fruit producers had built outposts of their empire along the highway, impressive white constructions fronting acres of healthy, well-watered crops extending to the foothills. If it weren't for the height of the Andes it could have been a *Provençal* scene, painted in dusty greens and purples and washed in evening sunshine.

Germán the younger woke up when we stopped at a crowded diner which served (claimed father and son) the best hot sandwiches between Santiago and Tierra del Fuego, and anyway they had always stopped there, since Germán Arturo (as my friend was called to avoid confusion) was a little boy; it was a family tradition. The two of them looked alike, but they were very different, in temperament and style, and their relationship was measured. I kept quiet, as I did not want to disturb its equilibrium.

The hacienda was called Los Lingues, after a type of tree. It was almost dark when we arrived. A servant showed me to my room, which was furnished with eighteenth-century prints, old lace bedspreads, heavy chests of drawers and antique silver. I opened the shutters, and looked out onto a veranda and a shadowy flowerbed smelling of roses. A second flunkey arrived with a silver tray which he placed on my dressing-table. On it were a bottle of Campari, a jug of freshly squeezed orange juice, a bowl of ice, a tall glass and a single yellow rose.

I poured myself a drink and sat in a velvet armchair facing the veranda. I had apparently arrived at the Chilean equivalent of a Bavarian schloss, half-spun out of fairy tales. Taking a handful more ice from the bowl, a fine bone china antique from France, I wondered how many times over the next months I would try to recapture this delicious luxuriance in a cold, wet tent.

The breath of Chilean colonialism filled the *salons*; there was no mistaking it. Germán Arturo and I ate alone in the seventeenth-century dining room at the candlelit mahogany table which could have sat thirty. He wore a tuxedo and I wore a cocktail dress borrowed from Rowena. The family coat of arms hung on the wall, and the table was laid with old French crystal, hand-printed plates and crested silver salvers. White-gloved waiters serving delectable food and a selection of wines from the 4000-odd bottles in the cellar remained inscrutable in front of an expansive Germán, still on a roll from lunch.

When I opened my bedroom door the following morning a table in the courtyard in front of it had been laid for breakfast, a small urn of flowers in the middle. Doña Marie Elena, wife and mother of the Germáns, was already sitting down, and she waved me to join her. She was a charming, forthright and extremely Catholic woman whom I liked very much, and she had already adopted me as a kind of protégée, which meant that she frequently felt obliged to grip my arm and deliver some ruthless truth. (Once, she stated plainly that I was too fat.) She always had staff flitting around her. There were several hundred staff, as the hacienda operated as a fruit-producer, a horse-breeding centre and an exclusive country house hotel, and there was always something going on, though it tended to do so quietly. Only the peacocks and Mr Fixit disturbed the peace.

I rode one of the horses later; they were all fine Aculeos with their manes cut short, like Stubbs' horses. Afterwards, Don Germán took me through some of the hacienda's ten thousand acres. He told me that the estate used to be far bigger. It had been split up and expropriated twice, latterly in 1972 during the Allende regime, in two of the many attempts to break the power of the landowners in the central valley.

'It must have been a gruelling period for you,' I said half-heartedly, but he only smiled a small, bitter smile.

The power of the central valley élite, a constant theme of Chilean colonial history, was constructed with the bricks of Spanish empire-building, the *encomiendas*, grants of indigenous men and women who were obliged to pay 'their' *conquistador* (called an *encomendero*) services or tribute in return for patronage, protection and Christian instruction. The Crown did eventually try to abolish or limit these *encomiendas*, but it failed. By the seventeenth century the hacienda had evolved and was established as the predominant social and economic unit of the Chilean central valley; each was a self-contained entity, and a rigid social structure developed around them. Later, *inquilinos* (service tenants) appeared within that structure. It would be difficult to overestimate the extent to which this neofeudal landowner-worker system imposed by the Spaniards has shaped Chilean society. The landowners consolidated their power base in the central valley, initiating a national centralization which was never dislodged, not even as the country extended north and south. It might have been the shape of a tapeworm, but it was as centralized as a wheel.

Feudal tradition was still so entrenched during the nineteenth century that in the 1854 census many *inquilinos* wrote the name of their hacienda in the 'Nationality' box. The clannish élite

148

clung on, but in the twentieth century it became increasingly difficult to ignore the incompatibilities of feudalism and democracy, and by the 1960s land reform was a major issue all over the continent. In Chile the movement was not just a social reform, it was economic too, as the land was desperately under-productive; it was nitrate and copper which had transformed the economy, and agriculture had been neglected. The largest haciendas were divided up. This was a massively controversial business, and revolutionary groups seized land forcibly while the right-wing élite were outraged and centrist politicians struggled to devise effective redistribution.

Frei tried and Allende tried, and to a certain extent the pattern was broken. But the dictatorship reversed their policies, effecting a reconquest of the workers by the élite in a macabre quasi-recreation of the pattern established by the Spaniards in the sixteenth century.

Germán Arturo suggested that we both stay another day or two, and of course I agreed. We played a lot of tennis, and rode the horses, or just tipped our chairs back in the gardens, a servant always positioned behind a bush with an eye on our glasses. We ate our meals outside, at night next to the fountain, around a table lit by three candles in an old gold candelabra. We usually had dinner with Germán's parents. They were delightful company, she very quick in her speech and observations, he laconic and mischievous. At Los Lingues I looked through a window onto a very particular aspect of Chile. Life there was a manifestation of a continuous and very old tradition – the oldest tradition, except for that of the indigenous people. Once or twice someone talked about what had been taken away from them, and how much they had clawed back. I couldn't bring myself to question too closely; among the Chilean upper classes it is the most keenly felt subject. But Los Lingues had survived, and they had survived – they always would.

Chapter Eight

Yes, I regret not having been tougher on the Marxists.

Colonel Manuel Contreras Sepúlveda, Pinochet's Intelligence Chief,
asked in 1989 by a journalist if he had any regrets

When I got up the next day Germán was ready to leave.

'Work,' he said gravely.

One of the many cousins who appeared regularly at Los Lingues was driving south, and he offered me a lift. I packed quickly, we all said goodbye, and that was it – I was off.

I planned to make Curicó my first stop. It was a small town in the central valley only an hour or two further south, and it was at the heart of a major wine region. The cousin dropped me at a turning off the Panamerican and continued his journey alone; I picked up a *colectivo* into town and checked into a hotel. My room had a kind of quilted wallpaper, spongy carpet and no windows, creating the effect of a padded cell. Curicó itself, I discovered when I ventured outside, was old-fashioned and provincial: shopkeepers wore white coats and fetched goods from deep wooden drawers and polished shelves, and a pharmacy where I bought a tube of toothpaste had rows of tall glass jars filled with bright liquids and white powders in its cabinets. It was a world away from Santiago.

I found out where the wineries were, took a small bus through a few miles of fertile agricultural land and turned up at Miguel Torres, a small company which exports more bottles on a pro rata basis than any other Chilean producer. The Miguel Torres team, acknowledged to be innovators in the industry (they were the first to introduce temperature-controlled fermentation to Chile), arrived from Catalonia in 1978 when the military government was freeing up the economy. Many foreign investors followed their lead. Even Baron Eric de Rothschild has his share of the Chilean grape.

A young man with a yellow shirt and a grave expression showed me around the cellars. Beyond the French oak barrels they were storing racks of the much-applauded Torres *méthode champenoise* – the only bottle-fermented Chilean champagne produced in commercial quantities. I had already learnt that there wasn't much of a wine culture amongst domestic consumers in Chile, but champagne appreciation was worse – it was non-existent. I saw from the boxes and tins on the supermarket shelves of the rich districts in Santiago that champagne is perceived as a glamorous status symbol and that packaging is more important than taste, and I searched for a long, long time among the rows of *demi-sec* to find any *brut*.

I walked around Curicó in the early evening, restless and wishing I were back at Los Lingues. It was a shock to be alone again, actually. There were some nice churches, but I wasn't in a church mood. On impulse I went into the offices of *La Prensa*, one of the oldest newspapers in Chile. The editor was thrilled to see a foreign visitor, and showed me round the newsroom.

'We still print with hot metal. But in two months we're changing to a computerized offset system. After ninety-three

151

years, the time has come,' he said with a benign smile.

The hacks shrank behind their manual typewriters and looked hunted.

I was taken to meet Mr Oscar, executive editor and town historian. Mr Oscar sat in splendour in a palatial office on the first floor, surrounded by a set of bound volumes of *La Prensa*. He pulled out one of the books he had written on local history and stroked his neatly trimmed goatee beard.

'Curicó,' he told me enthusiastically, 'is small, but it is like an Italian renaissance republic town – independent and self-contained. Have you seen the square?'

I had. It was edged by sixty palm trees, and there was a curious cast-iron bandstand, raised off the ground by legs ten feet long, with a ladder for the musicians. It was the only one of its kind in Chile (said Mr Oscar) and was copied from New Orleans in 1905.

We got on to earlier history. The Curi people occupied the land before the Spaniards hoovered it up in the eighteenth century. Mr Oscar presented me with a book he had written about this, and wrote a lengthy dedication.

As the national park in the mountains was only fifty miles away, I had assumed the bus journey wouldn't take long. This was a serious misjudgement, and I arrived at my destination after five sweaty and frustrating hours. The trouble began even before we left Curicó, when ninety-seven other people got on the bus (I counted them) including a large group of excitable scouts, pronounced scoots in Spanish, carrying paraffin lamps and their pack banner. A dozen of the ninety-seven sat on the roof, and once we left the Panamerican regular roof-banging indicated that they had dropped something which the hapless driver was required to stop and retrieve.

The road was poor, and our speed slowed to ten miles an

hour. The portion of the landscape I could see through the small area of window uncluttered by scoots or luggage turned from vineyard to forest. It was hot. Several scoots went to sleep in the luggage rack. The frequency with which we stopped was quite incredible, given the absence of any evidence of human life on the road, but I was wedged into my seat and could not observe what, if anything, was going on. A knot of scoots suddenly took an interest in the book I was reading. It was by John Shelby Spong, and it was called *Rescuing the Bible from Fundamentalism*. It was an excellent book, but I had considerable difficulty in conveying this to the scoots, who seemed to think the Bible was the exclusive province of Catholics anyway.

After four hours I saw the stiff green hat of a *carabinero* travelling slowly along the bus. We had arrived at a police control post, and the policeman was checking all ninety-eight identification documents. This was almost too much for the human spirit to bear. As he worked his way towards me, the only non-local on the bus, I heard people sniggering and trying to draw closer (this was not physically possible). He held out his hand for my ID, and, with Kalashnikov delivery, spoke into the hush.

'Where do you live?'

'In England.'

'No – where do you live in Chile?'

'I don't live anywhere. I'm travelling.'

'I insist that you live somewhere.'

I gave him Simon's British Council business card, which exerted his mind for some minutes. After a lot of scribbling in a notebook he shut my passport, and I put out my hand to take it. He slipped it into his top pocket.

'You can have it back when you return.'

I was too hot to argue, especially with ninety-seven pairs of eyes fixed on me and a scoot taking photographs. Later my neighbour told me that the policeman kept my passport because he wanted to make sure I didn't go into Argentina from the park. The fact that it would take me four days on a horse to do so meant that this was an unlikely scenario, but I wondered why he cared where I went anyway.

We were eventually disgorged in a clearing in the foothills flanked by tracts of forest and a volcano. People were rippling around charcoal braziers, tents and small food stalls, and a dozen tall horses scuffed the sandy ground next to a cypress tree. I found the rudimentary hotel, took a single room in one of its two candlelit cabins, and went for a stroll. It was a Saturday night, and everyone under thirty-five in the province apparently headed up there for the weekend.

'Hey, gringa!'

A large, smiling man of about my age loomed towards me.

'Join our party! Look! A gringa in the park!'

I was conveyed towards a small group of people, each one kissed me, and the large man handed me a dagger with which he had speared a piece of meat sliced from a flank suspended over a fire. The whole party was from Molina, the nearest village, and they had brought their tents up for the weekend. The group changed shape like an amoeba as new friends arrived and old ones peeled off; Alfredo, the large man, functioned as a kind of human nucleus, and he shouted and laughed all night, tirelessly producing bottles of cold beer from some cache in a cool box in the bushes. A guitar appeared, and they began to sing. Alfredo leapt up.

'I'm in love! I'm going to get MARRIED!' he shouted.

Everyone shouted back, and it wasn't until we were all dancing in a circle to celebrate the forthcoming event that I realized it was me he intended to wed.

The cabin overlooked the Claro river, and I was woken by two children and a large dog splashing around in it. I decided to go for a walk, and found Alfredo lurking on the bridge. We set off together, and after a few miles climbed down to the waterfall called *Siete Tazas* (Seven Bowls) where the river ran into a stack of seven rock basins in a narrow gorge, and three miles further downstream Alfredo took my hand and led me to a shelf above a bigger waterfall where the river plunged a hundred and fifty feet and trees were growing out of the cliff wall.

The clouds dissolved. I no longer felt homesick for the hacienda, or indeed for anywhere else. We passed a small farm with a white flag flapping from the gate. 'Bread,' said Alfredo, pointing at the flag, and he went in, returning with a large blackened loaf under his arm. There were parrots in the tallest branches of the trees, and with his mouth full of warm fragments of bread Alfredo told me stories, festooned with graphic detail, about the pumas he had seen in the forest during his highly eventful childhood. The park was called Parque Inglés – English Park – by a nameless observer who visited the area in September when the grass was so green and smooth and the trees so luxurious and abundant that the traveller thought he was in England. Alfredo was a great talker. I learnt that he owned a restaurant on the main square of Molina; he even told me the turnover and profits of the business, confident that I would be impressed by his financial status. Would I like to settle in Molina?

'Er, well, I . . .'

'Don't worry, you don't have to make any quick decisions.'

That was a relief.

'We can talk it over this evening.'

When I got back to the cabin I sat with a beer and wrote out the numbers one to thirty on a piece of paper, to plan the month ahead. The only commitment I had was the *rendez-vous* with the two friends from home in a couple of weeks. It was intended as a holiday together; a staging-post for me.

Apart from that, the plan was simply to pick my way south, but as I crossed off the days and wrote little pencil labels of where I might spend them I realized how much ground I had to cover before my Antarctic goal. I had to go.

As there was no bus, I was forced to hitch. Alfredo wouldn't leave me. I waited for two hours on the edge of a makeshift volleyball pitch where twenty people were playing in bare feet. A van emerged from a thicket just as Alfredo went to buy ice-creams, so I never got to say goodbye. But I thought perhaps it was best.

I sat in the back of the open van until we reached the police control post, where I collected my passport from my friend, and down on the Panamerican once more I stood on the tarmac in the early evening sun, still fierce enough to burn. I got a lift to Chillán in a juggernaut carrying twenty-eight tons of iron. As soon as I saw it on the horizon I knew it would stop for me, and I knew it would be slow. I had calculated that I could get to Chillán before dark, but once again I hadn't taken into account the extraordinary slow speeds at which I often moved in Chile. But I found a hotel late at night.

The buildings of Chillán, a colonial town, are modern, like all the buildings in a long portion of southern central Chile, as even if the old ones survived the earthquake of 1939 they were finished off by its successor in 1960. In that year, two hundred miles of Chilean coastline sank six feet into the Pacific. After a day sitting in cafés at the market and dipping my feet in thermal springs near a bleak out-of-season ski resort, I decided to see if I could continue the trip by train. There was nothing to detain me further in the central valley; the landscape I had been travelling through hadn't changed a great deal since the outskirts of Santiago, and I was impatient for the dramatic transformation ahead. I wanted to get to Concepción, a major city a little further on and the start of the south proper.

*

I found out that a train did run from Chillán to Concepción, but everyone thought it was peculiar foreign madness that I should take it in preference to a bus, claiming that it took much longer. How long could it take them to convey me seventy miles?

When I arrived at the station I found the old arched ticket windows boarded up and an employee sitting behind a computer dispensing tickets in a new office. It took seven minutes to issue a ticket: the specially-written programme was so slow it constituted a technological achievement. I wondered if they had done it to emulate the speed of the trains.

The route followed the east bank of the river Bío Bío right up to Concepción. Thick clumps of grass, sprouting between the rusted gauges of a pattern of tracks, revealed the dereliction caused by the dogmatically applied deregulation and self-financing policies of the late 1970s and 1980s. Both freight and passenger rail carriage had declined dramatically since they reached their peak in 1973, and between 1975 and 1985 the number of railway staff had fallen from twenty-six thousand to eight thousand. The network hadn't been administered particularly effectively before the dictatorship, however, and naturally a thin rural population meant that branch lines were expensive to run. One study had shown that it would be cheaper to buy all the villagers in a certain province a car than maintain their rail service.

The river, half a mile wide and streaked with sand flats, was more than a physical feature: it was probably the most potent symbol in Chilean history, for generations constituting the southern boundary of Spanish territory. The *conquistadores* were consistently pushed back up to the Bío Bío by the Mapuche, and the lands to the south were not brought under the control of the governor in Santiago until towards the end of the nineteenth century, after hundreds of years of violent struggle. The previous day I had read a story on the front page of a national newspaper concerning a plan to dam the Bío Bío which was provoking widespread opposition; although the project had become an important symbol of the Chilean green movement, the emotive power of the Bío Bío in the national consciousness was stirring passions well beyond the confines of the environmental lobby.

The Mapuche, a people of the Araucanian tribal group, were the only Amerindians able to resist the Spaniards throughout the long haul of colonialism. Their heroism is enshrined in the sixteenth-century poem *La Araucana* written by the Spaniard Alonso de Ercilla y Zuñiga and cited as America's first epic. Mapuche bravery still functions as an emblem of national pride: Allende spoke of the warrior Lautaro in his first speech as President. But Ercilla's peers and descendants officially sanctioned the mutilation and enslavement of the Mapuche. By 'mutilation' I do not mean that they were wounded in battle. I mean that they had their ears, noses, feet and hands cut off and their eyes gouged out. The Mapuche were systematically deprived of their lands by theft and discriminatory legislation for generations. Little has changed. The majority of Chileans remain indifferent to the distress of the marginalized, impoverished Mapuche and their culture, and to call someone an '*indio*' is a great insult. And actually the Mapuche weren't and aren't warlike by nature. They just happened not to go for the idea of their own genocide.

The mackerel sky melted after Quilacoya, and the sun set over the glassy water. On the near bank a wooden boat crept through the reeds.

The cheap hotel I had intended to stay in at Concepción had apparently dematerialized, and as it was late (the journey had taken four hours) I was compelled to take a room in a more expensive one nearby, optimistically called the Ritz.

Concepción, the country's third city and capital of the major zone of heavy industry, looked, when I left the Ritz the next morning, like a northern French manufacturing town in the 1950s. In the main street, near the hotel, there was a large and weatherstained statue of Juan Martínez de Rozas, an adopted son of Concepción and with José Miguel Carrera and Bernardo O'Higgins a dominant force in the early struggles for self-government. Martínez de Rozas was deported by Carrera and died at Mendoza on the other side of the Andes in 1813. O'Higgins, the illegitimate son of an Irishman who had risen in the service of Spain to become Captain-General of Chile and Viceroy of Peru, was to become the first ruler of independent Chile.

Napoleon's invasion of the Iberian peninsula in 1807 and his usurpation of the Spanish throne precipitated a heady rush towards independence in the South American colonies. The first junta was formed in Santiago in 1810, but personal and political rivalries sapped the country's power to unite in opposition, and the strife of the next seven years included a period of renewed royalist supremacy called *La Reconquista*.

The real liberator of Chile, warmly supported by O'Higgins (but not by Carrera), was the Argentinian general José de San Martín, who, in 1817, led his famous Army of the Andes over the mountain passes to defeat the royalist army at Chacabuco and subsequently, in April 1818, to set the seal on Chilean independence at Maipú. O'Higgins, meanwhile, had been elected Supreme Director, and had set about the creation of the Chilean navy, which was to take San Martín and his troops northwards to the liberation of Peru.

San Martín now enjoys the distinction of a blue plaque not far from Mornington Crescent, marking the house where he lived during a sojourn in London.

Independence didn't make much difference to most

Chileans, or to the country at large, except for the opening of the ports. The social structure remained unchanged, as did the hacienda system. O'Higgins sought to institute reforms, but with no great success. The instigators of freedom were irreconcilable, and a chaotic period of government changes and even civil war ensued: O'Higgins was forced to abdicate in 1823, and he left for Peru, never returning to the country he had fought so hard to liberate and dying in exile, like many of the great men in the history of South American independence.

Carrera was executed at Mendoza in 1821. I saw the note he wrote to his wife on a scrap of paper on the day of his death. It was smuggled to her in a timepiece, written in brown ink in a neat, tiny hand. It read, '*Miro con indiferencia la muerte; y solo la idea de separarme para siempre de mi adorada Mercedes y tiernas hijos despedaza mi corazón.*' ('I face death with indifference. What breaks my heart is the idea of being separated forever from my darling Mercedes and our dear children.') If it broke his heart to write it, I wondered what it did to hers, reading it after he had died.

Despite the turmoil of the period, independence was less disruptive for Chile in the longer term than for many countries on the continent. It settled, relatively speaking, in the early 1830s and became one of the most stable South American nations, often referred to as 'the aristocratic republic'. The 1833 constitution remained in place until 1925, except for a brief interruption in 1891 – an outstanding achievement, and not just by South American standards.

It was grey and cloudy that day, sky and buildings merging into one drab whole, and destitute people curled in doorways reminded me of London. A middle-aged woman wearing a red dressing-gown on top of a coat looked up at me as I passed, and our eyes met as a slow rivulet of her urine crept towards my boot. I was about to go into the cathedral, but as I walked through the porch I remembered a story Salvador had told me at the lido. It was about a man called Sebastián Acevedo who had set fire to himself on that spot in 1983. He had repeatedly asked the authorities to stop torturing his twenty-two-year-old son and twenty-year-old daughter, but they didn't, so he poured petrol over himself, as he had warned them he would, and incinerated himself in the cathedral doorway.

When a large wooden cross was raised in his memory, the military sawed it off at the base.

I decided to call on the Regional Director of Tourism for advice. He insisted on furnishing me with a guide, though I didn't really want one. I couldn't bear the idea of a whole drizzly day in the city, so I told the guide I was interested in the surrounding region as well and went to Hertz, who, reliable as ever, came up with Rocky IV.

Hortense, my twenty-three-year-old guide, showed me round the rather boring gardens of the university before we were allowed to leave town. 'Here,' said a graffito, 'was born the immortal Mir.' The once-powerful Movimiento de Izquierda Revolucionaria (Movement of the Revolutionary Left) was founded by students at Concepción University in 1965. It was a Castroite group committed to violent revolution, and among other things it promoted land seizures, especially by Mapuche, and it was soon driven underground. The *miristas* rejected the Allende regime as 'a reformist illusion', and were particularly active during his leadership. But they were hunted down with brutal efficiency by Pinochet's henchmen, and fatally weakened.

The art collection at Concepción is much vaunted, and determination gleamed in the Hortensian eye as she led the way. I'm afraid I didn't much care for the paintings; they were very bad. Hortense and I were getting to know each other, however, and by mid-morning we had abandoned the city centre and called in to the decrepit housing project where she lived with her parents so that she could change out of her uniform into a pink mini-skirt. We headed for the coast then, Fine Young Cannibals blasting out of the cassette deck and Hortense in dark glasses leaning over to toot the horn at the boys.

At Talcahuano, the fetid port servicing Concepción and the industrial zone, we went on board the *Huascar*, a Peruvian iron-clad which sailed into Iquique on 21 May 1879 at the beginning of the War of the Pacific and was met by Captain Arturo Prat and two small, wooden Chilean ships. The latter didn't last long, but Prat, undaunted, charged onto the *Huascar* and fought until they killed him. The battle has become a central feature of Chilean history and Prat a national hero – probably *the* national hero; towns and villages from Arica to Puerto Williams are bedecked with statues of the Heroes of Iquique and bisected by many thousands of A. Prat streets. This is surprising, seeing that Prat was, in reality, a fairly nondescript naval officer who sacrificed his life rather pointlessly. But the climate was ripe for a hero, and Prat was the man. When he died a Peruvian newspaper said the Chileans had gone mad and become idolaters of a new religion called Prat, and the word Pratomania was coined, while Chilean hacks came up with comparisons with Leonidas at Thermopylae and Nelson at Trafalgar. Prat has subsequently been transformed into whatever the *Zeitgeist* demands – there is even speculation in the press during election campaigns as to whom he would have voted for 'if he were still with us'.[1]

---

1. I acknowledge a debt to the Pratologist William F. Sater and his book *The Heroic Image in Chile* (Berkeley and London, 1973).

Small groups of excitable middle-class families enjoying a day out pushed their way around the *Huascar*. They were less interested in Quiriquina, an island skulking in the bay. Darwin was landed on it in 1835. One hundred and forty years after him, monopolized then by a naval training camp, it was used as a torture centre. I read an account of this centre by a Protestant lay preacher called Camilo Cortés who was held there. When he had recovered his health he became the unofficial prison chaplain. He said his faith became real in prison.

The skies obligingly cleared as we crossed the new road bridge over the Bío Bío, and we started down the coal coast, stopping to eat baked clams at a table on the sand between Coronel and Lota, overlooking the bay where, as the waiter reminded me cheerfully, the British warships *Good Hope* and *Monmouth* were sunk in 1914. Later in the afternoon, at Lota, the heart of the coalmining community, we walked alongside rows of wooden terraces, the second storey extending out on stilts forming a kind of industrial cloister, and thin black dust clung to the leaves of the etiolated trees silhouetted underneath the hallowed black wheel of the mine itself. Hortense's grandfather had been a miner; he had died of a lung condition when he was fifty-one.

Coal had transformed the region in the 1860s. It was low-grade stuff, but it did the job. The number of employees at the Lota mine had fallen dramatically over the previous decades. Before nationalization in 1972 it was owned by the Cousiño family whose winery I had visited in the Maipo valley; they controlled the area around Lota feudal-fashion for many years, and at the end of the nineteenth century built a large palace and park there. The palace was destroyed in the earthquakes, but the park, designed by two British landscape gardeners, continued to be tended as if the family were still in residence. Carlos Cousiño, buried there in 1931, was an unpopular employer with the reputation of a slavedriver, and as we touched the damp walls of a configuration of caves within a hillock Hortense whispered stories about devil worship.

The coal towns were different from anything else I'd seen in Chile. They were grimmer than the copper communities; dirtier, and more familiar to my European eyes. I had a real sense that the long and lush central valley had ended, and that I had entered a harsher environment where people had to work harder. It came as quite a shock, and it suddenly seemed to me that I had covered a great distance to get there.

We left town as a long high-pitched siren brought a shift to an end, and the road penetrated miles of pine forests, for long stretches uninterrupted then suddenly and ominously punctuated by charred red scars and logging plants. The Chilean forestry industry was the success story of the 1970s, especially after a new afforestation law in 1974 granted the loggers fiscal exemptions. Heavy investment saw the natural hardwoods increasingly giving way to the Monterey pine, introduced to Chile, where it grows faster than anywhere else in the world, in the nineteenth century.

Hortense caught the bus back home from Arauco, and I continued south alone. She had to meet her boyfriend, whom she revealed was a Mormon (though apparently not a very conscientious adherent). There were a lot of them about. On the road south I gave a lift to a middle-aged woman who immediately launched into a speech of missionary zeal about the one true god. She and her associates, she said, had set up on their own – the other religious organizations were all 'dead'. I asked her if she'd mind if I switched the radio on. I couldn't stand any more of that.

I stopped at Cañete at dusk, checked into a small hotel in the main street and then followed the suggestion of the tourist man at Concepción and called the curator of the Mapuche museum. She told me to come straight over.

Through the window of her old wooden house I saw two women of about my age weighing into a bottle of pisco while engaged in what looked like a spirited conversation.

Gloria was in her mid-thirties, and single. She had one of the best jobs in the Chilean Arts Department, a wide range of interests, and she was liberal in outlook. This kind of woman is not often observed in rural Chile, and it was my good fortune to meet her. She must have been surprised when I turned up, but she didn't flinch, and both she and her friend Cecilia simply took me on as one of them. It felt like coming home.

Cecilia, who had the corkscrew curls of a Pre-Raphaelite, worked as a teacher; she was married with two children, and lived nearby. Gloria was less striking: there was something old-fashioned about the way she looked, like a Forces sweetheart. Neither of the women was from Cañete; they had moved there with their jobs from elsewhere in the south. They seemed to like it well enough, though I got the impression that they relied on each other a good deal. When I answered their questions about myself I didn't see the blank amazement I often noticed on the faces of my interlocutors. They only asked a few questions, too; they didn't interrogate me, like most people. We sat around the table in the neat house and talked about our families, the community in Cañete, my journey – all kinds of things, and they told me that when I arrived they had been planning a ski-ing weekend. We laughed a lot; they loved to laugh.

Gloria's house was on one of the outermost streets of the small lattice of the village. Cañete still had a kind of frontier feel about it. The streets were made of mud, and the houses were wooden. The few shops were poky. It had a makeshift appearance which belied its history: it was founded on the site of a Spanish fort in 1558, in the Mapuche heartland. At that time Mapuche territory extended north of Santiago up to Copiapó and south as far as Chiloé. The horse, brought by the Spaniards, transformed the lives of the indigenous people and they copied metal spurs and stirrups with wooden replicas. Between 1598 and 1604 they destroyed every Spanish settlement south of the Bío Bío.

I went to Gloria's museum the next day. It was the only Mapuche museum in the country, and it was on its own in the lumpy fields, large, cool and airy. After she had briefed two of her staff about arrangements for a school visit, she showed me round. She was a very good guide. I was more interested in what she had to say than in the exhibits.

'The sub-groups within semi-nomadic Araucanian society shared a broadly similar culture, though they were never united, either physically, politically or culturally. They were spread around central and southern Chile, and also Argentina, and together with the Inca and the Chibcha represented the most important Andean cultures at the time of the Conquest. Estimates of their numbers at that time are weak, but we can say at least that there were between half a million and a million of them.'

Other academic sources went as high as two million. Yet the authoritative *Handbook of South American Indians* says, 'The Araucanian is probably the most scientifically neglected tribe in the hemisphere'.

Most Araucanian sub-groups had been extinguished. In the ethnic minority section of the 1992 census three choices were offered for the whole country: Mapuche, Aymára or Rapa Nui (the Polynesian name of Easter Island). The country was like a richly dyed piece of fabric whose colours had been bleached out.

Gloria introduced me to a Mapuche musician. I listened to him sucking air into a long thin wind instrument made of cane; it sounded like a trumpet, and was called a *ñolkín*. He said he used to play it during hockey matches. His first language was *mapu-dugun* ('language of the people of the land'); Mapuche land (*map*), which in their communal and collective culture belongs to everyone, is a vital part of the Mapuche person's identity, a fact which casts a particularly tragic light on their history as most of their land was stolen from them. From the sixteenth century many thousands of Mapuche in their northern territories, already penetrated by the Inca, were taken from their own land as forced labour for *encomiendas*, the trusteeships dished out to the Spaniards. Within a hundred years of the arrival of the white man the northern limit of Araucanian territory had been pushed down to the Bío Bío.

The musician embarked on a laborious explanation of a folk song which included mysterious references to 'the island'. I looked on all my maps later: no island.

'Yes,' said Gloria when I asked her about it. 'It's sort of off the map in every way. A thousand people live there – that's a lot for rural Chile, you know. It's called Isla Mocha. I excavated on it once – the Mapuche lived there. There's no public transport to it. It's like Chile was fifty years ago.'

My plans evaporated. Gloria thought it was quite a joke, and took up my new expedition as a personal challenge. We toured the village, finding out which of the three privately owned single-propeller planes which constituted Mocha's only link with the mainland was planning a trip. One of them was leaving immediately, so Gloria wrote a note to her friend Nina, who was the headmistress of the school on the island (there were no telephones). The plane returned that evening with an invitation to stay at Nina's. Another plane was leaving in two days, and would take me for the equivalent of ten pounds; this meant I would be on Mocha for the much-publicized national census.

While I waited I drove through the forests around Lake

167

Lanalhue and on to Contulmo. The road was very bad, and so dusty that I had to keep the windscreen wipers on. Lanalhue was the first lake I saw. It was a stirring moment, as now only the Lake District, large though it was, lay between me and the glaciated south.

Contulmo was colonized by Germans in 1884, and the teutonic architecture revealed that they had brought their culture with them and passed it on to their Chilean-born children. Beyond the village I followed a narrow lane along the shore of the lake, stopping after an hour outside the isolated Posada Alemana, a congenial old hotel with its own section of beach, owned by a descendant of the German colonists. It was far enough from the capital, I supposed, not to have been spoilt by squads of rich *santaguinos* seeking a holiday spot. The manager was a cheerful man wearing a peaked cap who claimed to be ninety-three, and he offered me *onces* in the dining area, under an awning and over-looking the lake. *Onces* (elevenses) are taken at five o'clock. There are several theories about their origin, but I believe the word was coined as a code for the eleven letters of *aguardiente* (clear brandy). It may have begun in the factories, where the workers liked to sneak off for a snifter at five without revealing their intention to the bosses, or perhaps behind the net curtains of little old ladies in the capital, anxious to preserve their genteel image and drink their brandy out of teacups.

Onces are no longer associated with alcohol; they are 'tea'. A maid served Liptons and apple *küchen* on a linen tablecloth embroidered with homely German proverbs. While the old man was reminiscing a boy at the water's edge rang a handbell, and twenty carp swam up and ate bread out of his hand, exactly as it happens in Kurosawa's film *Dreams*. They moved right up onto the sand, most of their bodies out of the water, and the superannuated manager never even stopped talking.

168

On the second evening, the last before my departure to Mocha, I was invited to a birthday party – Cecilia was thirty-five. It began at ten-thirty at night. Six of us sat around a circular table drinking pink panthers, a special cocktail made in a liquidizer from pisco, orange fanta and condensed milk. I thought with a stab of our birthday parties at home, and how different they were.

Chapter Nine

The Brazilian anthropologist Darcey Ribeiro estimates that more than half the aboriginal population of America, Australia, and Oceania died from the contamination of first contact with white men.

Moritz Thomsen, *The Saddest Pleasure*

Streets full of water. Please advise.

Robert Charles Benchley, in a telegram to his editor on arriving in Venice

The day I left for Mocha was damp and cold, and everyone told me cheerfully that it would be worse on the island. I waited at the airstrip all morning with the venerable Cessna's pilot, and when the weather cleared we left, levering in a pair of thuggish eight-year-old twins who were so similar that the configuration of dirt clung to their faces in the same pattern.

The plane smelt of shampoo. By the time we reached the beach a small smudge had appeared on the horizon; when the earliest Araucanians looked over and saw the island, they were spooked, and they said it was where you went when you died. They constructed a whole community of the dead over there.

170

It took half an hour to get to the outcrop of islets at the southern tip of Mocha. The island itself was an eleven-mile spine of virgin forest, rising to almost three thousand feet at the highest point and surrounded by a coastal plain, itself fringed with sandy beaches. The pilot twice tried to land on a strip of grass near the tip, banking sharply over the ocean, but a cow was asleep on the runway, so we set off for another airfield, where a crowd of people were waiting for a different plane.

Fifteen horse-and-carts were parked behind a wooden fence, the latter sagging with the skinned carcasses of cows, heads resting on the grass and filmy eyes staring from ribena tendons. The owners of the carts, about to dispatch their beef to the mainland, stood in a group nearby, men with high, flat cheekbones and shiny black hair, wearing heavy ponchos and cracked boots.

The pilot now looked on me as his personal responsibility, and as the headmistress' house was several miles away he took me first to a farm where we installed ourselves in a large kitchen with four women who sat knitting and commenting on island affairs like a Greek chorus. Somebody, the pilot said, would show up who would take me to Nina's. I thought this was rather a desultory plan, but as no one else did I kept quiet and drank my tea. The chorus discussed me as if I weren't there. They spoke about a North American woman who had come to Mocha five or six years before. They all remembered the smallest details about this person.

'She had a small cassette player she plugged into her ears,' said one.

'Do you know our apples?' said another woman, suddenly addressing me and pointing to a tree right outside the window.

'Do you sell them to the mainland?' I asked.

'Sometimes'.

171

'What else do people do here, besides sell apples?'

'Nothing much!' said the first woman, and picked up her knitting again. I opened the carpetbag to take a map out and study the topography of the island, to work out where I was going. A bottle of shampoo had spilt, hence the smell in the plane.

Drake stopped on Mocha in 1578 when he was circumnavigating the globe in the *Golden Hind*. The locals mistook him and the rest of the shore party for Spaniards, and arrowed them; Drake was wounded in the face. Francis Fletcher, a priest on board who wrote a narrative of the voyage, enthused about the gold and silver on the island, and suggested that Mocha stood in relation to the mainland opposite like a protective door, as the Isle of Wight does in England.

The Isle of Wight did not leap to mind.

A horse-and-cart lurched into the courtyard and one of the women stood up, signalling me to follow.

There was one road, and it went about two-thirds of the way around the island. An occasional low farmhouse stood back in the misty fields, and women in aprons looked up from their washing troughs and waved soapy arms.

We stopped by a clump of trees.

'This is Nina's! Behind the trees!'

I climbed down, and the woman threw the carpetbag after me.

The house was long and low, and it had a wide porch stacked with old bikes and wellington boots. The headmistress was standing at a window, and when she saw me she broke into a big smile. By the time I reached the front door she was there.

'Welcome!' She took the bag, and led the way to a kitchen where a number of saucepans were permanently maintained at boiling point on a giant wood-burning stove. Chickens pecked around the stone floor in between the intermittently spread sealskins, and Tía María, a resident aunt, pounded a glob of dough. Nina's two children sat at my feet and stared.

Nina had arrived on the island with her husband and children three years previously.

'I'm afraid all the professionals here come from the mainland. The *mochanos* don't have access to training,' she said, lighting candles as the thin sunshine drained away. Besides power, there were a lot of things they didn't have on the island, like a doctor, for example. They did have eight motorized vehicles, but they had to bring petrol over in small cans on private planes. They didn't used to have any crime either, but thieving had recently made its ugly appearance among them. The farmers made a living, but only just, as the cost of transporting produce to the continent was virtually prohibitive, and besides beef the only real export was garlic.

It rained hard all night before the day of the census, and at seven o'clock in the morning, when we walked to the school, now the census headquarters, it was through deep muddy puddles. Nina sat behind a child's desk assigning groups of houses to the island's state employees, converted into census takers, and they stuck printed discs to their lapels and set off, most of them on horseback, tucking their chins down into their buttoned-up coats. I was handed over with a bundle of census forms to two men bound for the remotest zone and we were conveyed to a cold southerly point in a police jeep. The tide was low, and we walked across the sand to a smaller island and our first house, a wooden one built on a spit of land permanently blasted by a brutal wind. One of the officials, an amiable post office worker, struggled through his questions next to a baking tray of small and shiny trussed pink birds while a pig outside headbutted the door and complained noisily.

The policeman abandoned us and we began our trek up the west coast, where the forest lay closer to the plain and the wind had the whole Pacific to build up speed. The houses, built in hollows among the sand dunes, were small and cluttered, with sombre 1950s furniture and nylon lace doilies. The censors were required to read out a list of consumer durables and tick those found in each household, and so they doggedly did, asking people whose toilet was a hole in the garden and who had never had electricity whether they owned a video, microwave, music centre or cellular telephone. At least in the transport section the National Bureau of Statistics revealed that it was not entirely out of touch, as after a list of more sophisticated forms of transport it had printed *carretón* (horse-drawn cart), and the *mochanos* brightened up when they found something to say yes to.

What they all had in abundance were apples, and an apronful was pressed on me as we left each house. I was not permitted to refuse this gift, as each orchard was different (they claimed) and I had to try them all. I was soon dragging round a sack of apples that would have provided me with enough roughage for a year. I started trying to feed them to the cows, but they didn't want them either.

People were asked if they could read and write, and most of those under fifty said that they could, and although the young *mochanos* hadn't received much education, they had all completed more years of schooling than their parents, which constituted progress, at least. A twenty-five-year-old with a physical handicap had received no education at all.

The last house required us to climb several steep sandbanks. These people did not even own a *carretón*. Three men lived there with their common-law wives and extensive progeny; one couple and their four children slept in the kitchen.

A cluster of dirty and barefooted children followed us until we emerged on a headland overlooking a wide beach of honey-coloured sand. During the long walk home over bright green moorland spotted with animals it began pouring with rain. A decent track covered the very last stretch, built by the munificence of the national petroleum company; they had found gas on Mocha and had been obliged to construct a basic infrastructure to facilitate their labours. The gas has not been exploited; not yet.

Nina, her husband and I sat up late most nights in the dark drinking pisco close to the fire. I shared a bedroom with Tía María and little Salome. A cow tied up outside usually kept me awake. One morning, idling outside a neighbouring farm-house with a trail of children who had attached themselves to me as if I were the Pied Piper, I heard a rumour that bad weather was drawing in, and that people anticipated a couple of weeks without contact with the mainland. I thought I had better get out while I could. Nobody knew when a plane might come, they simply told me to wait at the airstrip and see, so I walked there, passing four farmers engaged in the consumption of *ñache*, a popular dish consisting of freshly drawn lamb's blood, lemon juice and vegetables. I waited for six hours, and a plane did land, eventually, and later it took me back to Cañete and a very amused Gloria.

She had introduced me to the local schoolteacher, an elderly man who had lived among the Mapuche for fifty years, and he had offered to hike around with me for a day. He lived in Quidico further down the coast, and I drove there early in the morning to meet him. It was not an enjoyable journey, as Rocky and I were frequently forced off the deeply rutted road by logging trucks.

Shortly after setting off on foot together through the dewy, fertile fields a line of *huasos* appeared on horseback on an eastern ridge. *Huasos*, the Chilean equivalent of the gaucho, the South American mounted herdsman, were described by

George Pendle as 'the human expression of the vast and desolate pampa'. They came down towards us wearing short ponchos, black wide-brimmed hats and knee-length boots with elaborate metal spurs. 'Rodeo,' said the teacher disapprovingly, and we changed direction.

We came to a Mapuche house (a *ruka*). It was only a half-*ruka* really, as the wooden frames which used to be thatched to the ground like a wigwam were only used for the roof, meeting a simple stone wall. A barefooted woman greeted the teacher with an embrace, and shook my hand, watched by three small children with their mouths open and a few geese pecking optimistically at the hardened mud. A man left off harnessing a pair of oxen and came to talk to the teacher about the latest development in a local dispute about land rights, and I loitered in the background feeling uncomfortable.

We sat cross-legged on the grass later to eat sandwiches we had brought filled with *manjar*, a Chilean staple consumed in prodigious quantities from the desert to the icecap. *Manjar*, if you will believe it, is sweetened, boiled condensed milk, and looks like caramel. I hated it.

A young Mapuche wearing a cap with a batman logo walked past and nodded, flicking a switch irritably at a horse pulling a wooden-wheeled cart. Later, in a small courtyard between two dry-stone rooms, the teacher introduced me to a very old and very stately woman with a large frilly collar reminiscent of the Inquisition and two long plaits tied together with a turquoise ribbon. A small group of young women and children watched impassively from the doorway of one of the rooms while we were taken into the other, my eyes watering from the smoke of a fire glowing in the middle of the mud floor. The room was bare except for a table and three shelves piled with clothes.

'I,' said the old woman imperiously, 'am *machi*.'

Gloria had told me about *machis*. They were spiritual leaders and healers. The woman told a long story about her calling, which occurred in a dream when she was twelve. At fourteen she rode alone to the cordillera and was initiated. Months later I read sketchy details about *machi* initiation ceremonies in a leatherbound book tied up with pink ribbon at the British Library. It spoke of it as if it were ancient history.

Gripping my arm, our *machi* took a silver breastpiece with a double-headed eagle at the centre from underneath a pile of clothes. She wrapped a thick woollen shawl around my shoulders and pinned the breastpiece on top, finishing off the ensemble with a round head-dress with dangling nickel discs, a rosette and long ribbons. Finally she led me into the courtyard and stood me next to a wooden ladder about five feet high with roughly hewn steps. It represented a kind of altar, and was set up outside her hut when she was consecrated. I felt a bit of a prat, actually; I had the feeling she was making fun of me.

I did try to find out about the altar and where its steps led, but besides mumbling and not finishing her sentences she kept lapsing into *mapu-dugun*, so it was a struggle, and the teacher had opted out, placidly squatting in a corner and smoking his pipe. We did establish that although the Supreme Being was omnipotent, he was not, handily, concerned with the moral order, nor did the state of souls after bodily death depend on his reward or punishment. He was appealed to for material favours.

'Do you have any children?' she asked me suddenly, looking right into my eyes. Three of hers had gone to live in 'the city' (Temuco), and she was sad. The Mapuche still live within a sub-economy of survival, and, predictably, many young people abandon their roots and head for the urban centres, assimilating within the *huincas*.

The Mapuche suffered acutely during the dictatorship.

According to the 1978 report of the United Nations Ad Hoc Working Group on the Situation of Human Rights in Chile, 'On the day of the coup, the big landowners, the land barons, the military and the *carabineros* started a great manhunt against the Mapuche who had struggled and gained their land back.' Of all the accounts I had read of that period, a heartbreaking one for a people whose hearts had already been broken many times, one lapidary sentence never left me. A Mapuche child recalled the day her father was taken away, the last day she ever saw him.

'*Mi mamá*,' she said, '*se enojó porque no se puso los calcetines*' – 'mum was annoyed because he didn't put his socks on.'

The natural first base of the Lake District proper was Temuco, a large town still regarded as a frontier post, though it isn't a frontier to anything except the lakes. After a long, hot and dusty journey on unspeakably bad cross-country roads to Los Angeles, a town on the Panamerican, I followed the tarmac gratefully south to Temuco, where I deposited Rocky IV at Hertz as arranged and checked into a cheap hotel next to the market, a sprawling, vaguely threatening market lined with pyramids of melons, hung with dripping carcasses and exuding exotically dubious smells against a background of high-energy noise. I lingered for the mild hit of the spice rows and later acquainted myself with Temuco, a colourful town where most activities appeared to take place in the streets rather than inside buildings. I imagined that its inhabitants didn't have much time for events in Santiago. Neruda said, 'Temuco is a pioneer town, one of those towns that have no past, though it does have hardware shops.'

The next day I caught a bus into the mountains. The purpose of the trip was the monkey puzzle. Quintessentially Chilean and indigenous only to a narrow Andean zone, the tree had acquired the status of a national symbol, and was much cherished. Neruda had written an ode about it. I remembered monkey puzzles very well from the suburbia of my childhood where they operated as the outdoor equivalent of the aspidistra. They were emasculated there; I wanted to see a whole forest of them. So it was that I fitted myself into the crowded weekly bus like the last sardine in the tin – though we at least were all the same way up.

Two hours later the forty people standing in the aisle got off. Not a single building was in sight, even in the far hills. A sack of potatoes was passed from the very back of the bus and left on the edge of the dirt road. Everyone got back on.

The vehicle quivered, and then stopped, at Melipeuco, a scruffy village on the edge of volcanic parkland. Nothing was happening in the village, least of all transport of any kind to the Conguillío-Los Paraguas park. I set off to the police station, an isolated 'frontier post' so beloved of the Chilean authorities, where I found the incumbents scrutinizing lottery tickets. Policemen usually helped me; they often didn't have anything else to do. The young man on duty was a friendly type, and we sat on the step of the police station chatting for an hour in the watery sunlight.

'Do you think anything will pass?' I asked.

'Yes, sure'.

'I wonder if they'll agree to take me.'

'Sure they will,' he said, patting his rifle.

A forester took me. No one was shot. As there was a tree-stump where the passenger seat should have been I sat in the open back of his beaten-up Chevrolet as we travelled through the black lava-fields and eyed the double craters of volcano Llaima. The forester later told me cheerfully that they usually erupt every five or six years, and hadn't done so for eight. Pampas grass had grown strangely out of the lumpy surface, and the river had forced its way through the debris, creating cliffs striped with volcanic ash, basalt, mud and dust.

A row of araucaria pines, the trees I knew as monkey puzzles, appeared like a line of umbrellas on a ridge. I believe those which adorn small front gardens in the UK are a different type from those around Temuco, but they are Chilean; the seeds were taken to Britain by a seaman in 1795, and the trees in the park were instantly identifiable with one particular specimen from my childhood, which I could still see, through my aunt's net curtains, in her postage-stamp garden in Weston-super-Mare.

The forestry service, Conaf, had organized a campsite next to the largest lake in the park and overlooking the Sierra Nevada, a high and snowy mountain range. After parting company with the forester I enquired about cabins, but they were all full, so I decided to have lunch in the small café, walk through the beech and monkey puzzle forests for the afternoon and hitch out of the park in whatever direction was offered first – there would be plenty of daytrippers in February.

During lunch it began to rain hard. The pintails disappeared from the lake and the parakeets from the trees. I hadn't thought to bring my waterproof gear when I left Temuco in the sunshine. The sky became a solid grey block. I gave up any ideas of walking and when I had paid for my lunch I stood on the road to hitch a lift. I waited for two hours, and not a single car passed. Everyone who was going to leave had left early because of the weather, and the daytrippers had never appeared. The rainwater trickled down the back of my sweatshirt and made me shiver. I searched for monkeys in the branches of the trees, to see if they had made it (the shape of the branch supposedly makes the tree difficult to climb, and vexes the monkeys). But there weren't any monkeys. My hands went a funny purple colour. I felt very, very miserable.

After an hour a Conaf ranger walked past, and he laughed

at me, dripping under a monkey puzzle.

'Come and wait at the information centre,' he said. 'We'll radio to see if there are any vehicles about. You'll catch pneumonia here.'

I stood letting my clothes steam next to a log fire under a copper chimney hood as half-a-dozen campers without waterproof tents crept miserably in to dry their clothes. It became increasingly clear that there was no hope of getting out of the park that day. The ranger spoke on the radio. An unoccupied room was located at the back of the information centre, and a down sleeping bag materialized. At least I wasn't going to die. More people arrived next to the fire, mainly desperate mothers with wet little children. There was a kind of Hispanic Dunkirk spirit about that day. Later another ranger gave a slide show on the fauna and flora of the park. It turned out there were pumas lurking near the lakes. The Conaf men were always helpful, and loved answering questions and solving problems. They all wore brown trousers, part of a uniform obviously designed to make them look like trees. Seeing how desperately underfunded the organization is I was surprised at how much its motivated staff achieved. Wherever I was in Chile, I was always pleased to see them, and they seemed to be the same everywhere, whether in the desert, the forest, or on a glacier. They helped keep it all joined together, in their own way.

Long before Conaf men the park was the home of the Pehuenche, the People of the Araucaria Pine. For centuries the monkey puzzle constituted their livelihood – it provided food, wine, weapons and fuel – as well as operating as a cultural and spiritual symbol. The remaining Pehuenche were fighting for the right to stay on their lands; those who lived at Quinquen were demonstrating in front of the Moneda palace in Santiago that very month to protest about their proposed expulsion by a timber company. Their land had been sold to a private concern in 1918, but their grandparents had refused to leave. Massive-scale logging followed regardless, and despite recent state prohibitions and other governmental intervention the future of the Quinquen region Pehuenche and their traditional way of life is still insecure. I could go into these disputes in great detail, but you know the story, and its themes of moral turpitude, greed and a dominant culture. You have heard it told about many countries, in both hemispheres, probably so often that the words no longer register.

The roof in my room leaked during the night, and there was fresh snow on the Sierra in the morning. The sky was the colour of sulphur. The families left. Most of them were wealthy professionals from Santiago whose well-scrubbed children already knew a few words of English. Their cars were full, so I waited around in my damp clothes. I realized that from now on I wasn't going to be able to do whatever I wanted, whenever I chose. I had to take the climate into account. And it was going to get much worse.

At Temuco I reclaimed my gear in the nasty little hotel where I had left it, had a regrettably cold shower and washed my clothes. As I carried them back along the institutional corridor which smelt of rotting melons and looked like it belonged in a gulag I heard a phrase from a Beethoven piano sonata. It had escaped from a room off the corridor; the door was ajar, and someone inside was playing a record. Despite the poor quality of the sound the intense languor of Claudio Arrau was unmistakeable. It was the first time I had heard him in his own country (they had declared a national day of mourning when he died, a few months before my arrival), and I rested my head on the peeling wall of the corridor, embracing my wet clothes and listening to this stranger playing a Beethoven sonata on a record player in a crummy Temuco hotel room.

My clothes were still wet early the next morning when I

travelled south east to the heart of the Lake District. I felt tired and shivery, and had caught fleas from a child I had taken on my lap in a bus.

The Lake District is the most popular holiday destination in the country, and Chileans speak of it as their most beautiful asset. It was certainly beautiful, replete with volcanoes, green fields and the amaranthine loveliness of the evergreen forest. There were some resorts, but I was sufficiently high-minded to think that they wouldn't tell me much about Chile, so I stayed on the bus till Panguipulli, a village at the northern end of a lake of the same name. Six men were shifting water-melons from a heap on the ground to a heap in a truck, throwing them to each other. I began sneezing, my legs ached and I could feel my morale draining away; determined, therefore, to keep still for a few days, I went on to the smaller and, by Lake District standards, remote village of Choshuenco. The bus that conveyed me there, along the eastern shore of the long lake, was like a mobile tin furnace, and besides that after two hours a sack of flour fell off the luggage rack and split on a passenger's head, releasing clouds of white powder which made everyone cough.

Choshuenco consisted of two long dirt streets lined with wooden houses and gardens growing runner beans and blue hydrangeas. The three guesthouses were full. There were no more buses. There was allegedly another hotel just outside the village, on the black sand beach, so I carried the carpetbags to it, certain that I would be obliged to carry them away again.

They had a room. It was a large house on its own beach, with a wide balcony overlooking two wooded hills which formed a V as they came down to the water. The eight guest-rooms and two shared bathrooms were simply furnished, and someone had put twists of polished wood on the tables and windowledges. The large windows faced the lake and the Choshuenco volcano at the end of it, and the sun contrived to

183

shine through mine all day long. The family who owned the hotel were quiet and friendly; it was their home, too, and they kept a fire going in the enormous fireplace in the dining room and a jug of cold pisco sour on the bar.

I had to call London one day. I reversed the charges at a hut in the main street which called itself the telephone office. The person I had to speak to needed to telephone me back later, so I asked the woman in charge of the hut if I could receive a call there in the afternoon. She said that would be fine. I asked what the number was.

'One,' she told me.

'One?'

'Yes, one.'

'Is there a code?'

'No, just ask the operator for Choshuenco One.'

A group of kayakers were staying in the hotel and one of them, who was Swiss but lived in Dallas, had broken a rib, so he was hanging around looking dejected while his friends kayaked. I went for a day-long walk with him to a waterfall. He said it was just like Switzerland – the cows, the flocculent clouds in a blue sky, the green fields broken by trees and hedgerows, and the streaked mountains behind.

I had dinner with the kayakers next to the fire one night, and stayed up late, and then I had to let myself out at six-thirty the next morning to catch the daily bus out of the village. My flu-like symptoms had been getting worse despite rest and comfort, and I had a persistent pain behind my eyes and a permanently blocked nose. When the bus arrived shortly after seven it was already full, and I stood for three hours, slowly squashed against the back wall as even more people got on, and there I snivelled and succumbed to the lethal combination of self-indulgence and guilt.

I had to reach Puerto Montt that night, ready to meet my friends from London at the airport early the next morning. It meant a long day's travelling, with several changes. On the last bus a woman crane-operator from Seattle carrying a bag of pastries sat next to me. She wanted to offload her tent, so she gave it to me, with a pastry.

'Look,' she said later with her mouth full of apple turnover and her finger pointing at a sign. 'We're there.'

Puerto Montt was a landmark in my journey. It was where the name 'Panamerican' ceased to apply to the highway; Pinochet's dream road, the little-travelled Carretera Austral, took up the baton at Puerto Montt and went south. The roads were symbols of a more general transformation. From the northern borders of Chile almost two thousand miles away you can travel easily right down to Puerto Montt, as long as you don't go off at a tangent into the mountains. You could drive the whole way at once if you wanted, in a straight line. Provided you stay on the coastal plain you have a sense of being plugged into a national network, but at Puerto Montt the plug comes out, and to the south the country hardens into a continental icecap and crumbles into an archipelago. Few people live down there, and fewer visit.

I went first to a pharmacy near the port, and described my symptoms to the saturnine pharmacist. He said he thought I had flu, and I asked if he could take my temperature. He rolled up his sleeve and said, 'We take temperatures rectally here,' removing a thermometer from its sleeve as if he intended to do it straightaway, next to the toothbrush display.

The next morning I picked up Rocky V from Hertz and my friends from the airport. The friends had flown from Santiago and had already been in Chile for a fortnight. We had known one another for twelve years, and I felt as if I had arrived at some small oasis of the spirit, a psychological service-station before the next long leg of the journey. We travelled north

185

around the shores of Lake Llanquihue, through Germanic streets of wooden turreted houses. In Frutillar, the Teutonic heartlands, I saw a group of old men in a bar hunched over copies of the *Condor*, a German-language newspaper printed in Puerto Montt. Germans colonized southern Chile extensively in the 1850s and over the following decades. Perhaps partly as a result of that earlier connection, during the Second World War Chile was the only South American country not to declare war on the Axis. The development of modern Chile owes a good deal to the Europeans who arrived during the nineteenth century, notably the British, Germans and Slavs. In the case of the British, the majority of immigrants belonged to the middle and upper classes, and their surnames still feature prominently among influential and aristocratic types in Santiago.

We asked a farmer's wife if we could pitch our tents on her piece of the Lake Rupanco shoreline, and she agreed with a majesterial smile. Someone occasionally passed on the track above us – a man walking next to a pair of oxen pulling a cart, another riding a white horse, another urging three cows to the milking shed. Four pigs came down to grub around among the remains of our tortillas, followed by a goat and a flock of geese. My friends had brought mail from home, and it included a batch of Christmas cards. It was mid-February, but I put them up around the tent for the night anyway, and the goat ate them.

We struck camp the next day and drove to Petrohué National Park, where we walked up the Casablanca volcano. It wasn't very high, and at the top we had a picnic, above the treeline in the centre of a 360-degree horizon of mountains. There were over thirty lakes and lagoons in the park, and the slopes around them were coloured with fuchsias, the clear dark pink of stained glass. The day after that we travelled down to the eastern shore of Lake Llanquihue, the third largest lake in South America (286 square miles), and had another picnic in a field with sheepskins drying over the fence. Llanquihue was more like a sea than a lake. It was overlooked by the perfect cone of Osorno volcano, which Darwin watched erupting. Osorno is 8730 feet high and it is to volcanos what Krug is to champagne; it is the Taj Mahal of the natural world.

The *conquistadores* didn't make much headway down there in the southern lakes. When they weren't fighting them, the locals told them about a fabulous city made of pure gold in the far south, populated by white men. The Spaniards wasted years in pursuit of this city of their dreams. They knew roughly what the lakeland consisted of – Pedro de Valdivia wrote to Emperor Charles V on 26 October 1552 and told him he had been present at the discovery of Lake Llanquihue, and Juan Fernández reconnoitred the zone for the Governor in 1620. The natives east of Llanquihue were Huilliche and Puelche; some of them were farmers and fishermen, and others transhumant shepherds. For years they kept the pass over the Andes a secret from the Spaniards, who were particularly anxious to know of its whereabouts as it constituted the only land route open to them between their colonies in the north and south. A priest discovered it for them in 1708.

At Petrohué, a settlement on the banks of Todos los Santos lake, the road stopped. The water was brilliant aquamarine, and the forest fell to the edge of more than twenty miles of shoreline. We got on a boat leaving for the small island in the middle, sunk within a giant rim of volcanoes. They made the whole lot a national park in the 1920s – the first in Chile. There were more alerce trees then. The alerce is a slow-growing conifer (*Fitzroya cupressoides*) exclusive to Chile, much overlogged for its excellent wood and now a protected species. The alerce at Petrohué still shelter the little Chilean shrew opossum, one of only two marsupials found outside

187

Australia and the rarest mammal in the country.

Indigenous people called the western tip of the lake Place of the Small Black Flies (Petrohué). This displayed a fine sense of understatement. We stayed in the only hotel, and for several hours concentrated on the destruction of these tabanid horseflies, coining several more expressive names for their home.

It rained all night, and a thick mist descended over everything except a greyish-blue block of matt water. We had been planning to take a boat across to Peulla with the tents and hike around the country between the lake and Argentina, but the weather conditions meant that this was out of the question. Being in Petrohué in those circumstances was like spending two days as a hostage in a wet NCP carpark. We decided to return to Puerto Montt. I was beginning to realize that the effects of bad or freak weather in Chile increase exponentially, like circular ripples emanating from a pebble tossed into water. The road out of Petrohué (the flies had evacuated) was closed. A busdriver who arrived at midday reported that it had reopened, but one of the newly formed rivers across the road was 'tricky'. We set out. The volume of water rushing down from the hills was overwhelming. It was an opaque mid-brown, like chocolate milk, and spilled over itself as it hurtled across the rocks and vegetation to join the rising river. At one point a small queue of cars stood pathetically on either side of forty-foot wide rapids gushing over the road (and boldly described as 'tricky' by the busdriver). The owners of the cars were in conference. A grader had just created a new road upstream, and collective confidence was being worked up to tackle it. We watched them cross one by one, some taking a run-up and careering through the waves, others moving so slowly that submerged exhaust pipes almost caused fatal stalls. We felt our stomachs tighten at each crossing, and then it was our turn, but with double traction Rocky cut straight through, and we continued in the pounding rain, past lone churches built of alerce shingle tiles and painted bright colours. They all had tall pointed roofs and looked as if they might have been designed to feature on an Austrian chocolate box. At Puerto Varas the front was deserted, and looking at the railings in front of the expressionless water through gaps cleared by windscreen wipers reminded me of the south-west of England when I was a child, when we drove to Clevedon or Portishead on another rainy summer Sunday and ate an ice-cream in dad's first car, which had one long bank seat in the front, occasionally spotting holidaymakers trying to redeem the irredeemable with binliners, and we always argued on the way home.

It rained on; it never stopped raining. Woodchip volcanoes on the dock at Puerto Montt changed from pale yellow to a rich, dark rust. We settled into a café with sawdust on the floor and windows steamed up on the inside. It was just the day for a long, indulgent lunch, and the Brylcreemed waiter in the black jacket with shiny elbows facilitated the happy event. I fancied myself as something of an expert on *paila marina* by now, and my friends, hardly conservatives in the matter of food themselves, raised their mutual eyebrow at the heap of unidentified tentacled, swollen or blood-red shellfish that arrived, gurgling and alcoholic. We drank a lot of cold Chilean Sauvignon blanc, and rubbed our favourite arguments threadbare.

In the morning it was raining. The streets flooded, cars sat in water up to the wheelhubs and public-spirited individuals moved benches across the deepest rivers to form footbridges. The locals appeared in bright yellow souwesters and trousers or thick woollen ponchos with a knitted bow at the neck. Everyone talked about the rain, and we returned to our waiter for lunch; he shouted with delight when he saw us.

*

189

My friends left for Santiago. They had found a bottle of pisco that was fifty per cent proof. Their holiday, they felt, had been a learning curve from thirty per cent pisco through to fifty. This was quite an astute observation, as Chileans are very conscious of the strength of a pisco, always seeking out the higher end of the scale and scorning the lower echelons, which they seem to think are produced exclusively for the faint-hearted and foreign, though these two categories are effectively synonymous.

We said goodbye at the airport, and I drove back into town alone, conscious of a familiar heavy feeling like a brick below the breastbone. It was a feeling I associated with Sunday evenings. I dropped the jeep off and walked around town, eventually following the sound of taperecorded bells to the cathedral, which was bright red and made of alerce wood in 1856, making it the oldest building in Puerto Montt. The tourist leaflet optimistically announced that it was modelled on the Parthenon. A mass was about to begin, so I went in, for comfort. There were six of us in the congregation, and one was asleep. The priest shook my hand on the way out. While we were talking, a carton of wine I had bought to nourish me during a long rainy evening alone in a dreary guesthouse room fell out of my bulky rainjacket and bounced on the flagged floor.

Chapter Ten

The island of Chiloé is celebrated for its black storms and black soil, its thickets of fuchsia and bamboo, its Jesuit churches and the golden hands of its woodcarvers.

Bruce Chatwin, *What Am I Doing Here*

In Petrohué I had run into Chris Sainsbury, an English tour guide working in Puerto Montt. I already knew of him, as several people had told me to look him up; he was a kind of gringo landmark. We had passed a very agreeable evening at the hotel bar in Petrohué. Chris had a gap coming up in his work schedule and was planning on spending a week on Chiloé, his favourite part of the country and one to which he returned even when he wasn't guiding. He had suggested that I join him. I was pleased that he asked; I had taken to him straightaway.

Damp or actually wet clothes had become a normal part of life, as sand had in the north, and I was beginning to get the point of the jokes told in Santiago about the residents of Puerto Montt having webbed feet. Despite heavy rain, on the morning we left a crowd gathered around a building near my hotel. Investigations revealed that the Bishop of Puerto Montt was sprinkling holy water around a new fried-chicken-and-chips takeaway shop.

I met Chris in a café near his office. He was reading a thriller when I arrived, and almost as soon as I sat down he asked me if I had any books to swap. He was drinking beer at ten in the morning, which I thought was probably an auspicious start to our trip; there was something of the roué about him which made me feel comfortable. Chris was in his forties, with blond hair, a squint and spindly legs. He was knowledgeable on a wide range of topics, and highly imaginative. About twenty years previously he had taught English for two years at a minor public school in Oxfordshire, and when he left the school presented him with a book token for £1.50 and the local pub with a gold lighter.

The large island of Chiloé to the south of Puerto Montt occupies a special place in the Chilean imagination, one of the few locations in the country familiar to northerners and southerners alike. Unlike Easter Island and Juan Fernández, Chiloé is near the mainland and cheap to visit, and it is also in possession of a colourful and idiosyncratic mythology and vestiges of a rich traditional culture.

The roll-on, roll-off ferry took half an hour, and we leaned over the rail into the wind. To the south, in the wider body of water they call the inland sea, Humboldt penguins, southern sealions and dolphins were swimming around in little groups. Wet-suited shellfish-catchers rolled over the edge of small boats and sank, connected to their air-supply in the vessel by a simple air-compression tube. When I remarked on the primitive nature of this arrangement Chris said that he could remember when air-compression was operated by a hand-turned winch.

The bus rolled off the ferry into the green Chilote hills, the fields at their feet spotted with thatched meat-smoking cook-houses. The inlets, staked out to trap seaweed destined for

Japan, were for many generations the home of the canoeing Chono, who paddled around a 300-mile strip of archipelagic Chile. They disappeared a long time ago, and not a single word of their language has been passed down. One of the very few facts known about them is that Jesuit missionaries baptized 220 Chono in 1612. The Jesuits had just arrived then, and they constituted a powerful presence until they were expelled from the continent in 1767. They left churches all over Chiloé.

The Chilotes were militant royalists and they opposed national independence until they were forced to submit in 1826. Eight years after that, Darwin toured the island extensively, and he was fascinated by it (though he was much, much more interested in animals, rocks and plants than in people). He found one house 'which was the extreme point of South American Christendom, and a miserable hovel it was'.

Like most islanders, the Chilotes were great seamen. They built a boat called *La Goleta Ancud*, and in 1843 sailed it south to the Magellan Strait, where it claimed the tail of the continent for Chile twenty-four hours ahead of a French vessel bent on the same mission. The captain of the *Ancud*, however, was a Bristolian, like me.

On the pier at Ancud, the most northerly settlement on the island, fishermen were lugging baskets of sea-urchins up the steps. These urchins looked like rambutans, red balls spiked with green bristly hair. The hair covered a hard shell, and the fishermen sat down at the top of the steps and tapped them, slicing off the top like a boiled egg and cutting out the fleshy, dark yellow tongues. A small translucent crab was lurking among the tongues.

'It's symbiotic,' explained a fisherman with a green hat. 'It lives inside the sea-urchin. Very delicious. Look.' He picked up a crab, placed it under his top lip, allowed it to crawl round his gums till it reached the back of his mouth, then flipped it between his back molars – and crunched.

The double-spired cathedral at Castro was like a wedding cake iced in cornflower blue and salmon pink. The Franciscans built it during the first decade of this century, and although the Italian architect had meant it to be made of brick, the Chilotes executed his plan in wood clad in corrugated iron. As it turned out they knew best, as if it had been brick it would certainly have fallen down during the 1960 earthquake. The style of the interior was standard European Gothic, except that it was made entirely of wood, even the pillars and arches, and it was disorientating to see something so familiar cast in a different medium.

Castro is one of the oldest colonial settlements in the country. Some of the houses in its neat streets had monkey puzzles in the front garden. Planting a monkey puzzle is a big decision. Once you've got it, you aren't allowed to chop it down. (If you chop an alerce down – the *Fitzroya* conifer – and get caught, you go to prison for ten years.) It was not always so: as recently as 1987 Pinochet approved a decree permitting exploitation of the monkey puzzle, though Neruda had said, 'Anyone who hasn't been in the Chilean forest doesn't know this planet'.

After we had checked into a boarding-house and Chris had checked into a bar I went to the small museum, where a wooden bicycle made in the 1950s was leaning against a corridor wall. Apparently lots of Chilotes owned such a thing. They only work if you go downhill. When I asked the museum attendant what you did if you wanted to go back up, she looked at me pitifully.

'You put it over your shoulder and walk,' adding as an afterthought, 'Are you foreign?'

Without further encouragement she delivered a spiel about an elf called a *trauco* which lurked in the bushes after dark and was responsible for any pregnancy which occurred on the island out of wedlock. The Chilotes enjoyed wheeling out their cast of mythological characters.

Chris was a great travelling companion. He sat happily in bars all day, reading, and whenever I wanted to talk I would find him, and he would close his book and chat until I left again. I spent the days doing whatever I pleased and the evenings in his convivial company, often listening to anecdotes culled from many years work around the globe as a photographer for Operation Raleigh, the adventure charity for young people. Chris' greatest asset was his wit, and he made me laugh all the time. He had somehow backed himself into a waterlogged corner in Puerto Montt, and was stuck. He talked about writing a historical book about Chiloé, but I wondered if he ever would. He was like a character from a Graham Greene novel, or if he had been born a hundred and fifty years earlier he might have been a Bernardo O'Higgins, wandering the world with a bottle of wine in his hand, inadvertently conquering countries as he went.

Almost everything in Chiloé is particular to it, including the food, and the *pièce de résistance* in this last department is *curanto*. We ordered a portion between us one evening and a small mountain was placed in the middle of the table, partially obscuring Chris from my view. The dish was invented by fishermen who went off to remote spots. They took with them supplies which could last weeks, like smoked pork, smoked sausage, dried vegetables and potato dumplings, supplemented them with shellfish, wrapped it all in *nalca* leaves, a kind of giant rhubarb plant, then buried it between heated stones under a fire so the whole lot would stay warm for a day or more. This very Polynesian culinary style was probably brought to Chile in some form by the islanders who roamed the Pacific centuries ago. You have to search hard these days to find someone on the island to cook the dish

195

underground for you, and it has metamorphosed into *curanto olla*, prepared in a saucepan without the leaves and with a piece of chicken and a few boiled potatoes added, the shellfish steaming above the rest in a kind of bain marie. (Potatoes, incidentally, are indigenous to Chiloé, and Chris was convinced that they originated there, not Peru – a theory put forward by several early scientists and supported by Darwin.) *Curanto* is served with a cup of rich broth. It is unimaginably delicious, but not to be tackled by the faint-hearted.

On the second day we went to Chonchi, a small sprawl of wooden houses an hour south of Castro. A few of them were on stilts. I had walked around a lot of these *palafitos* in Castro. To start with, the owners avoided the irritation of having to buy land: they just paid a small concession to the state, which owns the coastline. Secondly, 'moving house' for these Chilotes meant pulling the stilts out of the mud and towing the house to a new site. Thirdly, why commute to work when you can park the boat under the front room? In Chonchi the municipality had even had the decency to instal a row of streetlights in the water.

Under the stilt houses in Chonchi four children were collecting minnows from the bottom of a boat in a rusty tin can. The boat was called Borman. I wondered if this was another Chilote secret.

I had found, in Santiago, a picture postcard by a photographer called Paz Errazuriz. It showed two hugely fat people hunched over what was apparently their bar in Chonchi. It was an old-fashioned zinc bar, and a row of bottles stood behind their heads. They were obviously man and wife, and they were staring straight at the camera, expressionless except for what might have been a glimmer of amusement, even contempt. It was such a beguiling image that I dragged Chris off on a pilgrimage to find this couple. The card stated that the name of the bar was La Sirena, and although it had changed its name to Bongo, everyone in Chonchi knew it.

Plastic seats had replaced the wooden benches and melamine the shiny zinc, but I was sure it was the right place as the woman serving was an identical but younger version of the one on my postcard. When I showed this card, the old couple were produced.

'I suppose you've seen a lot of changes in the village,' I said to the old man. He thought for a while. '*No tanto*' – not so many.

Chris took a photo of me posing with the man; I wanted to recreate the card, with me in the wife's place. When I got home, months later, I stuck the photo in one of my albums of Chile, underneath the postcard. When I was writing about Chiloé I got the album out to look at it again. Someone – I never discovered who – had captioned my photo, 'He subsequently remarried'.

Shortly after this episode at the bar a hotelier ran out of his kitchen and onto the street to greet Chris, who, being a tour guide, was well-known (and well-liked) on the island. The Chilotes were keen on the idea of him getting married, and they were sorry to hear that he brought no news in that department. The hotelier remonstrated and dispensed consolatory tots of *licor d'oro* (liquid gold), a local speciality which always appeared in unlabelled bottles. It was mild, sweet and amber, and although it was translucent, the main ingredient was cow's milk.

Afterwards we waited for a bus back to Castro outside a shop where a boy was pouring petrol into wicker-clad wine bottles. On the journey we passed a salmon farm. Salmon – big business in Chiloé – have attracted massive foreign investment over the past decade. Chris said we could visit some friends of his who owned a farm, and explained how it worked.

'So you mean,' I said, 'that it's intensive cultivation of an introduced species?'

'Yes,' he said. 'But if we meet my friends I don't want you getting on your environmental high horse.'

I heard a lot about these salmon farms later from fishermen in Patagonia who told me that the companies rear the fish to smolt in cages in freshwater lakes before moving them to seaboard farms. This not only produces water contamination but also leaves a lakebed deposit under the cages and transmits disease to the indigenous fish. I couldn't help feeling indignant, whatever Chris had implied about my inappropriate western liberal soapbox. As with the infamous Bío Bío dam project, I was made aware of the growing tension throughout the 'South' between development (and the neo-liberal economics which had begotten it) and environmental protection. Lever Chile and other multinationals in the salmon trade deny that salmon farming causes pollution; but they would, wouldn't they?

We were lucky with the weather; the sun shone. (The island has a dreary microclimate, and wooden sledges are still used all year round to cross the mud plains.) We stayed in Castro for three nights, in a boarding-house with a restaurant decorated with embossed pictures of kittens. I was pleased to see that in the *South American Handbook* this boarding-house was designated 'F' (the rankings descended from 'A'). Generally, the lowest category in any town or village was an 'E' (I was very familiar with the 'E's), and staying in an 'F' constituted something of an achievement. Shortly afterwards I spotted a 'G' in the book, and was disappointed not to be able to enjoy its pleasures.

The mainland opposite Chiloé was still largely uninhabited, despite attempts at forced settlement during the dictatorship. It was patterned with fjords, and the *Dresden* had hidden in one of them in 1914 before sailing to its destruction in the peaceful bay of Robinson Crusoe Island. The man who ran my guesthouse in Puerto Montt had told me an elaborate story about his grandfather smuggling food to the beleaguered ship in the middle of the night. The captain had already outwitted his British assailants for several months and the *Dresden* had crept over a thousand miles up the Pacific coast.

'The sailors,' said the man at my guesthouse, 'were *this* thin,' and he demonstrated with his thumb and index finger an inch apart.

We took a bus north, and it wedged itself on a landing craft going to Quinchao, the largest of the islands between Chiloé and the mainland. The craft was a regular shuttle, but it still managed to dig itself into the soft shore, and it took the crew half an hour to unjam us.

Quinchao was green and undulating, with an occasional excrescence of shingle-tiled extravagance. The locals of the lesser islands were drawn to its capital, a tiny port called Achao, for everything they couldn't produce themselves, and a flotilla of brightly painted boats in varying states of disrepair jostled around the sloping jetty, loaded and unloaded by dark-skinned islanders anxious to get home. They moved their goods however they could: heaped in wheelbarrows, stacked in metal carts attached to bicycles, piled on wooden-wheeled wagons drawn by nags, heaved on handcarts, loaded in the back of pickups and pressed down on overladen shoulders. They brought sacks of flour, crates of Coca-Cola, bundles of shiny fish held together by a reedy cord, brown smoked fish stiff and flattened like table-tennis bats, wicker-clad bottles of pungent local wine, sheets of corrugated iron and baskets of onions with diminutive baskets of garlic lashed to the handle. Children carried industrial-sized packets of sugar, and shifts of salmon workers loitered in their uniform white wellingtons and lifejackets. A man threaded among the crowd with a tray of popcorn balanced on his head, dispensing small bagfuls wherever he could find a taker. Along the beach, an old man was pitchforking bright green seaweed onto his oxcart, and his son was standing on the mound, stamping it down.

I had washed my clothes and hung them out of the window of the boarding-house at Castro. A shirt had fallen off the sill, and I ventured into the back yard to retrieve it. This yard was a bottle bank waiting to be discovered, full of hideous shards. After recovering the shirt I was picking my way back when the ground collapsed beneath me. Once I was up I instinctively checked my wrists first, and then I looked down and saw a red map of Africa swiftly forming on one leg of my jeans.

I had fallen straight onto a broken bottle. I held the leg under a cold shower for twenty minutes, then made a tourniquet out of a T-shirt. The wound took weeks to heal, as it was right on the knee, and it left a thick and raised red weal, which I still have, my bodily souvenir of Chiloé.

There was a shingle house at Cucao with a sign outside saying '*se venden fósiles*' – fossils for sale. The village had only had a road for ten years, so there were still plenty of fossils. Before the road the villagers had to sail through two interconnecting lakes to get to the other side of the island.

Four hundred people live in the middle of the lonely west coast of Chiloé. They farm, fish and pan for gold in the river, and they do without most things, like electricity, for example. It was raining when we arrived. They had built Cucao around a big patch of a tiny light green fern, like a communal prayer mat. Chris bounded into a house with a sign in the window offering beds. When I got there he was sitting next to a stove in the middle of the kitchen, a can in his hand, and he was laughing. A haggard woman in a pinny stood with her hands on her hips trying not to laugh too.

'How many times have I told you not to come here without giving me advance warning?'

There were three rooms to rent; she slept on the bench around the stove when she had guests. Her name was Vera Luz – True Light – and she had four grown-up daughters. Her husband had been killed in an accident. She told me all this immediately.

'I've had to be the man and the woman in this house – double the work. I never stop working.'

She had hung plastic bags of water from the rafters, like the ones fairground goldfish come in. It keeps the flies away, or so they say down there.

I rented a horse that afternoon. There were plenty of horses on the island, and they didn't have a very enjoyable life. In a hamlet north of Castro I had watched a horse towing a car up a hill. The car had got to the bottom of the steep hill, but it couldn't get back up, and a farmer appeared with a horse and a long leather strap. He attached one end of the strap to the towbar of the car and another to a pommel on the horse's saddle, instructed the driver to sit in and drive, and himself mounted the horse and whipped it until both beast and car began to move.

'These hills are so steep,' he said to me afterwards, 'I have to use the horse all the time to get my own pickup to the top.'

My horse, who selected our route, took me through rows of shingle huts with tiled roofs which I eventually realized was a cemetery. They buried people in these little houses all over the island. Presumably it was partly a function of the inclement climate: you couldn't linger over your devotions in the open air if it were pouring down. A clammy mist swirled around the gravehouses; I could see where the myriad Chilote myths of dismembered spirits had come from.

There were six hippies in the cemetery. Cucao beach is a favourite hangout for young Chileans seeking to commune with nature. I had met one on the bus; he worked for the

201

Hong Kong & Shanghai Bank in Santiago.

There was a boy in the house called Christian. He was twelve, and he was always working, ferrying pails of water from the well, peeling potatoes, sweeping, running errands – he worked until eleven or twelve at night. He was very shy, and tried to run away whenever I spoke to him. It turned out that True Light had taken him in when he was abandoned by his parents. He had a number of half-brothers and sisters, and one of the girls had just had a baby. She was ten. True Light told me all this as she sipped *maté* tea through a flat silver straw. Maté is a bitter infusion made from the leaves of a shrub tamped down in a wooden bowl like tobacco in a pipe. I had grown to like it. It always seemed as if the ceremonial and laborious tamping, sucking and water-replenishing were as much a part of its attractions as the refreshment of the beverage itself, like a Chilean version of the Japanese tea ceremony.

Saturday was the first day of 'Cucao Week' (any excuse for a fiesta). In the afternoon the church on the fern green held a perfunctory mass and two rival huts swiftly set themselves up on either side of it, both offering live music and warm beer. All the men were pissed, lounging inside the huts or loitering next to their horses, wearing ponchos and ritually swapping bottles in the drizzle. The women stayed outside, clutching babies and looking anxious. Some of them sweated in small tents attached to the huts, frying *empanadas* over a fire.

I woke early the next day and sat in the kitchen with True Light. It was permanent Armageddon there. I listened to her incantation of misfortunes while Chris snored on, and tried unsuccessfully to extract information about the south west of the island, owned by logging companies and virtually un-inhabited.

Above Cucao, in the north west, there was a coastal

mountain range. I had kept the horse, and set out to explore these mountains with the horse-owner's young son. It was a sharp and sunny morning and the village was silent except for the southern lapwings, aural hooligans of the Pacific coast. To get to the beach we crossed a pedestrian suspension bridge over the river, a noble construction of steel cables and wooden planks which the elements had beaten into an arch. The boy was unaware that his skills on a horse outweighed mine by a wide margin, though he soon found out. My feet kept losing the heavy wooden clog stirrups. It wasn't very good for my wounded knee. It wasn't very good for my bottom, either, as the saddle was a thin affair made of metal, wood and leather and covered in several layers of threadbare sheepskin.

We dismounted and let the horses walk free when we reached the beach. Other horses were pulling in bulging nets, and Magellanic oystercatchers were picking razor clams from the frothy waves. Later, in the mountains, the boy took us on a circuitous loop through a dense bamboo forest, and I remember the primeval smells, the barberry and the yaps of invisible forest birds.

The bus from Cucao to Castro failed to appear that afternoon so we got a lift in the back of True Light's brother's pickup. The sun was shining on the lakes. At Castro the Salmon Olympics were in progress. These did not involve performing fish, but competitions between five teams of salmon workers, each representing a different company. The rest of the islanders, crowded on the quays to watch, had organized themselves into lines of cheerleaders. The teams raced around the bay in rowing boats, pulling in nets and depositing divers.

When we returned to Puerto Montt from Chiloé Chris took me to his local bar in the residential hill district of Bellavista. It was

203

in a small wooden hut at the end of his street, the inside kippered by smoke. A large man was standing behind the bar, and five women and two boys leant in front of it. There was an overwhelming smell of fish. 'Drink!' said one of the women, thrusting a filthy cup of wine at me. A plastic drum behind the door furnished the toilet. Chris was a regular at this bar, and he said that he had never seen a sober person in there. Often, by mid-afternoon, the owner and clientele were slumped on the floor, rendering entry into the bar impossible. We bought a litre of beer (it was only available in litres) and tried to maintain a conversation. It was a taxing occupation.

Several women came in and spoke quietly to the barman. He passed them dented newspaper-wrapped parcels from under the bar and they handed over crumpled banknotes. One engaged in more protracted negotiations. The owner reached under the bar and flopped a salmon on top. He chopped it up and gave two large and unwrapped slices to the woman, who concealed them under her mac and left.

As we left ourselves I saw that the glass was missing from the door panels, and remarked on it to Chris.

'Yes,' he said, 'that hazard, at least, has been removed.'

Chapter Eleven

The ice was here, the ice was there,
The ice was all around:
It cracked and growled, and roared and howled,
Like noises in a swound!

Coleridge, *The Rime of the Ancient Mariner*

The greatest practical difficulty of my trip was Antarctica. After travelling hopefully down numerous culs-de-sac, both in London and Santiago, I had reached the conclusion that the only way I was going to get there was with the Chilean Air Force. In Santiago I faxed letters of reference around to judiciously selected air force mandarins and waited. Nothing happened, so I did it again, and I organized meetings with them too, explaining gravely in their cavernous offices that my journey would remain forever unfinished if I didn't make it to Antarctica. I tried to conceal a threat that if I didn't go it would look as though that bit of Antarctica wasn't Chilean after all. One day a general told me over the telephone that I was invited to travel to Antarctica in a Hercules aircraft. When this might take place, and where I should find the Hercules, took a very long time to establish. I was eventually instructed to present myself at a base in the far south on a certain day at the end of February.

This base was just outside Punta Arenas, so I took a commercial flight down there from Puerto Montt. It meant I was spoiling my plan of a nice logical journey from top to bottom as I was now going straight to the southernmost point of the mainland, jumping a third of the country. But I couldn't start asking the air force if they could change the date of the Antarctic trip. I would have to fill in the gap later; the only point of having a plan, I reasoned conveniently, was to allow the contingency of things to change it.

It was a cloudless day and the archipelago looked like a set of geoglyphs on a blue field. I amused myself by picking out shapes – a small llama, a boomerang, a set of geometric figures. We flew over Patagonia, khaki and spotted with ochre pools. It was very flat. Finally we circled the Magellan Strait, the same dull silver as the plane's wing. The Strait and the cold waters around the tip of the continent evoked the names of great voyagers: Ferdinand Magellan in the *Trinidad*, Francis Drake in the *Pelican*, which he renamed the *Golden Hind* while he was down there, Pedro Sarmiento de Gamboa in various ships, Pringle Stokes in the *Beagle* (Stokes shot himself on board), Robert FitzRoy, also in the *Beagle* (he committed suicide later) – and the list goes on. But it was the Mariner's spectre-ship I saw when I looked out of the thick pebble window towards the Southern Ocean: 'We were the first that ever burst/Into that silent sea'.

The sky was huge down there. As I walked down the steps of the plane I thought, You've reached the bottom of the world, and for some reason I thought of the street I grew up in and the long row of red chimneys I could see from my bedroom. I was surprised, because the air was warm, but I caught a bus into the centre of Punta Arenas and when I got off and turned a corner a wind made me falter as I walked. I checked into a private house offering rooms; it was small, and clean, with no locks on the doors and a set of dentures in the toothmug. For the first time in weeks I unpacked completely. Mould had grown in pleasing patterns on T-shirts rolled up into the carpetbag too hastily while damp. I washed all my clothes by hand, pegged them on the line in the garden and hoisted them up into the white and grey expanse, diminutive fragments of colour flapping energetically.

People from Magallanes, the twelfth and southernmost region of Chile, promote the theory that the country was first discovered by Europeans in the south, when Magellan appeared in 1520. That was fifteen years before Almagro rode down through the north. Magellan entered his Strait from the Atlantic, coming round the Cape of Eleven Thousand Virgins. In 1583 Sarmiento founded two settlements on the Magellan Strait, largely to protect Spanish territory from the British, but all the inhabitants of both places died except one, and it was a British ship which saved him.

A couple of centuries later scientific expeditions began arriving at the tail of the continent, and in 1843 John Williams, the Bristolian in the *Goleta Ancud*, claimed the Magellan Strait for Chile. Punta Arenas was founded in 1848. It was used largely as a penal colony at that time, and was totally dependent on Santiago. It was coal that really brought it to life, in the 1860s and 1870s. In this last decade sheep were shipped over from the Falklands – they could adapt to the climate, whereas sheep from the central valley of Chile itself couldn't – and a great Magellanic industry was born.

Europeans arrived to carve out a new life for themselves in that austere place, especially towards the end of the century. In 1892 the gold rush began. Export trade flourished, and by 1906 the territory of Magallanes was sending well over ten million pounds of wool annually to Britain alone. The community was impressively sophisticated: by 1896 – fifteen years ahead of the capital – it had electric street lighting. The numerous foreign colonies all published their own newspapers, and they vied with each other in their cultural activities. Large and beautiful houses were built, many of which remain, converted into offices, clubs and museums and recalling the solidity of Victorian London or Manchester.

The first decade and a half of this century were the golden years for Punta Arenas, and the two largest colonies were British and Croatian – the Brits, naturally, in the managerial posts. But when the Panama Canal opened in 1914 ships didn't have to sail right the way round the continent anymore, and the docks at Punta Arenas went quiet. People didn't know what to do about it, and their newspapers grew thin and morose. Between the wars a large number of British families left. But the Croats proliferated.

The first Anglican baptism on record in the settlement took place in 1891, and St James' church appeared in 1895. At that time the Anglican Church in South America operated as a two-pronged venture: one prong provided chaplaincies for British residents and the other organized missions among the indigenous people. The evangelical tradition of this second prong has never been abandoned. A month or two later in my trip the Anglican bishop in Santiago told me that he had decided, on a point of principle, to instruct the flock to tick the 'Evangelical' box on the national census form rather than 'Protestant'.

In Punta Arenas I went to a service in English, my first since mass at St Mark's in Regent's Park the day before I left home. It was very low at St James' – several thousand feet below St Mark's. Over the ubiquitous Anglican cup of tea afterwards a friendly young man said to me, 'You came on a very formal day. Sometimes – like today – we're more traditional than usual, to keep the old expats happy.'

The sermon (with handouts), concerned fasting, and it was

good, though I couldn't imagine Father Tom daring to suggest a fast in Regent's Park. John Hervey, North American pastor of the Anglican Church in Punta Arenas and the man responsible for the sermon, kindly asked me over to his house for an 'informal talk'. When I arrived he was behind his desk in a cosy office at the bottom of the garden. He thought the Catholics had their backs to the wall. 'Twenty per cent of Chileans are Evangelical Protestants,' he told me. 'There is tremendous religious upheaval here. The country has been very well evangelized by Protestants, and as a result the Catholics are putting the heat on.'

This Catholic 'heat' was being generated by an institution if not in crisis then at least deeply divided. The Church in South America had spent several decades trying to decide whether its responsibilities lay with the here-and-now or the after-life. To a certain extent it was a debate provoked by the Second Vatican Council, which in the early 1960s turned the global Catholic spotlight onto social concerns – more specifically, onto poverty, teaching the uncomfortable lesson that the rich and influential have a responsibility towards the poor. A hundred and fifty South American bishops met at Medellín in Colombia in 1968 and committed their Churches to a more active role in national life. The progressive priest saw himself as a protagonist in the struggle to liberate people from their daily misery, and the theology of liberation which he espoused acknowledged the complex reality of the human condition, something which many people felt the ossified structures of Catholicism had never even attempted.

Even before the 1960s, although religious practice in Chile had consistently been identifiable with support for the right, the Church had allied itself with the Christian Democrats, who represented social Catholicism and reform. After 1958 it moved further still towards the centre, and involved itself in secular projects. So it was understandable that the ideas of the

Second Vatican Council settled easily in some parishes west of the Andes.

Many South American churchmen went much further than the Vatican had intended, however. Front-line staff – those facing the pain of the South American slums every day – became increasingly alienated from the hierarchy. Liberation theology, which taught that spirituality and social oppression are inseparable facets of human existence, was much mistrusted, and as a result the most visible characteristic of the Chilean Church after 1964 was fragmentation. Liberation theology, I was repeatedly told, was always more popular among the priests than the bishops. The US administration equated it with Communism: by 1980 this prejudice had become so enshrined that the Council for Inter-American Security was quite explicit about it. Its policy proposal that year, perceived by some to be associated with the Latin American policy of the Reagan administration and known as the Santa Fé document (though its real name was *A New Inter-American Policy for the Eighties*), stated: 'US foreign policy must begin to counter . . . liberation theology as it is utilized in Latin America'.

Tensions within the Chilean Church were greatly exacerbated by the prospect of a Communist or Marxist regime. Most of the bishops spoke out against both ideologies throughout the 1960s. Despite the fact, however, that in previous decades the writings of Marx and papal encyclicals had each stated a total rejection of the other (and Castro was excommunicated in January 1962), the concept of Christian Marxism was taken very seriously in some quarters, and by the end of the 1960s many people had hope for an eventual rapprochement of Communism and Christianity. But as the middle political ground collapsed in Chile at that time, the Church polarized still further, much as the country did. Just how little liberation theology had impinged upon many Catholics was revealed in a survey conducted among regular attenders of mass through-out the country in 1971. Two-thirds of them said they wanted the priest to speak only about the life of Jesus and the importance of Christian love and never to mention issues relating to poverty, injustice or the necessity to participate in efforts to change social structures. This was the most depress-ing little nugget of information I ever uncovered about Chile.

For the first half of Allende's presidency both the Church and the Marxist-Socialist coalition worked positively for coexistence and cooperation, encouraged by a 1971 apostolic letter indicating a softening of the Vatican line on Marxism. Cardinal Silva publicly endorsed the nationalization of cop-per, for example, and Allende told the *New York Times* that he believed the Church was going to be on his government's side. When Castro made his famous extended visit to Chile in 1971 he said in his farewell speech that there were 'many points of coincidence' between 'the purest concepts of Christianity and Marxism'.

Towards the end of its curtailed tenure the Popular Unity administration proposed educational reforms which the bish-ops didn't like. (Education was an extremely sensitive issue, as to a certain extent Catholics saw their school system as the last hope of Christian influence.) The reforms were never passed, but the tensions were never resolved, either. The country was in chaos by that time, and while the Church didn't officially move from its position of tacit support for the regime, by the time the coup came many of its members – not only the right-wingers – thought it was necessary. There was a widespread feeling in the country that something had to happen; nobody knew, then, how much it was going to cost.

At the far end of the cemetery in Punta Arenas a corrugated iron fence overlooked the steel grey Magellan Strait and a ghostly Tierra del Fuego on the horizon. The ever-accreting gravestones and elaborate mausolea (the names carved on them revealed the city's cosmopolitan past) were interspersed with hundreds of twenty-foot high tumescent bushes cut to a rounded tip, a fine example of the most *outré* Freudian topiary.

Although Magallanes is Chile's largest province it is home to less than 1 per cent of the population. Vast expanses of ice and steppe separate it from the rest of Chile and a thick slice of it is simply omitted from most maps. North of these wastes there is a vague and unspoken perception that the country proper ends at Puerto Montt. The citizens of Punta Arenas deeply resent what they call 'the ignorance of northerners'. I lost count of the number of times people told me irritably, 'In Santiago, you know, they think that down here we have penguins in the plaza and Indians on the streets'.

I had the telephone number of an elderly man of German descent whose father had played a key role in the vanishing act of the *Dresden* in the Chilean fjords, and when I called he invited me to tea. The house was in a quiet street in the north of town, and a neatly dressed man wearing a tie and hand-knitted cardigan opened the door.

'*Wilkommen*. Welcome. *Bienvenida*!' I was afraid he was about to launch into 'Cabaret'.

I was introduced to his wife and, during the course of the afternoon, a range of children and grandchildren. There was a kind of yard at the back of their home, and nine cars or jeeps in varying stages of decay were wedged within its brick walls.

Gerd swiftly got onto the topic of the Word of God. I asked what his religion was. I had long since given up saying, 'Are you a Catholic?' when the subject arose; it seemed very likely that my interlocutor wouldn't be.

'I am a Jehovah's Witness,' he said.

It wouldn't have surprised me if he'd told me he was a Palestinian falangist.

There was a bar upholstered in cream vinyl in the lounge with a tall ceramic *bierstein* on top. Albert Pagels, Gerd's father, was a Lutheran from Rügen Island in the Baltic. He had arrived in Punta Arenas as a young quartermaster in the merchant navy in 1903, and stayed, making his way first by hunting and goldpanning and later by providing field experience on foreign scientific expeditions. He appears frequently in Carl Skottsberg's *The Wilds of Patagonia*, published in 1911. He was a self-taught man, serious and eminently capable. Shortly before the First World War broke out five German cruisers arrived in southern Chile under von Spee, and one of them – the *Dresden* – was soon in urgent need of expert local knowledge to dodge the pursuing British. The German authorities got in touch with Albert Pagels, and what he and a handful of others achieved in concealing the massive cruiser from the enemy for ten weeks and keeping its supply line open has entered the annals of German naval history. Pagels twice refused to be bought off by the desperate British, and although a mere civilian, he was awarded the Iron Cross, First and Second Class, in 1919.

Albert had been in Germany during the Second World War, and although he had never joined the Nazis, he had been proud to help 'Germany'. Gerd was devoted to the memory of his father, and behaved as if he were oblivious to the embarrassing matter of what 'Germany' represented at that time. I asked him if he would be proud to help Germany (where he had never been).

'Yes! Most certainly yes. Even my children feel German, though they don't speak the language. My youngest son feels more German than Chilean.'

A pregnant granddaughter appeared with a plate of *sopaipillas* (squarish doughnuts) and a dish of cherry jam. Unfortunately, said Gerd, she was not a 'Bible student', as he referred to the Witnesses. None of the family were, though he had stuck to the faith for 37 years, and he said, in English, 'I am alone in the trenches'.

After the invitation to Antarctica was delivered the logistics of the trip had involved, over a six-week period, a succession of inconclusive telephone calls from sweaty phone boxes and hand-written faxes to generals, as well as the expenditure of a good deal of nervous energy. Everyone in Santiago had told me I'd never get there, and their words mocked me as I haemorrhaged money, time and mental health on the project. I had come to feel that the whole trip would be left dangling if I didn't get to the southernmost point of what Chileans think of as their country.

The problem was not a lack of goodwill, or of authority: I was an official guest of the air force, and nobody disputed it. The problem was communicating with the right people at the right time to make the necessary arrangements. Often I had walked three miles to a telephone at the appointed hour of eight in the morning to find it broken or that the person I needed had been called away.

As soon as I arrived in Punta Arenas I had begun groping around, if one can grope on the telephone, for a departure time: air force scheduling was erratic under any circumstances, and when it had Antarctic conditions to take into account it was almost a minute-to-minute business. The uncertainty made me agitated. In addition, there had been no mention of equipment. A set of thermals had been languishing at the bottom of the carpetbag since the journey began (and had been carted doggedly through the Atacama desert) and I had a professional jacket and boots: that was it. I asked, over the phone, what I should bring.

'Oh, just pack your woollies – and don't forget your camera!' said an amiable sergeant as if I were going to Skegness for a winter break.

I was finally instructed to present myself at Air Base Chabunco at eleven o'clock one Tuesday morning. Only then, with a celebratory flourish, did I allow myself to rip the cellophane packaging off the thermals.

I turned up at the windy airfield overlooking the Magellan Strait at nine-thirty, almost paralysed by anxiety. At least the airman at the high-security gate had my name – or something approximating to it when pronounced in Spanish – on a short list. I was told to wait at the civilian airport a mile away, and a lieutenant drove me there in a jeep.

Other members of the party trickled in. The first were two builders employed in the construction of the first Antarctic church. What mattered most down there to the Chileans was assertion of their national identity, because that, as they perceived it, validated their claim to the land. The Catholic Church was an integral part of that identity, despite the fact that hundreds of thousands of them had rejected it.

A dapper army officer on a business trip followed the churchbuilders into the terminal. He was being sent to investigate a military plane which had crashed on the runway at the main Chilean Antarctic base two days previously, and later he told me enthusiastically about this crash and the perilous conditions in the Antarctic. The next person to come in was a petrochemical engineer from ENAP, the national petroleum company, who was supervising the construction of a diesel pipeline from a maritime terminal to the base, and he was accompanied by his beautiful seventeen-year-old daughter. Arrival six was a young woman from Valdivia who knew someone in the air force.

We sat around. The army officer flossed his teeth. A captain appeared and said there was a problem with an engine. There were only two civilian flights that day, both to Santiago, and I watched the airport fill and empty, fill and empty, like a cowshed at milking time. A kiosk opened during these brief

215

periods of activity offering a listless selection of confectionery and a limited range of reading material. Popular magazines in Chile of the *Hello!* variety were much like their counterparts everywhere else in the world except for their titles: one magazine which I often observed people reading was named *Things* and another *Very Interesting*.

Seven hours passed. Assuming that Hercules planes are not equipped with a Ladies I had put all the thermals on in advance. These included ankle-length longjohns and a long-sleeved vest. By lunchtime I was in danger of passing out from heat exhaustion. In the middle of the afternoon I was standing outside, taking some air, and through the glass doors I saw an official appear in front of my hopeful fellow-travellers. They leapt up. I rushed in. The man had asked them to move so that the cleaners could sweep that area of the airport. It was the most exciting thing that had happened all day. The fraying cord of hope unravelled a little further at six when the captain came back and said there was another problem, this time unspecified, and told us to go home and come back at six-thirty in the morning. The sergeant in charge of the church-builders was driving them to their boarding-house in town, and I decided to instal myself in a room in their lodgings, working on the assumption that the plane wasn't going to leave without them.

The churchbuilders weren't particularly interested in Antarctica. What they were interested in was when they might finish their work there, the football champions Colo Colo and the marital status of the young woman from Valdivia. To pass the evening they hired a video called *Retorno al Futuro II* which the obliging family who owned the boarding-house watched with us in their living room; a ten-year-old son insisted on the presence of the family chicken in the room.

Something went wrong with the television screen, causing the subtitles to disappear, so the churchbuilders prevailed upon me to provide a simultaneous translation of their video.

The next morning we went straight to the door of a Hercules built in the United States in 1980. A perishing wind cut across the airstrip, stinging our faces, and a jeep arrived loaded with cargo for Antarctica, including a vacuum cleaner and crates of Coca-Cola. The young woman from Valdivia turned up, controversially, with the dapper crash-inspector. We boarded, and strapped ourselves into red webbing fold-down seats.

Even when the plane took off I was convinced it was going to develop engine trouble, and turn back, and that all flights would be suspended indefinitely and I would never see the seventh continent and never finish my Chilean journey. The cabin did actually fill with acrid smoke, but nobody looked very worried about it so I supposed it was normal. We advanced over the gunmetal Strait, the sky, more enormous now, streaked with salmon pink and petrol blue clouds. The Strait was so narrow that I began to appreciate Magellan's achievement in finding it. Tierra del Fuego followed shortly, then water – the Pacific, and the Atlantic.

A contingent of air force personnel had come with us. The plane was very noisy, and every single person except me had brought protective ear-phones. The bastards could have told me, I thought. I asked to go into the cockpit. It was large, up a ladder, and there were seven people in it. After chatting to a couple of them for a few minutes I noticed an elderly man wearing dark glasses hunched in a seat sunk into the wall. His hands were jammed into the pockets of an expensive-looking black wool overcoat with gold decorations on the shoulders. He was sitting absolutely still, his skin pale against the black fabric, and he looked deadly, his jowelly face expressionless. *My God*, I thought, *it's him*. But it wasn't Pinochet. It was a naval captain rejoining his ship, anchored in Antarctica.

There was a man in the cockpit who had been living at

Teniente Rodolfo Marsh, the largest Chilean base in Antarctica, for two years. He was very enthusiastic about it. 'It's a paradise,' he said. 'No crime, and no danger. My children are innocents.' He had three young children, and he took them to the continent once a year to expose them to microbes. The entire family caught a cold as soon as they landed in Punta Arenas. They had everything at Marsh, including a school. There were a couple of hundred residents in the summer and about ninety in the winter. Antarctic service is voluntary, and there is no shortage of takers.

Back in the body of the plane the lower orders of the air force larked around with redundant red webbing and blocks of polystyrene. When one of the blocks flew across the cabin and hit me on the shoulder a representative followed in pursuit, and he sat down next to me and introduced himself, speaking loudly right into my ear. He was from the desert north, and he said, 'I'll never get used to the cold, not if I live here till I'm a hundred and one'. It didn't take us long to get onto the subject of the Falklands War and Chilean assistance to the British RAF. 'We painted the crown off a plane at our base, and we gave your men our flying jackets. It was very funny seeing them with our name tags. You know, "Gonzalo" is thought of as a small, swarthy bloke. When I saw a tall, blond Englishman in a jacket labelled "Gonzalo" I really laughed a lot.' The troops often spoke like this. The officers did not. I wheedled a fighter pilot round to the subject once, and he said, 'I saw many things. I do not speak them.'

As we came down the sea reappeared, its surface pierced with icebergs. Everything was shining. It was like entering another universe; a surreal one, beyond us. Some of the icebergs were ice-blue. So that was where the locution 'ice-blue' came from.

We crossed Drake Passage and approached the South Shetlands, the Antarctic archipelago named by Scottish sealers at the end of a tapering tail of land flicked out from the amorphous white continent. The petrochemical engineer looked up from his *Reader's Digest* and pointed out King George Island. As we got nearer I could see that it wasn't all white; part of it was dark earth. It was summer in Antarctica. But most of it was white. There was so much white land, fluted like corduroy and plated with glaciated slopes, glittering and reflecting the sun. There were some ice cliffs, but mostly the land sloped down to the ocean, which crusted into ice in a wide band all around the island. A collection of brown pinpricks appeared, and it made me laugh out loud to see the Lilliputian base set down there on the snow.

We landed in a roar. When the door was opened a glacial blast swept into the Hercules, and as I set foot on Antarctica, my heart singing, a man dressed like a yeti approached me.

'Mrs Sara Wheeler? Welcome to Antarctica. I am Commandante Leopaldo, and you are my responsibility on this icy continent.'

He looked as though this were an onerous task, so I tried to be friendly, to break the ice, as it were.

The base consisted of clusters of portacabin-type buildings, all raised several feet off the ground, with flat roofs and small, square windows. We entered the mess, one of the largest; the lobby was busy, as it took people ten minutes to divest themselves of their outer layers of clothing. The floor was splotched with puddles. The mess was as well-heated as my flat at home in the winter, and air force personnel sat around in T-shirts in a lounge area, chatting or reading mail. Leopaldo fetched me a coffee. After a quarter of an hour of small talk we got dressed up again, went outside and walked down to Fildes Bay. The circumpolar sea consisted, to some three hundred yards out, of millions of chunks of neon blue ice, and a sinister grey Armada vessel was anchored beyond them.

There was a bank a few hundred yards from the shore – a

bank that dispenses money, like the ones you find in every high street. The manager, open-collared, leapt to his feet when Leopaldo ushered me in, and he kissed me before typing my name on a certificate indicating that I had been given one thousand dollars by an Antarctic bank (I had not). In the meteorological station nearby I was shown the studio of Radio Sovereign FM. On Friday evenings it broadcast a quiz show. All the questions were about Antarctica, and other bases took part, although they first had to find someone who could speak Spanish. The Chinese had recently won, and they arrived at Marsh that same night to collect their prize, which was a specially baked cake.

'*En Antártida*,' said Leopaldo, '*no hay fronteras*' – there are no borders.

I was shown the hospital, a larger metal box on stilts where two appendicectomies had been performed and several children had been born. They were very proud of this hospital, and it was frequently used by staff from neighbouring bases – even Argentinian staff. There really aren't any borders in Antarctica, and Antarctic politics, which revolve around territorial claims, international no-mining legislation and environmental protection, and which are complex, tense and often hostile, are played out not in the icy continent but in government buildings of the First World's capitals.

The Chileans behaved very confidently down there. Usually they were shy in international situations. But they were nearer home than anyone else on King George, better equipped, and there were more of them, so it was natural that they should feel confident. They were very conscious too that what they were doing was important for Chile.

Expatriates in Santiago often told me that they found Chilean nationalism an offensive characteristic. They complained about people being narrow-minded, and were frustrated by the general lack of interest in anything beyond

Chilean borders. Such things are more noticeable to residents than travellers – though I did observe a limited field of vision, even among educated Chileans. As in the case of Argentina-hating, a sense of inferiority seemed to be lurking in the shadowy hinterland of the national consciousness, and I wondered if it didn't breed a kind of insecure nationalism. Self-obsession and insecurity were apparent in the disproportionate and repetitive media coverage generated on the rare occasions when anything Chilean enjoyed international success. I grew tired of reading about the Chilean iceberg on the stand at the Seville Expo. The newspapers were excessively parochial – the front section of the leading quality broadsheet, *Mercurio*, was filled with vacuous shots of the aristocracy at cocktail parties. 'Geophysical isolation,' said one of my history books, 'means that a nation is more than usually obsessed with itself.'

I was shown the furnace where combustible rubbish is burned and the welded tin drums in which non-disposable rubbish is flown back to the mainland. I was shown the post office, the state lottery office and Leopaldo's house. His wife was baking a fruit cake. We could have been in a middle-class suburban semi almost anywhere in the developed world. Not only did its occupants enjoy the likes of powerful central heating and a microwave oven, but they had also decorated their home with lace doilies, flying ducks and framed family photographs.

Later we walked over shattered ice pools and climbed a rock; at the top we watched eight chinstrap penguins waddling placidly around the rookery. Below I could see the church, at that time resembling a blue bandstand, and next to it were the churchbuilders, who waved, their heads sticking up out of a giant container bearing the words '*capilla antártica*' (Antarctic chapel) in a docker's scrawl.

Leopaldo pointed at the sun. 'We have a hole,' he said, 'in

221

the ozone,' as if this were some kind of Chilean achievement. The hole which opens annually in the ozone shield fifteen miles above the earth's surface in Antarctica causes too much ultraviolet light to reach southern Chile. I heard many stories about animal blindness in Magallanes, and I read in a local paper that the incidence of melanoma in humans in Punta Arenas is above the global average. But this was too downbeat for Leopaldo, who didn't want to discuss the matter, and he mentioned lunch and led the way back to the mess in silence.

Leopaldo disappeared once we were inside, and I never saw him again. A squadron commander called Carlos appeared to have taken over his heavy burden; perhaps I was considered too much for one person to cope with all day. Carlos looked like he had just been defrosted after twenty years in a medical school freezer. He was rather more approachable than his predecessor, however, and we got off to a good start over a steak lunch served by a man in a red dicky bow. I noticed how he and everyone else addressed me immediately in the familiar '*tu*' form.

After lunch we had another coffee in the lounge, where small groups of men were playing cards and looking bored. Carlos showed me military maps of the zone. Antarctic territory claimed by Chile is perceived as an extension of the mainland. It is a segment measured in degrees, like a slice of a cake, and the Chileans take care to ensure that it features on every map – even small badge maps of the kind that boy scouts sew on their parkas. It covers twice the area of mainland Chile, and they call it *territorio chileno antártico*; land earmarked by the other six claimants was referred to on Carlos' map as *pretensión británica* or *reclamación australiana*. Antarctic territory is even incorporated within the administrative subdivision of the country: the Twelfth Region is called *Región de Magallanes y de la Antártida Chilena*.

Chile and Argentina base their Antarctic claims on medieval

222

bulls and decrees inherited from Spain. Official Chilean documents dealing with Antarctica make a great deal of a note handwritten by Bernardo O'Higgins early in the nineteenth century referring to Chilean territory down to the South Pole; this note was discovered languishing in British Foreign Office vaults in 1918. Chile made formal declarations to the international community in 1940 in order to assert its territorial rights in Antarctica, and it was one of the original signatories of the 1959 Antarctic Treaty, ratified by twelve nations in 1961. The Treaty, which recognizes that Antarctica shall continue forever to be used exclusively for peaceful purposes, remains the core of international Antarctic politics. Besides legislating for environmental protection and the exchange of scientific data between contracting parties, it stipulates that no new territorial claims may be asserted, or existing claims enlarged.

Chilean policy towards Antarctica is probably the only area of national life that remained unchanged in 1970 and 1973. Similarly, one of the few things Chile has ever agreed with Argentina was to take a common line against Britain twice in the 1940s by reinforcing the concept of a South American Antarctic (although they even squabbled about that later). Pinochet flew down there in 1977 and declared that it was merely a continuation of mainland territory. Six families were sent to Teniente Marsh in 1984 to institute a 'permanent' settlement; like Argentina, Chile has been criticized for the 'non-scientific emphasis' of its Antarctic presence.

Carlos folded up the maps and told me we were going out. He took me off in a specially adapted landcruiser, and a few hundred yards from Marsh a large orange caterpillar tank appeared in front of us with six Chinese men in orange snowsuits perched on it. One of them got down and embraced Carlos. They had rumbled over from the Chinese base, which was called Great Wall. The embracer came round to my side and pumped my hand enthusiastically with his big furry glove.

We drove on to Great Wall, a cluster of rusty portacabins painted red. National Working Committees of Young Pioneers had been busy setting up monuments in honour of nothing in particular. In the porches (the front doors in Antarctica were like the doors of industrial freezers) small armies of plastic flipflops were lined up in neat rows.

We walked to a ridge, accompanied by a single skua, a brown goosey gull which was eyeing the fur cuffs of Carlos' boots. The north side of King George Island is one of the few parts of Antarctica not permanently under snow, and patches of the exposed soil were covered in wiry lichen.

'That,' said Carlos, pointing to a pale green, heathery tuft, 'takes a thousand years to mature.'

On the other side of Marsh, later, we stopped the landcruiser at a small stream. A man joined us from the Russian base. It was called Bellingshausen after the first man who ever saw the continent. (It was in 1820, and he was looking for the Pole.) 'We are very proud of this river between our bases,' said the Russian in Spanish.

'What's it called?' I asked.

'The Volga,' said the Russian immediately.

'The Mapocho,' said Carlos simultaneously, and they both laughed.

Each country transports its culture to the bottom of the world when it sets up in Antarctica – the good and the bad. In Bellingshausen the piles of rubbish, the acres of mud, the puffy faced men with silver teeth, the ghostly outlines of the metal letters CCCP which had been clumsily jemmied off doors, the abandoned machinery of failed scientific projects, the one minuscule and inadequate Lada – well, they were Russian all right. The base contained six 'souvenir shops'. These were recognizable by the word SHOP painted in tar on doors leading to tiny rooms set aside for profiteering. The Russians had carried souvenirs thousands of miles to flog them – dollars only – to tourists from the luxury cruiseships which docked from time to time in the ice flow. In one of the shops a blonde woman with bright blue eyeshadow was selling fur caps and amber necklaces. 'Russian amber can cure diseases,' she said with a gleam in her eye.

In the snowfields beyond we saw a tiny orange figure kneeling against the white. He was a Chinese scientist working on a project involving ice and its microscopic air bubbles. The air was taken off and examined in laboratories in Washington (Beijing wasn't up to it), and it revealed what the atmosphere consisted of thousands of years ago. 'Air archaeology,' said Carlos.

By the time we reached the Uruguayan base (half a dozen corrugated iron hangars) we had picked up two Brazilian lieutenant colonels, a Uruguayan vulcanologist and a French doctor. We got out of the landcruiser and began walking to a lake. A steep ice cliff on the far side was streaked green and grey by antediluvian volcanic ash and covered with a lid of dazzling snow six feet deep, and at one end of the lake an ice cave arced perfectly, its fringe of sharp icicles catching the sun. It was a tough walk, up and down snowhills, arms outstretched.

'There's a river beneath us,' said Carlos cheerfully, 'so keep your arms out to stop being sucked under if the ice breaks.'

These conditions were benign, of course, compared with the interior of the continent. Jean-Louis Etienne was co-leader of the 1990 International Trans-Antarctica team, which travelled 3741 miles on foot across the seventh continent. In the middle of the journey he said, 'Sometimes it is like Antarctica has no soul ... it is not a place for man. But other times ... I feel like I am in a big, wondrous temple.'

We had to cross another river, an open one about two feet deep which ran from the lake, and one of the Brazilians gave me his spare pair of dayglo snow goggles and a piggy-back.

The cave turned out to be a tunnel patterned with perfect circular indentations like beaten white metal, each exactly the same size.

> It was a miracle of rare device,
> A sunny pleasure-dome with caves of ice!

Water and oversized icecubes flowed through the tunnel, but we walked along the edge, meeting a curtain of icicles at the other end. I went ahead with the vulcanologist, and Carlos and the rest went back to Artigas for a cup of tea. The soft snow again made walking hard work, but from the top of the hill beyond Antarctica appeared in all its glory, refulgent in the late afternoon sunlight. As their shadows lengthened on the rippling Southern Ocean the icebergs took on an incandescent quality, and I watched a single snow petrel fly among them, gliding through its private symphony. There was no sound at all except the occasional metallic tap-tap as the vulcanologist, a hundred yards away, scraped snow into a specimen tin. I did not need to take a photograph, and I could not: I knew that moment would always be with me, and I did not want to betray it with a picture.

On our way back to Marsh we left the landcruiser again and hiked over to a beach of volcanic basalt pebbles on Drake Passage, sliding down ice slopes on our bottoms. Little pieces of quartz glittered around the ice pools, and an Antarctic dove perched on a whalebone before floating off and hovering against the bright blue sky. At the edge of the water a harem of southern elephant seals dozed and flicked their tails, their skin and fur peeling off horridly like wallpaper, and then a bull almost twenty feet long inflated his snout and trumpeted at us, revealing a soft lipstick pink gullet. Out on a small headland Antarctic fur seals and their pups lay comatose in little groups, exuding indifference, their heads flat to their bodies and their eyelids drooping occasionally in a languorous blink.

The last thing we did was climb a hill with a clear view beyond the island. Another white landmass filled the horizon. I looked over the small buildings of the small base in the foreground, and I thought, That's an ice-desert bigger than Australia. It was the highest continent, as well as the driest, the coldest, and the windiest. But it wasn't that. Nobody owned it – that was the thrilling thing. Seven countries might have 'claimed' a slice for themselves, and there might be pushing two hundred little 'research' camps, but the continent wasn't really owned by anyone. It was like seeing the earth for the very first time, and I felt less homeless there than I had ever felt anywhere. All the sordid failures and degradations of humanity and the morass of personal anxieties we struggle to live within shrank to insignificant specks as I looked out over the Antarctic snowfields.

A Pole came to Marsh for tea. The Polish base, Arcktowski, is one of the smallest on the island, and rather poorly equipped; 'but they're used to roughing it, in Poland,' Carlos said. This Pole was a lively man with masses of black hair, and when I first saw him he was laughing wildly with three or four Chilean officers. Although I had observed that all countries freight their cultures down there, the harsh conditions limit their application. Antarctica is a leveller; they're all in it together. The Pole's Spanish was ropey, and I asked him how he communicated with his colleagues at the other bases. He laughed and said in Spanish, 'We speak *antártico*. It's our own language – grown by us, like a plant in a cold greenhouse!'

227

Chapter Twelve

When God created the world he had a handful of everything left –
mountains, deserts, lakes, glaciers – and he put it all in his pocket.
But there was a hole in this pocket you see, and as God walked
across heaven it all trickled out, and the long trail it made on earth
was Chile.

Drunk, to author, Isla Navarino, March 1992

Back in Punta Arenas I applied myself to the task of renewing
my visa, which was due to expire in three days. After being
shunted from one municipal building to another I was
signalled towards a table stacked with forms outside a men's
toilet. I sat down and started to fill one in, grudgingly
determined to meet the exhaustive requirements of another
Chilean bureaucrat. The visa renewal form demands two
colour photographs in which you must be holding a sign
bearing your full name and passport number. I had anticipated this event by having the said photos taken in Santiago;
they came in fours, so I had mailed the other two to my
mother, thinking at least she would be pleased to receive
concrete evidence that I was still alive. She wrote to me shortly
afterwards asking if I had been arrested. It was clear that she

wouldn't have been surprised either way: the paragraph concluded, 'Aunty Gladys' leg is no better'.

When I reached a question on the form asking the size of my boat I put a dash. When I came on to a complicated section on nets I realized I was renewing my place on the fisherman's register. It turned out that the right form, when I located it, had to be signed by the governor, so I was obliged to leave it at the office, arranging optimistically to pick up the new visa when I got back from my next mini-trip. I left the officials huddled round fifteen lurid DDR stamps on a double-page spread in my passport and glancing up at me with narrowed eyes.

I called into the post office, and found my name on the *poste restante* list. Waiting post in Chile is separated into male and female recipient lists, but in Punta Arenas they had achieved the feat of a third category. This list was labelled 'Pseudonyms and numbers'. Why would anyone write to a number? How did they know if a name was a pseudonym or genuine? How did a recipient prove he or she was a number? Also, after my name on the female list I read, 'Finney, Albert'.

Largely due to the efforts of the Regional Director of Tourism in Punta Arenas I procured a plane ticket for almost nothing to the south of Tierra del Fuego. I later learnt that it was because a senior airline official had spread it round that I was 'pretty'. This revolting state of affairs was a familiar one by this stage of the trip; it was never sufficiently revolting, however, for me to reject its fruits.

The plane was a Canadian Twin Otter, and I boarded with ten islanders, citizens of the southernmost permanent settlement in the world (Antarctic bases don't count) – though I can't say it showed. Tierra del Fuego is a group of islands across the Magellan Strait from the Chilean and Argentinian mainland, divided by a vertical line between the two republics. It was spotted by Magellan in 1520, and he named it

Smokeland after the wispy columns he observed rising from the natives' fires; his peremptory patron, Charles V of Spain, however, wished it to be Fireland, and so it was. It wasn't until Drake arrived half a century later that Fireland was discovered to be an archipelago. Properly, the toponym belongs to the group, but it is commonly used to refer to Isla Grande alone, the largest island in South America. The Twin Otter was propelling itself south of this main island to Isla Navarino, in turn usually known by the name of its only settlement, Puerto Williams.

We crossed the north of Isla Grande, splashed with opaque green lakes ringed by mineral-tinted bands of earth, and continued over the dark blue vastness of Useless Bay, and then Dawson Island appeared, wobbling through the heat of the Twin Otter's engines. In 1973, after the coup, every surviving minister in the Allende government except Carlos Briones was tied up in a small plane and taken to Dawson Island. It was a good place to choose to make them feel forgotten, cold and isolated, a Chilean Siberia.

Shortly afterwards we followed the Almirantazgo Sound along the coast of the big island, skirting the Darwin cordillera, tipped with frosted snow and stretching into the distance, sunlight bouncing off the isolated lakes. The highest mountain wasn't identified until 1962. The plane slid over a glacier in an air current and landed at a diminutive airstrip overlooking the Beagle Channel.

Isla Navarino, a Chilean possession, lies below Argentinian territory, separated from it by twelve miles of water. Three small islands called Lennox, Picton and Nueva directly off its east coast almost caused a war between Argentina and Chile in 1978, six years before the Falklands. They had been arguing for a hundred years about which of them owned the islands, and in 1977 international arbitration assigned them to Chile. Argentina refused to accept the decision, and troops on both sides mobilized. The object of desire was not so much land as sea. Besides fish, there was oil there, and oil was what both republics needed.

The Pope eventually persuaded the two governments to disarm and settle. Fourteen years had passed since then, but I had noticed a residual national anxiety over this southern territory. In Punta Arenas I had asked people if they thought Argentina might try to take the three islands again. My diary notes, 'Everyone, no matter what their background, is convinced that the Argentinians are going to have a go again – if not the three islands, then another bit of southern Chile. It feels like a place on permanent alert, and when I heard shouting in the street outside the house this evening I thought it was an invasion, and put a new film in the camera. But they were celebrating victory in some local football match.'

The present settlement at Williams exists largely as a deterrent, and it is dominated by a naval base. It acquired its peculiarly British name in 1953 in honour of John Williams, the Bristolian captain of the *Ancud*, the ship which claimed the Magellan Strait for Chile in 1843. The small settlement which existed prior to the base was called Puerto Luisa; its residents were descendants of English missionaries, and they ran a sawmill and farmed. Williams has been made the capital of Chilean Antarctica, its location outside Antarctic boundaries notwithstanding.

The houses were low, with corrugated iron roofs, and the roads dirt tracks carved out with puddles. It was all very bleak, and I felt a long way from home as I stood in the rain trying to decide what to do. There was one guesthouse in what they called the square; it was rather an apathetic attempt at a square, with a low concrete wall sheltering a few dead shrubs. In this guesthouse, however, I was enthusiastically welcomed (I was the only guest) by the owner, Mario, and his wife; it was 29 February and Mario's birthday, so he immediately invited

231

me to his party, due to begin imminently.

Mario took his birthday very seriously, running around the house and garden making the final preparations for the celebration. I guessed he was about forty-four, and he had lived on the island for twenty years. He had done all right; he had an entrepreneurial spirit, and the guesthouse supplemented an income from various agricultural interests. His wife, a figure of Chaucerian ribaldry and feisty spirits, presided over the household while knitting in her chair next to the wood-burning stove or pursuing her five-year-old son, Julio, a delightfully wicked little boy whom I took to greatly, though he allegedly told his mother at the end of the week that he didn't like me. Entrepreneurial spirits have to be understood in context down there, and once the guesthouse had been set up it was clear that both Mario and his wife felt that they had discharged their responsibilities towards it. They were wholly disinterested in whether I intended to stay one night or one year and unembarrassed by the absence of any kind of heating in the bedrooms, which meant that they were like freezer rooms in meat-packing factories.

I enjoyed their attitude to life. It followed a strict policy of *laissez-faire* – except when it came to birthday parties. The guests began to arrive, and Mario fussed around them. Knots of people stood in the garden, drinking from plastic beakers and hugging the bonfire. I was introduced like a cabaret act. Everyone wanted to invite me to their home or show me some special feature of the landscape, and the week was quickly booked up with projected outings and dinners. Later in the evening Mario made a fulsome speech thanking his good and loyal friends for sharing this special day with him. We ate meat grilled over charcoal and drank the popular mixture of wine and Coca-Cola, although I noticed that as it got later they abandoned the Coca-Cola, and soon it was two hours past midnight and I had forgotten to ask anyone to marry me.

*

At the brutal hour of seven-thirty a rusty juggernaut tooted outside the house: my first trip, to collect wood and deliver it to a police station at the western tip of the island. The house was silent and strewn with the debris of the party, which had moved indoors when the fire died. I had forgotten the driver's name, and his mate's, but it didn't seem to matter, and we set off in good humour, three clouds of breath condensing in the high cab.

After half an hour the driver slammed on the brakes. 'Beaver!' he said, pointing to a crocodile skin spatula disappearing into a bush. Often too in the undergrowth we disturbed fat upland geese, which looked brown and ordinary until they panicked, taking off towards the water and revealing their striped white wings.

A sign welcomed us to Puerto Navarino, which consisted of a police station, a small jetty, two houses owned by the navy and two derelict farm buildings. I believe it was the place once called Laiwaia where, in 1867, missionaries established an indigenous farming settlement. It might seem odd to locate a police station in an isolated spot with no one to police, but it was directly opposite Ushuaia, the southernmost town in Argentina, and this was a paranoid island.

Two young policemen in mufti came out of the station and climbed into the back of the truck. We drove further west, and they began loading logs. I walked around the deciduous forest, already deep red, the silvery trunks covered in a pale primrose lichen. The prevailing south-westerlies had beaten them into surreal shapes, like distended letters of the alphabet.

On the coast grass had grown in unnatural humps over piles of shells and ash, and I found a bone fish spear in an exposed pit, finely carved into a double point. I have it sellotaped to a corner of my word-processor now; I suppose it belonged to a Yahgan once. His tribe were nomadic (the name is western-ized. They called themselves *Yámana*, which means 'people') and for generations paddled their canoes from the Brecknock peninsula to Cape Horn, but as they were hunted and marginalized by European colonists and their descendants they concentrated themselves in the canals around Isla Navarino. The spoke five mutually intelligible dialects, to-gether constituting a linguistic group unrelated to any other: for family connections so distant that a sentence would be required to express them in English, the Yahgan had a word, and they enjoyed verbs such as 'to come unexpectedly across a hard substance when eating something soft' (like a pearl in an oyster). To express specific periods of the year they used phrases like, 'the time when the bark is loose'. But they had no words for numerals beyond three.

The last pure Yahgan, Abuela (Grandmother) Rosa, died in 1982.

The Yahgan were distant relations of the Alacalufe (the westernized name of the *Kaweshkar* tribe) who canoed further north, from the Magellan Strait to the Taitao peninsula. They were nomadic too, and they could count up to five (though 'five' was synonymous with 'many').

The third significant indigenous tribe around the Strait were the Ona, known to anthropologists as 'foot Indians' as opposed to 'canoe Indians'. Divided into two branches, called Haush (or Aush) and Shelknam, they lived on Isla Grande, and hunted the guanaco. One of their ideas was that foetal development required repeated coitus. Even by the exacting standards of the conquerors of the Americas the Ona suffered a particularly brutal extinction.

Darwin hadn't been very impressed by the people he saw in Tierra del Fuego. He wrote, 'Viewing such men, one can hardly make oneself believe that they are fellow-creatures, and inhabitants of the same world.' I wonder what they thought of him, or what they would have thought about a country which sent its working-class children down the mines and up the chimneys and into the textile mills until they collapsed under the looms.

I was struck, too, by Darwin's conviction that the primitive lifestyle of the Fuegians constituted evidence of a stunted sensibility, or even of no sensibility at all. He wrote of them, 'How little can the higher powers of the mind be brought into play! What is there for the imagination to picture, for reason to compare, for judgment to decide upon?' (Was he fingering his copy of *Paradise Lost* at that moment? He usually had it in his pocket on the journey.) Laurens van der Post frequently illustrates the folly of failing to understand that the imagination can be triggered in many different ways. I often stopped in a still place and thought of the moment in *Venture to the Interior* when van der Post drinks in a particularly scintillating African landscape whilst listening to Bach's St Matthew Passion. He remarks to his companion, a man who loves Africa profoundly, that it was a shame Livingstone couldn't hear that music when he walked by there.

'I expect he heard the same thing, in other ways,' replies the companion sharply.

Later, in the undergrowth behind the police station, I discovered a camouflaged bunker and a heap of empty cartridges. I realized how real their apprehension must be, with such concrete reminders of 1978 in their back gardens. I lay down on the grass next to a small wooden bridge, contemplating this permanent state of tension, and I must have fallen asleep, as I was woken by a warm breath on my cheek, and opened my eyes to the inquisitive stare of a white pig with large black spots.

A policeman cooked lunch later, and after we had eaten we stretched out in the sun while the four police horses frisked on the beach. The policemen showed me round the station ('the oldest in Chile'), and when they said it was hard in the winter, these lieutenants of the Cold War, I ventured to ask what they did in those months. They quickly listed numerous activities, the most arduous among them feeding the horses.

As the sun moved towards the ocean and the truck driver muttered about leaving, the head policeman said to me, 'Why don't you stay with us? I'm driving to Williams on Tuesday morning – stay till then. You can live in the mess, and ride the horses . . . whatever you like . . .'

'But I haven't got any things with me.'

'We can lend you a toothbrush.'

It was a beguiling idea. I had never seen such a beautiful spot.

'We'd love some company,' said another policeman.

My main worry (I had lived in the same clothes for three days often before) was that I had nothing to read. The head policeman showed me the small library, to solve this problem, and I selected from back issues of *Police Review*, *A Legal Guide to Autopsies* and *An Anthology of Erotica (illustrated)*. (Out of boredom I did actually read several copies of the *Police Review*. Months later the Navarino policemen sent copies to me in London as they came out, addressed to my telephone number.)

So it was that I was a guest of the Chilean *carabineros* for three days and two nights; my visa actually expired while I was enjoying their hospitality. The head policeman, José, was in his early forties and had a wife and two sons in Punta Arenas, but when he got out his photo album to show me, all the pictures were of him; it was his way of asserting his identity, I suppose, and a more honest one than many others. One of his two subordinates, Mauricio, was twenty-three and tall with Transylvanian good looks, and the youngest, called Piglet by the others, was thin, cheeky and highly strung.

The mess window overlooked a skyline of Argentinian

236

mountains, bleachy white and sharp as cleavers. At night the lights of Ushuaia flickered beyond the mute black strip of water. The small black-and-white television was permanently on in the dining area, tuned in to an Argentinian station, *faute de mieux*. It was ironic that the rationale for this outpost was to guard against Argentinian hostility yet its occupants spent all evening watching Argentinian dancing girls. Over dinner on the first night José said his piece about the shocking absence of censorship on Argentinian television. Ten minutes later he was goggle-eyed in front of a soft porn film.

The policemen treated me like a little queen. They tried to prepare extra special meals for my benefit, which was particularly touching given the primitive nature of the kitchen and the pathetically limited ingredients available. José, an intelligent man who would have been an officer had his family had enough money to get him trained, held strong opinions on a wide range of unsavoury topics such as military control and the evils of trade unionism, but I closed my ears, and couldn't help liking him. They took me out on expeditions, anxious that I should see everything. If my boots were just a little damp they insisted on lending me shoes even though they were much too big, and I had to fight to be allowed to wash the dishes.

On the second day we went to pick mushrooms, and they taught me which ones were safe. I wasn't a good student: I noticed that most of the mushrooms in my basket were rejected by Mauricio when he prepared lunch. We ate them with a bright orange spherical fungus picked off the beech trunks. Afterwards, Mauricio and Piglet took me with them on patrol to Wulaia, a bay to the south west.

'What are we patrolling for?' I asked as we guided the horses through gorsey bushes.

'To see if there are any Argentinians, I suppose,' said Piglet.

'Well, what are we going to do if there are?'

237

'Umm . . . go back and tell the boss, I guess.'

The bay looked towards the Murray Canal and the un-inhabited Hoste Island, a series of peninsulas linked by fragile strips of land sprawling among the cold Pacific waters. Wulaia was a potent name in the history of the indigenous peoples of the Beagle Channel and the interlopers who came to disturb them. Captain Robert FitzRoy of HMS *Beagle* took four Yahgan with him on the long journey home, and after three of them (one died in Plymouth) had enjoyed the sophisticated pleasures of nineteenth-century England he conveyed them back to their channels and left them at the small, peaceful bay of Wulaia. They had spent about three years in British company.[1]

More than a quarter of a century later, on 6 November 1859, a small British mission held its first church service at Wulaia. Eight foreigners were present and they had mustered an impressive congregation of three hundred. The mission cook, Alfred Cole, had remained on board their ship, the *Allen Gardiner*, which was anchored opposite the little church. As Cole listened to the tuneless, enthusiastic verses of the first hymn from across the water he noticed movement outside the church, and then he saw all his colleagues butchered by a party of men led, it seems almost certain, by Jemmy Button, one of the three who had been presented at the Court of St James' during his stay in England.

The twentieth-century Chileans had named an island after Button.

Back at home, Fuegian missionary work already had a bad

---

[1] The story of the canoe people's residence in England, including their audience with William IV and Queen Adelaide, is well documented. For a brief introduction see Chapter 61 of Bruce Chatwin's *In Patagonia*.

reputation, and its supporters were accused of naivety and worse. After news reached London in 1852 of a harrowing and ultimately fatal endeavour on Navarino a leader in *The Times* demanded the end of Patagonian missions. But it never came. The Anglican Mission established itself in various parts of the islands during those years, and from 1906 to 1920 its members worked in another corner of the west coast of Navarino, called Douglas Bay. We rode on to this place, one of the most desolate on earth, and Mauricio said, 'I think you are the first here, from your country, since those *protestantes*.'

I sensed that he was about to ask me why my compatriots had come, so I quickly developed a vigorous interest in the flora to head the question off; there were few things I would not have done to avoid answering it.

We lay there in silence, capturing the last of the late afternoon sun, the dog pushing his nose under our chins and the horses stamping, steam dissolving off their coats into the sharp air. The Beagle glittered, lumpy steamer ducks careered over the rocks, redundant wings flapping irritably, and as I thought of Darwin's judgments again a moment came into my mind from Lucas Bridges' *The Uttermost Part of the Earth*, one of the best books ever written about South America. He was sitting only a dozen or two miles from that spot at a similar time of day almost a century ago.

Talimeoat was a most likeable Indian. I was much in his company. One still evening in autumn ... I was walking with him near Lake Kami. We were just above upper tree level, and before descending into the valley, rested on a grassy slope. The air was crisp ... A few gilt-edged, feathery clouds broke the monotony of the pale green sky, and the beech forest that clothed the lake's steep banks to the water's edge had not yet completely lost its brilliant autumn colours. The evening light gave the remote ranges a purple

239

tint impossible to describe or to paint.

Across leagues of wooded hills up the forty-mile length of Lake Kami, Talimeoat and I gazed long and silently towards a glorious sunset. I knew that he was searching the distance for any sign of smoke from the camp-fires of friends or foes. After a while his vigilance relaxed and, lying near me, he seemed to become oblivious to my presence. Feeling the chill of evening, I was on the point of suggesting a move, when he heaved a deep sigh and said to himself, as softly as an Ona could say anything,

'*Yak baruin.*' ('My country'.)

At sunset, on my last night, we went on a final trip: they so much wanted me to see a beaver (my glimpse of a tail, apparently, didn't count). There were many clearings of leafless and chiselled trunks enfolded within the luxuriance of the forest, but although we saw their wigwams and their swimming pools as we sloshed through the mud, we didn't see a beaver. The policemen did show me old Yahgan canoe runways at the water's edge. I had never seen a Yahgan canoe, but I saw an Alacalufe version in Punta Arenas. It was about ten feet long and made out of evergreen beech bark. This boat had arrived at the town's sandy point in 1903, together with one other, and the people in it said that they had come from the canals to petition for the return of a five-year-old child who had been stolen by sealers. They got the kid back, and the public notary bought the canoe from them for posterity, dispatching its occupants home on a sailing ship.

At twilight the clouds hung low like white canopies illuminated from below by a pink spotlight. The mountains turned shades of indigo and the mirrored water darkened, cracked by trails of ducklings. On the highest peak of Hoste Island a slender column of rock jutted upwards just before the perpendicular walls of the summit.

'That,' said José, 'is what the locals call the monk entering the monastery.'

When I woke on the last day there was a three-feet long beaver on the end of my bed, staring at me and baring its horrid little yellow teeth like an old man's toenails. About five seconds passed as we looked at each other, then I heard sniggering outside in the corridor. I wiggled the beaver with a toe. It was stuffed. I shouted abuse through the door, and Mauricio and Piglet laughed for fifteen minutes.

After breakfast and a good deal of shuffling around José cleared his throat.

'*Sarita*, we'd like to present you with something.'

Piglet stepped forward and thrust a slice of wood into my hands which he had been holding behind his back. They had sawed it off a beech trunk, glued the three silver badges of the police force in an arc at the top, painted on it '*carabineros de Chile*' and inscribed this in Spanish: 'Puerto Navarino, the tip of Chile and the southern limit of the world, reached only by true persons of sacrifice, bravery and loyalty to a cause, and these people include our friend Sara Wheeler. This plaque is from her devoted friends among the *carabineros*.'

I looked down at it, and they stood in front of me with their coy smiles. José, who had a Pinochet sticker on his wardrobe door and whose politics made Pol Pot look like an innocent, said quietly, 'Thank you for trusting us.'

He shook my hand, and he touched my heart, too. I suggested photos, and they rushed off, changed into their uniforms and stood like woodentops, unsmiling, next to the *carabineros* sign outside the station.

Back in Puerto Williams I reappeared at Mario's guesthouse; there were still no other guests, and I doubted if anyone had noticed my absence. I said hello and walked back into my room, which was just as I had left it, bed unmade, three days previously.

People were so used to nothing happening on the island that it rarely occurred to them to do anything themselves. There was seldom anyone on the street before ten, and at Mario's it was difficult to raise anyone before eleven. Nobody washed up there until there was no clean crockery left in the kitchen. It was very endearing.

I walked through the sphagnum bog and beech trees to a lake in the heart of the island, towards the Navarino Teeth, an uneven gum of gleaming lower canines. When I stopped on a high ridge to eat some bread and salted cod I had bought for lunch, for a minute I sat within two feet of a female guanaco who had climbed up from the other side, her smooth tawny fur damp with sweat and her dark hooked tail vibrating.

The fish was like a salted cricket bat.

At Ukika, a tiny settlement where the descendants of the Yahgan – all mixed blood now – live in dainty cabins, a man in metallic green football shorts was painting a wooden canoe on the beach. They couldn't dive for shellfish like their grandparents even if they wanted to because a plankton known as the *marea roja* meant that all the filterers were poisonous. Their grandparents' killers were imported western diseases and the European settlers themselves, who sliced off their ears after murdering them, presented the ears to the authorities as proof and collected a reward. The *marea roja*, the man in the green football shorts stopped to tell me when he saw me picking up a crab from the sand, his tone of voice indicating the importance of the matter, doesn't affect the *centolla*. This crustacean, called a king crab in English, is an economic staple of the island, as famous as the Juan Fernández *langosta* and as expensive in Santiago. One had been soaking in the bathroom sink at Mario's for two days.

At six o'clock in the evening Luis appeared at the door of

the guesthouse. I had met him at the birthday party; he ran the local shipping agency.

'There's a group of your countrymen at the yacht club.'

I hadn't seen a Brit for ages, and I missed them. In the Toyota van on our way to the club I learnt that all twenty-one had sailed in from New Zealand on a yacht which they were taking round the world. They were standing in the bar when we got there, laughing and drinking, pleased to be on land, and Luis smiled at our very British introductions. The captain invited Luis and me for dinner on board. The yacht was called *Creighton's Naturally*, the name of the company which sponsored it when it raced, and we ate spaghetti. The idea was born of raising a football team, and Luis offered to fix up a local opposition. Once the idea set into reality, their jokes betrayed them.

'We'll have to stipulate a handicap: they play in bare feet!'

'Pete, they live in bare feet!'

'You'd better close your porthole tonight, or you'll get an arrow in your ear!'

Everyone laughed. All through the country, when I had been asked what foreigners think of Chileans, the question had been followed by, 'They think we're wild *indios*, don't they?'

I always vigorously rejected this painful (for them) perception of their identity, but here were educated Europeans joking that Chileans were not yet sufficiently socially developed to wear shoes. I glanced at Luis – fortunately he hadn't understood. He was leafing through a copy of the *Sunday Sport*.

The next day Luis arranged a fleet of beaten-up vans to take us all to the hard dirt pitch on the edge of the forest. I took little Julio along with me. The Creightons hung a ship's banner and Union Jack over one goal, but they looked hunted when the Williams team ran onto the pitch, mean in matching strip;

243

the Brits were playing in boating shoes, and their leftwinger hadn't touched a ball since 1954. Julio kept trying to run away. Our boys were slaughtered nine-one, and I was proud of them: this was true British grit, and they had facilitated the most southerly international ever played.

I hitched a lift on a supply boat taking a coffin to Cape Horn. A passenger had died on a luxury North American cruise ship, and we were transporting the coffin to the ship and then returning to Williams, a round trip of about sixteen hours. The *Ñandú* (Rhea), a hundred-foot supply boat, left Williams at dawn, just when the colours exploding through the pearly sky were deep and vivid. There was a German seaman on board who had been living in Chile for ten years. He was wearing a stained peaked sailor's cap, and he chainsmoked. After standing on deck next to me in silence for five minutes he gestured aggressively towards the dense southern beech forest at the eastern end of Navarino.

'See those trees? The government's sold vast tracts of forest in Tierra del Fuego recently to Japanese paper companies. Jam today, hunger tomorrow. It's the same as the fish. They couldn't sell off fishing rights quick enough. The foreigners moved in with their sophisticated equipment and it didn't take long for the waters to be overfished and the Chilean fish industry paralyzed.'

He lit another cigarette, then went on 'Just look at how beautiful it is here. The Garden of Eden. Nothing like this in Europe. But they don't know how to protect it – to protect themselves, their future.'

The empty coffin was lying conspicuously down the middle of the main cabin covered in a candlewick bedspread, and everyone self-consciously avoided it. Chileans will use a diminutive for anything, and as if to prove it the sailors referred to the body for whom our cargo was destined as '*el muertito*' (the corpsette). As the journey continued, however, we forgot the coffin, and shortly after we had passed two small penguin colonies I noticed that the sailors were playing cards on it.

The German seaman pointed out a tiny island called Snipe which caused a major row between Chile and Argentina before the 1978 crisis (they seem to have disputed everything at some time or another), and soon afterwards we passed Picton, Nueva and Lennox themselves. They were always spoken of together, like a music hall act. So that's what they were, those famous names of modern Chilean history: small, inhospitable lumps of wind-tortured desolation, permanently surrounded by damp mist and a growling grey sea.

In the stretch of leaden water between Lennox and the Wollaston islands, the latter dripping from the end of the continent like drops of water from a leaky tap, I went up to the bridge. The black, curved back of a whale broke the surface straight ahead (it was a finback, one of the biggest) and the captain made a joke about the Britishness of the Malvinas.

'Our air force was grateful for Chilean help,' I said.

That shut him up.

'Isn't that right? Chile helped Britain, at your bases?'

After an awkward pause this civilian sailor said,

'We don't talk.'

I was again amazed at the acute public awareness of the need for secrecy over events in 1982. Chile was, admittedly, officially neutral in the Falklands War, but the Argentinians must have known what went on, ten years later. Perhaps I, a child of the 1960s, didn't appreciate the depth of patriotic secrecy fostered by war. It was very near home, for them.

Two more islands appeared out of the mist, the last visible remnants of the longest mountain range on earth – 4300 miles from the Caribbean down to the Horn, and it doesn't stop there, it just goes underwater. It began to rain, and I was summoned below deck for lunch. The *Ñandú* had begun to seem very small, as if it were shrinking, and it was no longer gliding smoothly. I didn't feel much like lunch, but as their only guest I was ceremoniously placed at the head of the table; I simply didn't know what to say to get out of it. Now I knew what George Bush had felt like immediately before his display of emetic diplomacy in Tokyo. The captain and five of his crew set about a four-course meal culminating in pieces of meat the size of shoe-soles. Someone made a joke about the British constitution; I could see they were warming up for a treat.

Hornos itself, an island rather than a cape and as dark and lugubrious as the others, was meanly spiked with dwarf beech trees and coated with tussock-grass. We dropped anchor there in tumultuous winds and waited for the ship we were supplying, squinting through binoculars at the few lonely buildings above the cliffs. Out on deck the German seaman, confounding the laws of nature by keeping his cigarette alight, shouted into my ear, but the only phrase I caught above the squall was 'corruption at the highest levels'. I had it all planned, if the *Ñandú* started sinking. I was going to hold on to the coffin. Remember *Moby-Dick*? It was the empty coffin which saved Ishmael when the *Pequod* went down.

The cruise ship appeared and three of its Philippino crew lurched over in a Zodiac inflatable. We could have docked directly with the ship if its captain hadn't wished to protect the sensibilities of his elderly US passengers, claiming that our cargo, now wrapped in a fluorescent orange tarpaulin, would be less conspicuous if loaded from a dinghy. I gripped the rail and through a curtain of rain watched the coffin being lowered, and just as one end banged into the Zodiac, the crew of the *Ñandú* straining at the ropes and waves slapping the leaning deck, I was sick.

As the ship moved back into the mist the German appeared

proffering a mug of *café a punto* (spiked coffee). One sniff of whisky sent me straight back to the rails, and the next five hours passed in delirium as I sank into a slough of misery and thought of an anecdote recounted by the halitosic Frenchman with the *Légion d'honneur* in Juan Fernández involving a troopship he had taken to Singapore on which six men died of seasickness.

At ten at night we docked for half-an-hour at Puerto Toro on the east coast of Navarino. An agitated shoal of people darted around on the quay, lit up against the tar blackness by the *Ñandú*'s bright lights. They scrambled over themselves to load boxes, chairs, children and dogs. Toro was inaccessible by land, and it was time for the eight kids to go back to school in Williams.

When we left, the children leant over the rail as adult faces lined with anxiety dissolved into the darkness. The crew all decided they were hungry, and the German set about making a goulash, his cigarette set between his lips at a jaunty angle. I retired quickly to my bunk below deck.

Chapter Thirteen

If one doesn't get birthday presents it can remobilize very painfully the persecutory anxiety which usually follows birth.

Henry Reed, *The Primal Scene as it were*

I had to go north, but from Punta Arenas it wasn't going to be possible to continue very far by land, as the country soon disintegrates into an archipelago. The land simply runs out on you. I could have travelled over the Andes, through Argentina and then back into Chile further up, but I felt it would be disloyal to abandon the thin country at this stage of my journey, and anyway I wanted to sail through the islands. Someone had told me there were a thousand of them.

I flew back from Williams to Punta Arenas, horrified to see a familiar object laid down the middle of the Twin Otter. The North American cruise ship had docked at Williams and offloaded the now full coffin for speedy dispatch to the nearest international airport. At least I would be able to get a lift into town with the hearse at the other end.

Tucked into the car nicely next to the head of the coffin, I noted that my unwitting pursuit of this dead stranger was taking on a macabre fascination, and as I got out and watched the hearse disappear I wondered if I was about to follow the man's soul to Purgatory. As it happened, I believe I did.

I picked up my visa and spent a wet Monday running between cold shipping offices, trying to persuade intransigent officials to convey me up the coast in their vessels. A naval ship was leaving that night for Tortel; I had never heard of the place, but I saw on a map that it was suitably positioned in the middle of an empty white space representing ice. A man at the naval headquarters announced triumphantly, on my fourth visit, that he had secured me a passage on this ship. I returned later for the final details. Another man came into the room, and when he saw me he let out a kind of sharp hiss.

'But we can't take *you*.'

'Why not?'

'Because you're a *woman*.'

Later that afternoon I heard a naval officer who was present describing this incident to a colleague. 'Then,' he said, 'there was a very small explosion.'

The captain was not at any of the mess halls, or on his ship, the *Orompello*, or in the naval offices, and I was beginning to consider loitering outside the brothels of Punta Arenas. Finally I discovered another wing of the naval headquarters and asked the duty officer if this captain could be located. The man told me to take a seat in the waiting room, and disappeared with my passport. I sat on a bench between two marines.

'All bosses are bastards,' announced the marine on my left, kicking an innocent radiator. The pair of them had been put ashore for bad behaviour and were waiting to hear what their punishment would be.

'What I need is a good night out and lots of bottles of pisco. Fuck the bosses.'

This sentiment hung in the air as the three of us sat there, damp, miserable and planning our revenge, until the door swung open and a tall captain appeared, immaculate in crisp navy blue and polished gold. He stopped in front of me, saluted, clicked his heels and handed me my passport.

'*Capitán Lathrop, Señora, a sus órdenes.*'

The marines leapt to their feet and looked from the captain to me and back again with abject horror, obviously deducing that I was a plant. They stood like saluting statues as I shook hands with the captain, looked him in the eye and tried to compose myself. There is much truth in the cliché about men in uniform.

'Dismissed.'

He put the marines out of their misery. I cast around for my very best Spanish and told him it was my life's ambition to reach Tortel and that my only hope was aboard his ship. He in turn looked me in the eye.

'I would be delighted to take you, but the ship is very overcrowded and cramped, and there is no room except in the marines' quarters, and I could not under any circumstances whatever put you in there.'

That did sound rather gruelling.

I found that a gas-carrier was leaving for Chacabuco, but the manager of the shipping company that owned it told me, after I had waited two hours for him to return from his cousin's wedding reception, that it was against international regulations for such a vessel to carry passengers. My only hope, at five o'clock, was the regular cargo ship which left every ten days for Puerto Montt and which carried a few passengers in portacabins on deck. These places were taken weeks in advance, but with some desperate lobbying I procured a passage, and to celebrate I went for a farewell drink with William, one of the footballing yachtsmen. He had left the *Creighton* to continue his journey overland, and he had with him a British white-water rafter. It was 9 March, and all three of us had picked up mail from home that day. The boys were

250

crowing over their Valentine cards, and thought it was inordinately funny that I didn't have any. They went on to entertain me with stories about the rough passage I was to endure on my cargo ship for four days and rushed to their dictionaries for a translation of *Golfo de Penas*, the name of a notorious stretch of water I had to cross in archipelagic Chile.

'Gulf of Miseries,' cried William, delighted.

'Gulf of the Torments,' said the rafter with obvious glee.

Bloody men, I thought.

I caught the last bus to Puerto Natales, a port three hours away to the north whence my ship departed and the end, virtually, of the road. After that it was fjords, islands and icecaps. It was still pouring with rain, and the light faded on a dark blueish-grey and cadmium yellow Patagonian landscape. We stopped to pick up a man waiting next to a single cinnamon tree, the pair of them illuminated in a pool of light spilt through the window of a saloon bar. Most of the passengers on the bus were Natalians who had travelled from Puerto Montt via the long Argentinian loop. When the first lights of Puerto Natales glittered on the horizon against the background of Last Hope Sound the passengers shouted '*Las luces! Las luces!*' (The lights! The lights!), and it was a hopeful introduction.

It was wet in Puerto Natales. I checked into a wooden boarding-house with huge rooms and a woodburning stove in the hall around which people had draped damp clothes, and the sweet smell of wet wool drying opened doors in my memory. The owners of these clothes, I learnt later, were waiting for my ship. Everyone who came to Natales seemed to do so in order to get somewhere else. It was a basic kind of place: bars with steamed-up windows and dripping horses tied to telegraph poles in the wide mud streets. A lot of the men looked like John Wayne.

I took one organized tour during my six months in Chile. It

251

was a daytrip to the Torres del Paine national park, the only place in the country known to all tourists and travellers and one where it is essential to spend at least a week. An authoritative and normally po-faced book called *South America's National Parks* published in the United States by a company called The Mountaineers says this about Paine:

> Torres del Paine is not a mere park, but a park of parks, a destination of travellers to whom a park is more than a place in which to be entertained, but rather an experience to be integrated into one's life. Torres del Paine is the sort of park that changes its visitors . . .

'Resist the temptation to take a one-day tour,' the book went on to recommend. I didn't like being given that kind of advice, and took a small-minded pleasure in refusing it, although the fact was that I genuinely didn't have time to do the park properly because my cargo ship was leaving the next day. I rather hoped that to make up for my failure to devote a respectable period of time to the park, the tour would at least be spectacularly bad, but it wasn't. The guide was called Fabien, and he was young, helpful and very well informed. He drove me from Natales to the park in a Japanese car with two elderly Argentinians. These latter were themselves Patagonians, and a debate simmered for the first hour about the relative merits of Chilean Patagonia (of which Fabien was a native) and its Argentinian counterpart. I asked about the Patagonian boundaries – where it began and ended – and this provoked a furious exchange of views. It appeared that Patagonia possessed the ultimate in topographical mystique: like Tartary and Christendom, it wasn't pinned down by boundaries. It was outside the mundane administrative framework of provinces and countries; it existed on a higher plane.

I asked if they could sum up the difference between Chilean

Patagonia and Argentinian Patagonia in one sentence.

'Absolutely none at all except the Chilean bit has mountains,' said the Argentinian.

'Quite,' said Fabien, and that was that.

At the Milodón Cave between Natales and the park we saw a fibreglass replica of the fêted prehistoric Giant Ground Sloth, an apologetic cross between a dinosaur and a bear. The cave was rather beautiful. The Argentinians, I noticed, had acquired the habit of calling each other 'mammi' and 'pappi', as if their relationship had been subsumed in its entirety by their numerous progeny. Pappi videoed us standing next to the fibreglass model.

We followed the cordillera then, the landscape still rimed, and Fabien waved at ponchoed men on tall horses driving immense flocks of sheep. He pointed out large lone ranches, the focal points of vast tracts of dry yellow land. For several miles the sun shone into clear air, and the dull and dreamy colours sharpened. But then a dun wall of vapour appeared, and the hillsides swirled in the mist. Mammi never stopped talking, though she was obviously used to being ignored as she never seemed to expect a reply.

As soon as we entered the park we saw hundreds of tawny guanacos. These animals had got rather a bad press. Their habit of spitting when cross was so well-known in Chile that the water-canons used on protestors during the dictatorship were named after them. The rheas were more difficult to spot – but we did find some, ungainly quilted ostriches silhouetted against a pale granite mountain, the peak of which had a slate coating, like chocolate sauce frozen on an ice-cream cone. It wasn't until much later that the three granite towers (the *Torres* of the park's name – actually crystallized rock masses) solidified in the mist. One of them was over 7500 feet high.

'It makes me feel humble,' said Pappi.

At Lake Grey we walked across ribbed sand towards the

icebergs, and in the woods behind them we are box-leafed barberry fruits, the elixir of Patagonia, which cast their spell if you taste them and compel you to return. As we stained our lips red we listened to Magellanic woodpeckers, and once or twice the crimson crest of the male flashed between branches. Among the waterfowl of the Paine lakeshores Fabien had pointed out a fat bird called the Chiloé widgeon which sang a three-syllable chorus; when I listened properly I heard a finely tuned orchestra vibrating through the cold air, percussion furnished by the high-pitched squeal of a piqued guanaco.

As we drove back to Natales at sunset coots, flamingos and black-necked swans were gliding together on a small lagoon near Lake Sarmiento. A flock of the Chekhovian swans, breaking the silence with the synchronous flapping of their wings, flew towards the mountains, dark necks horizontal against the bruised sky. The clouds were backlit in a way now very familiar to me down there in the far south, and upland geese patrolled low over the yellow, green-tufted steppe.

Before the sun rose I crossed the gangplank of the *Puerto Eden*, a seven-tonner sitting gloomily on the dark Natalian water. I found my cabin, and lay down on one of the six bunk beds, breathing stale air. Two young Germans arrived.

'It's going to be a long trip,' said the woman. 'What are we going to do to amuse ourselves?'

'I can think of one thing,' said her boyfriend, embracing her.

I thought, I'm going to be lying here seasick for four days with people bonking in German all around me.

Alongside the cabin thirteen trucks were loaded with sheep, youngish cows and horses. They were packed tightly together, with no space to lie down. The sky lightened, and people milled around on the top two decks. When the ship's hooter blew the animals panicked, and the cows shat on each other's faces. Six dolphins saw us off.

The nice man who had found a ticket for me had put it about that I was a journalist, and the captain invited me up onto the bridge, apologizing that my berth was below deck with the 'small herd' (he was referring to the tourists, not the animals). I assured him I was quite happy, and he introduced me to the second mate.

'Peter Shilton,' said the second mate when he found out I was English. 'I am Peter Shilton.'

His real name was Patricio, and he was a sad character in his mid-forties, with Brylcreemed hair, dark circles under his eyes and a wife who had divorced him. He was embarrassingly kind, regularly placing tea, sandwiches and whisky on the ledge in front of me, explaining weather patterns, showing me tidal charts and poring over Admiralty maps to point out exactly where we were. Given my affection for Mornington Crescent I was disappointed to note that we were not going to pass Mornington Island. It was on an Admiralty route, and we were confined to commercial channels.

The captain wore dark glasses all the time, even when he raised his binoculars to his eyes, and this made him look sinister, an impression supported by his generous applications of pungent aftershave. His name was Trinquao, which conferred upon him a Rabelaisian flavour he did not deserve. The ship, he told me, was travelling a route commissioned by the government in 1978 when Argentina closed the southern border crossing. The border had since reopened, but Chilean truckers preferred the maritime passage, as it was cheaper.

The *Puerto Eden* waited for an hour in the shadow of a mountain until the tide facilitated her passage through the Angostura Kirke, one of the narrowest navigable routes in the Chilean waterways. To steer us through, the captain, a study in concentration, called instructions to the seaman at the helm

255

behind him. The water was as smooth as an ice rink, and the air as cold, but the sky was vivid blue, and the sun shone. Shortly afterwards we sailed past the silent expanses of the vast Alacalufe Forestry Reserve, and I thought what a nerve they had, naming their park after a people their forebears had systematically massacred.

A hundred people were incarcerated on the 340-foot *Puerto Eden* as well as the animals, trucks, two bulldozers and a few cars. Besides twenty-seven crew members there were twenty truckers, a handful of students returning to university, a large family who didn't stop eating for four days and about forty foreign tourists. The latter consisted almost exclusively of backpackers 'doing' South America. They were mainly German, with a few North American, French, Dutch, Australian and Swiss. I shared the two triple-decker bunks in my cabin with three Australian men and the German couple; the room was in a kind of portacabin on deck, next to the horses, and it had no windows. The ship's administrators had made quite an effort to make it almost as bad for us as for the animals. The 'dining rooms' were on the second floor of the portacabin, one for the truckers and one for us (as there were more of us, we had to use ours in shifts). The two rooms received completely different food, and the rotten-toothed truckers dined on steak and salmon while we, the rich orthodontized offspring of the West, were ladled greasy soups and watery stews. Breakfast consisted of two slices of stale processed bread with a slice of luncheon meat between them.

'This was sure worth getting up for,' said a Californian biologist the first morning.

What was worth getting up for was the view of the islands, and it was different every day. Stepping out of the fetid cabin was a thrill.

I spent the days on the bridge and the evenings with the travellers, and time slid by rather agreeably. There was one young man who was always alone; he looked different to the others, and they ignored him. He had shaved half of his head, and the hair that was left was long, blond and floppy, reminiscent of the post-punks of Camden Town. His Oxfam overcoat stood out next to the brightly coloured German outdoor gear, and he looked pinched and unhealthy, whereas the others exuded vigour. On the second night I shared a bottle of pisco with him. He was a British climber, and he had just spent five weeks getting to the top of Torre Central in Paine. That granite tower, over 7500 feet high and with a 3600-foot face, has only been conquered by thirteen teams since the first man stood on the summit in 1963. Paul had slept in a tent he had made at home in Wales which hung from one point on the rock, suspended over half a mile of empty space. When he got to the top he and his partner only stayed there a minute because they were afraid they would be blown away. They used half a mile of rope and had allowed themselves to take up one book each. Paul had chosen a physics text book. He had been sponsored by the top climbing equipment firms, but was planning on selling all his gear in Bariloche, an Argentinian resort, to raise cash for a ticket home. He was diffident, even difficult, and he chose his words carefully, the antithesis of the strident backpackers; although he wrote pieces for the climbing press he said he found it painful because for him climbing was an intensely personal experience. His vision was to marshal all his mind, all his body and all his spirit to climb higher. Over the next two days I coaxed stories out of him, the pupils of his eyes as small as the hearts of grey cornflowers in the sunshine of the top deck.

Months later I unearthed an account of Chris Bonington's ascent of the Torre Central, recorded in *The Alpine Journal* in 1963, before Paul was born, and I relived the thrill of the climb, not on a cargo boat in the Patagonian fjords but in the sound-dampened hush of the British Library Reading Room.

The ship docked only once, and that was at its namesake, Puerto Eden. At about noon one day twenty painted houses emerged out of the vapour, and half-a-dozen fishing boats came rowing out to meet us. They drew up alongside our ramp and loaded boxes of smoked mussels onto the ship (the deep-water ones they call *cholgas*), shouldering crates of beer from the hold in exchange. There were brown mussels in bunches too, strung together on reeds, and women as leathery as the *cholgas* humped them swiftly in the light rain. The first mate, who was much younger than Patricio, much quicker, and much more handsome, turned his head away and suppressed a smile as wads of cash were pressed from hand to hand, payment for illegally caught king crab.

The dozen Alacalufe in Puerto Eden are the purest alive. The settlement was on the first steamer route from the Magellan Strait up the Pacific coast, and this brought regular contact to the northern Alacalufe. They remained far more isolated than their relations to the south nonetheless, as their territories had little to offer the predatory Europeans and *mestizos*. One erect old man had come from the village to stand on deck in his wellingtons. The third mate, a short, wiry individual who had done well for himself and had a gold tooth to prove it, tried to engage him in conversation for my benefit, but extracted only monosyllables.

'He talks,' said the third mate later, 'like you, with an accent.'

Whenever we approached a difficult strip of water the dark-glassed captain appeared and stood on the bridge calling his instructions. Once we squeezed past a very small island presided over by a white statue of the virgin emblazoned with the words, '*Gracias Madre*' (Thank You Mother).

'The only virgin in the zone,' whispered the first mate.

The tourists quietened down as we saw from our maps that the long, rough route across the open water of the Golfo de Penas – the Gulf of Distress – was only an hour or two ahead, and wild rumours of atrocious weather reports circulated through the cabins. I thought of a line I had read in the diary of an Englishman shipwrecked in that gulf in 1741. On 25 December he records that he ate a pair of raw sealskin shoes for his Christmas dinner. The midshipman on the voyage was the teenage John Byron, the poet's grandfather; the ship was called HMS *Wager*, and it was on its way to plunder Spanish settlements on the Pacific coast. They had a horrible time on the shores of the Gulf of Distress. Byron went on to become a vice-admiral, but he was always dogged by miserable weather; the poet said of his grandfather, 'He had no peace at sea, nor I on land.'

Patricio came to my cabin with some blue seasickness pills, and I took them. A smoking volcano appeared just before we left the friendly islands on either side and sailed into the ocean, and a wandering albatross flew over the deck.

On the fourth day we woke to islands again: bottle green and intermittently disappearing into white mist, a landscape drifting in and out of consciousness. It was true that there are a thousand islands in archipelagic Chile. The gulf had not troubled us, and I learnt from Patricio that the name doesn't refer to distress at all. It was originally spelt *Peñas* ('cliffs'), and in the hands of British cartographers the tilde dropped off, leaving the incorrect *Penas*. I made a note to write to William and the rafter about this. At breakfast an air of mild celebration infused the dining room, muted only when we noticed a dead horse being winched overboard. Later, the islands melted into gradations of blue, from a rich cobalt to a light Wedgwood wash, and we lay on the decks like lizards after the cold, wet weeks of Patagonia.

*

Puerto Montt, where the ship docked, was much further north than I wanted to be, so I had to take a shorter trip by water back the way I'd come. The journey through the islands on the *Puerto Eden* had meant that I'd missed the whole of the Eleventh Region, the remotest part of the country, and although much of it was impenetrable I intended to tackle the slices that weren't. I didn't like the idea of retracing my steps, but it was unavoidable in southern Chile.

A ship was due to sail that night, so I bought a ticket, sat down at a café on the docks and read a local paper. There was a story on the front page about a twelve-year-old girl who had given birth to her father's child. She came from one of the isolated fishing communities I had sailed past. I often heard stories about the dark side of what looked like paradise. They seem to be told about remote settlements almost everywhere, but the nether regions of archipelagic Chile did seem exceptionally prone to such excesses: besides incest of every imaginable variant I was recounted stories of a range of highly imaginative forms of bestiality and other practices which would have done credit to a roll-call of Old Testament prohibitions.

Although the *Evangelista* was owned by the same company as the *Puerto Eden*, the two were as different as the desert and the icecap. The *Evangelista* was a passenger ship, capable of transporting four hundred people in comfort and offering reclining seats, televisions and a bar, and it was as empty as the *Puerto Eden* had been overcrowded: there were less than forty of us on board. For the first half of the twenty-two-hour voyage to Chacabuco, a very small port in the middle of the desolate and labyrinthine Eleventh Region, we sliced through thick fog. The other passengers were all men, and when they weren't sleeping they entertained themselves by staring at me.

I slept on the floor, in my sleeping bag. Late the next morning the clouds evaporated and sunshine reflected off the glaciers as gulls skidded along the water, so fat with fish that their wings beat the surface as they tried to take off. There was another gringo on the ship, a Swede in his late twenties called Pontius Bratt. He was writing a paper on economic reforms under Pinochet at a university in Santiago. When we arrived in Chacabuco it was dark, and we had to wait an hour to disembark. Chacabuco didn't have much to offer. Pontius and I found rooms above a bar lit by an orange light. There were two men in the bar, drunk beyond all sense of time and place.

I left early the next morning, before anyone else got up, and left the money for my room on the sticky bar. Another shabby, one-night hotel, passive provider of that delicious anonymity of transience.

I made my way then to Coyhaique, uplifted by the extravagance of the landscape, cleft by the coiled Simpson river. This was my final region of Chile, and it had been saving up the best till last.

I had a contact in Coyhaique, an Englishman called Mark Surtees who worked as a guide for a fly-fishing expedition company. We had spoken on the phone in London, where he spent Chilean winters in his other life as a freelance management consultant. I found him in a small house with an untidy garden, drinking maté next to a stove in the kitchen. When I walked through the low door and introduced myself he said, 'Hello Sara,' as if he had been expecting me that very moment. (In fact he hadn't had any idea when I would turn up, if ever.) He was about my age, and he was tall and chunky with blond hair, an entertainingly laconic manner and a Newcastle accent. I later discovered that at university, where he had read English, he wrote his thesis on Biggles.

'You must stay here,' he said imperiously. Occupation of the house was fluid in any case, and I never worked out which of the various people who came and went were official residents. Most of them came in through the window; the door often remained locked all day, despite heavy window traffic. It was great fun in that house. It was owned by a Uruguayan called Alex who also owned the fishing company, and it was called the Sheraton, a wordplay involving Uruguayan slang and the rats who were in residence when Alex and the other fishermen moved in. I felt bone tired, and slept for almost two days.

While I was based in Coyhaique I wanted to go south for three or four days, but it was difficult. The nether regions of the celebrated Carretera Austral, a road built by Pinochet when he dreamt of linking together the fragments of his thin empire, were largely untravelled. The *carretera* stopped abruptly, at nowhere in particular, before the land hardened into low continental icecap, so I intended to go down it as far as I could, loop into the interior and then return for a few days more rest and recreation at the Sheraton.

There was no bus for two days, and the one leaving on the third was already full. Everyone laughed when I suggested hitching. I broadcast a message on *Radio Patagonia Chilena* asking if anyone was driving to Cochrane, the only village of any size to the south; they were apparently not. Pontius Bratt materialized. We discussed renting a truck (Hertz, unfortunately, were not present) and while we were in the car-hire office an Alaskan came in, followed by a strawberry blond Austrian man. We decided to hire a small truck between us, and so it was that four strangers went on a sketchily-conceived trip.

The first manifestation of group dynamics was a squabble provoked during a preparatory shopping expedition by the Austrian's purchase of a carton of cigarettes. The Alaskan, who was called John, objected to smoking in the car. I was appealed to as arbitrator in this dispute, a matriarchal role to which the three of them often returned in the course of the trip and which I did not relish. A formal agreement was reached permitting smoking anywhere except bedrooms and the truck.

We set off early the next morning. The gravel road was so deserted that if we did pass another vehicle we waved chummily. We came to a small collection of corrugated iron houses under a Gothically rocky hill pierced with glaciers, and Pontius asked a woman with no teeth if we could buy bread. She took us to a dark little house where we picked crusty rolls out of a hemp sack.

Shortly beyond a river distinguished from the many anonymous rivers by its name, the river Nameless, we sat down on the steppe and had a picnic. The rolls were like golf balls, but our delight in the landscape and with life in general that day was unquenchable, and an Andean condor obligingly passed overhead, black against the brilliant sky.

There were corrals, and some horses, and there must have been people living undiscovered in the nooks of the highway, but we didn't see them. As the afternoon disappeared we arrived alongside the north Patagonian icecap, stretching for miles beyond the western mountains, and on the eastern side of the road a river became a lake, so blue it was vulgar. This lake got much bigger. It was called Lake General Carrera (though the part on the Argentinian side was called Lake Buenos Aires; they couldn't possibly share a name), and it was the second largest lake in South America. A small man appeared on the road next to it, wanting a lift, so we took him a few miles, and he told us he was a paramedic. He had walked for four hours to visit a sick man. Then the river Baker rushed at us, wild and emerald, flowing towards the south Pacific at over 300,000 gallons per second, curling through the rock, fizzing with white water, and we watched it for many miles in silence, until it turned black in the dark, and then, after all that, the moon was full.

The truck crunched to a stop on a bend at about ten in the evening. All three boys wanted to fix the puncture. None of them could, as the spanner for the wheelnuts was broken. We were six miles from Cochrane, where we had planned to stay, and it was too cold to sleep in the truck; we were considering our options (there were very few of them) when a van appeared. This was little short of a miracle, but although we borrowed a spanner and changed the tyre we knew that we would need another miracle the following day as both tyre and inner tube were so badly chewed we would have to find new ones.

Cochrane was celebrating its thirty-eighth anniversary. Thirty-eight was quite a respectable age down there. It was the last part of continental Chile to be colonized, so the wandering local tribes had a long reprieve. Ninety years ago the government encouraged settlers by granting concessions to three animal-farming companies, though these isolated settlements didn't coalesce into villages until the 1920s. Even Coyhaique, now the capital of the Eleventh Region, wasn't founded until the end of that decade. Sheep and cattle still constitute the economic base. Mark the fisherman had told me, 'Civilization is a thin veneer down here.'

It was inaccessibility which had preserved it. The whole southern archipelago consists of what was, to the north, the coastal mountain range, which south of Puerto Montt has been flooded apart from the mainland. The Andes meet the sea, and their lower slopes are richly forested.

We found a second-hand tyre in Cochrane. It was almost bald; Chilean tyres could win longevity records. A large and surprisingly well-stocked store on the square provided us with an inner tube. Three men wearing sheepskin on their legs were buying rope 'on account', and they pressed their inky thumbs on the bill before slinging the purchases round the necks of their horses, tethered to a redundant traffic light. We drove up a terrible track to Lake Cochrane, through a freaky grass plain like a golf course, and got out to climb the rocky outcrops above the part of the lake where the waters shone in a rainbow and met a solitary strip of beach. The rest of the lake was dotted with green islands, like decorations on a cake. Apart from one small hacienda at the back of the valley, the rocks overlooked an immense spread of untouched countryside, and it brought to mind the florid comparison of the country with the Garden of Eden which features in the national anthem.

It was quite hot, and John started to behave oddly; he said all Alaskans do when they feel the sun. He was several years older than the rest of us, a carpenter, and he was sensitive and introverted. He hated the Austrian, and told me one day that he had written in his journal (he was a typical journal-keeper) 'I feel as though I address everything I say to Sara and Pontius only.' When it came to splitting into pairs for the twin-bedded rooms I always went with him, to minimize his contact with the Austrian. Months later he wrote to me in London to thank me. It was a beautiful letter.

I could see what he meant about the Austrian. He was an accountant from Vienna, and had taken eighteen months off to do a world tour. He liked ticking off the places he'd been on a list he had made in a blue spiral-bound notebook. Whenever we went to a café he insisted on asking the price of every possible combination of foods ('How much would it be without the cheese?' 'Can I have just a plate of boiled rice?') and he had an unwavering conviction that the world in general was committed to fleecing him. You couldn't call what he did living. I travelled in parallel with him, but I shared a journey with the other two.

We returned up the Carretera Austral. At the confluence of two rivers a man with a stationary motorbike in front of a flock of buff-necked ibis flagged us down and practically forced us to load him and his broken machine into the back of the truck. Shortly after he had demanded to be dropped off we took a long, lonely route up the southern shore of Lake General Carrera, and again we were silent, then Pontius said, 'It is not possible for it to get more beautiful,' but it did, of course, and we climbed very high in the crepuscular light, the road a slender silver precipice above the luminous lake, and as the sun set we drove through configurations of rock as if we were travelling through pages of Dante. Around one bend half of the moon appeared over the top of an incandescent cliff, and all four of us started to laugh.

I woke up on my thirty-first birthday in a seedy hotel very close to Argentina, and John the Alaskan in the next bed tried to wish me Happy Birthday in Spanish, but by the time he had worked it out we had both lost interest. The hotel was in a village called Chile Chico (Little Chile) because of its sunny microclimate. In Cochrane our beds had been layered with quilts and blankets like double-decker sandwiches, but in Chile Chico they gave us two thin blankets each, and we didn't need more. The Eleventh Region is a mass of violently disparate climates, reflecting a violently disparate geography; it was very disorientating.

We had to take an excursion back along the road, to see our lunar landscape under the sun. We hadn't realized how precipitous this road was, and besides that there were freshly tumbled boulders along it. It had been open less than a year, and a man in a shop in Chile Chico told us later that it was often blocked; he referred to it soberly as an 'international highway,' a term used by Chileans for any dogtrack crossing into Argentina.

There had been a small settlement called Fachinal, now abandoned, and we had our picnic lunch on the boardwalk, striped with crystal water where old planks had rotted. Pontius Bratt produced a bottle of champagne for my birthday; it was typical of him. He had brought it all the way from Coyhaique specially. Pontius was one of those people who are so genuinely nice you don't mind them being near-perfect. He was tremendously bright, had won scholarships all over the world and was strong-minded enough not to take the high-profile high-salary jobs which would have been a natural progression. He had a great sense of humour, he listened carefully to other people and he had mixed feelings about his nationality, which is usually a good sign. I really enjoyed his company, but we forgot to exchange addresses, so I never heard from him again.

I knew they'd be thinking of me at home on my birthday, just as I was of them. I could go for weeks without feeling melancholy or lonely – months, on occasion; I lived off emotional reserves like a hibernating animal lives off its fat. But a small thing could provoke a fit of grief. I might look at the date on a calendar, or hear a few bars of a piece of music, or sometimes I would wake up in the middle of the night with a start, imagining that a close friend was in the room.

That evening we drove onto a little ferry which took two-and-a-half hours to convey us across the choppy water to the other side of the lake. We had a drinks party on the tiny deck with two cartons of wine and a communal cup made by sawing off the bottom of a water bottle. It was very windy, and as the boys sang 'Happy Birthday,' each in his own language, a wave hit them. We moved inside to an even tinier room, where I couldn't decide if I was drunk or seasick but feared it was both, and listened to a local in a startlingly conspicuous greatcoat rambling boringly about the differences between saltwater waves and their freshwater equivalents. There were

267

three passengers on the ferry, besides us and The Coat.

On the other side the Austrian drove for three hours in the dark, a terrifying ordeal for the rest of us as the road was the worst yet and he saw it as a challenge. Besides this, The Coat had asked us for a lift to Coyhaique, so there were five of us in the truck. Nobody wanted to sit next to The Coat so Pontius, John and I wedged ourselves in the back; it was much too small for three. Hares were zigzagging around in the head-lights, and the moon was so bright that the Austrian made a great joke of putting the sunvisor down.

We got to Coyhaique at eleven, and my other set of boys, the fishers, cranked themselves up for a party. I felt melan-choly, and they sensed it, but they tried to deal with it by giving me a lot of whisky, and at about two o'clock I went to bed and my birthday party adjourned to a strip club.

Chapter Fourteen

The sense of limitless freedom that I, as a woman, sometimes feel is that of a new kind of being. Because I simply could not have existed, as I am, in any other preceding time or place.

Angela Carter

After the weekend I went fishing with Alex. The black-necked swans were alone on Lake Frío. On the banks dragonflies darted about and woodpeckers pecked half-heartedly at the treetrunks. Alex caught several rainbow trout, and it made him happy; he had been tense, but the river conducted all his nervous energy away. He was the kind of person I always homed in on: he was out of control. He entangled himself with women then decided he didn't want them anymore, and when he drank too much he smashed up cars. He laughed exuberantly a lot, was depressed a lot, and was obsessive; he missed Uruguay, he was hopeless with money, and he got jealous if Mark spent too much time with anyone else. Alex badly needed approval, and, like Mark and I, he was prone to excess.

It took some effort to persuade him that we should eat two of his catches for our tea. My new friends often spoke disparagingly of people who 'killed' fish. It was all part of the culture. Like all fly fishermen, they looked upon anglers who caught fish any other way as a lesser species.

'It's like comparing martial arts with a street brawl,' Alex said.

Fly fishing was about being at one with the line, the rod, the river, the wind and the air temperature, and it was about second guessing what the fish were about to do – as Mark said, it was about 'being that trout'.

Like rock climbing, it was Zen.

Word got round that there were good salmon in a saltwater fjord near Chacabuco. It was the end of the season and the last client had gone, so the fishermen dropped everything and zipped through the Simpson valley. On the banks of the fjord two middle-aged ranchers hailed Alex and invited the two of us to join their boat. They were just the kind of people I had been told 'weren't real fishermen': they didn't use fly, and they loaded the boat with five bottles of wine, a bottle of whisky and heaps of salami and brie. They set up their rods with spinning tackle, wedged them along the side of the boat, switched on the motor and cruised around the lake in high good humour, shouting to other anglers and recalling impressively lengthy catches of previous expeditions.

The big Pacific salmon, which had probably escaped young from a farm, had come in to breed, and as they were nearly impossible to catch with a fly, and other anglers were hooking them in with spinners, I noticed that Alex and my other companions from the Sheraton, in another boat, quickly abandoned their principles.

Alex gave me his rod as the ranchers slid through the whisky. After a few minutes I felt a sharp pull on the line and a surge of panic. The three men shouted instructions simultaneously, pointed wildly at reel, rod and water, and then a pink and grey back arched out of the fjord and I struggled clumsily with the flailing rod and the straining reel, fighting to keep my salmon until one of the ranchers landed it with a gaffe. They were still shouting after they had whacked it over the head, thrust it, cold and convulsing, into my arms and lifted the spinner with which I had caught it to my lips, followed by the whisky bottle.

My salmon weighed eleven-and-a-half pounds, and it was the first fish I had ever caught.

Still flushed with triumph, I cooked the fish in the wood-burning oven that evening, with capers and black butter. It made up for having had scabies diagnosed that morning. My hands and lower arms had been itching for some time, and when I found myself awake for half the night clawing at my legs too I sought medical advice. Scabies, the doctor informed me crisply, are mites which live under the skin. They come out at night and run around.

Lurking in the shadowy recesses of my mind was the notion that scabies is a sexually transmitted disease.

'How does one acquire these . . . creatures?'

'From mattresses, normally. Very common around here.'

Well, I'd slept on a lot of mattresses. The treatment involved applying a special lotion and not washing for forty-eight hours. I was also told to boil my bedding, but the idea of boiling a sleeping bag on a primus stove defeated me. I procured an iron from a neighbour instead – it was an iron iron which had to be heated up on the stove – and ironed the bag to kill the mites residing within it who were waiting anxiously for my return. I also ironed the mattress I slept on at the Sheraton, and while I was doing so the postman appeared at the window. He looked surprised. I locked myself in the bathroom.

A skin parasite is hardly a social asset, and under most circumstances you might feel shy about possessing such a thing in the company of people you've only known a few

271

days, particularly after you've gone forty-eight hours without washing. But it seemed a routine part of life in the Sheraton, and I was so grateful to them for not making me feel like a leper. I learnt that in Uruguay a common cure for certain skin lice is kerosene. One of the fishermen, a peripatetic North American horticulturalist, knew a good deal about transmittable mites and diseases, having had most of them, and he generously dispensed his painfully acquired wisdom on the subject of my condition.

Mark and Alex wanted to go off to fish for a few days without any clients; it had been a long season. They invited me to join them, and one morning we loaded Alex's pickup with camping and fishing gear, waved goodbye to the North American parasite expert, and headed north.

All roads out of Coyhaique cross millions of acres of lush grass strewn with the husks of hardwood trunks, vestiges of southern beech forest cleared by the farmers who took the first land grants. Our road, the only one going north, was devoid of cars and of any sign of human life; it was a concept, the Carretera Austral, not a road. It was a dream made real, linking two-thirds of a tamed country with its lost tail and bringing communication to an unimaginably beautiful hinterland.

It was a part of Chile that touched my soul. As I sat in the back of the pickup I grappled with the notion that Pinochet was responsible for opening it up; he had seen construction of the road through, despite massive opposition even from his own team. He was still so present in Chile; I had often felt it, from the first day. Besides the fact that he actually was still around in his role as commander-in-chief of the army, featuring frequently in the media, he stalked inside everyone's head too. They often referred to him, by name or allusion.

I had come expecting a black-and-white country. For anyone exposed to the western media, Pinochet was a symbol of evil and opposition to his regime had become identified with the noble battle of right against wrong, oppressed against oppressor. Less than a week after the coup, the *Guardian* ran a story on its news pages which commented, 'For Socialists of this generation, Chile is our Spain.' But from my first week in the country I had met all kinds of Chileans – not only rich ones – who regretted Pinochet's demise and had no trouble at all in consigning the unsavoury facts to oblivion and telling me that he had been good for the country, and for them. On his birthday, several hundred people still turned up outside his house with flowers. Large sectors of the population had felt safer with him than with what they perceived as the alternative. He and his colleagues (he emerged out of a collegially-led junta) had always exploited public fear of a return to the economic chaos of 1972–3. The people had irrefutable evidence that leftist governments were a disaster, after all, and the failure of Allende's economic policy had become so enshrined that the massive external destabilization which exacerbated it had dissolved in the further reaches of national memory. They had forgotten a lot of other things, too. According to one of the most cautious academic sources, between 3000 and 10,000 Chileans were killed in the immediate aftermath of the coup. The Rettig Commission recorded less than 3000 deaths and disappearances, but a new national reparation and reconciliation corporation has subsequently added many hundreds of cases to that figure. Somewhere between 40,000 and 95,000 people were taken prisoner for some period in the first three years. Hadn't the *Pinochetistas* I met (43 per cent voted to keep him in 1988) read all those accounts I had read about torture and depravity and murder? Hadn't they met the woman whose three sons had been killed, as I had, or the hideously disfigured man who had set fire to himself in the village square to draw attention to the disappearance of his daughter, who at that moment was being raped by the eleventh man that day? Well, hadn't they?

Of course, the fact that he was no longer in charge showed that he had failed in his attempts to depoliticize them. He had a spirited try: during his rule, the longest continuing presidency in the nation's history, he banned just about everything he could think of. *Fiddler on the Roof* was prohibited because it depicted military abuses. He fuelled rumours of armed uprising and manufactured a wartime atmosphere. Even when the nation voted against him in the plebiscite of October 1988 it found he had ensured that the new president wouldn't be elected for fourteen months and wouldn't take office for three more after that. He had set things up so that whatever happened he would retain at least some power. His constitution, approved in a stage-managed plebiscite in 1980 and named *Constitución de la Libertad*, presumably in homage to Friedrich Hayek, the anti-Keynesian economist who wrote a book with that title and whose economic and political philosophy profoundly influenced the Pinochet team, remained in place after his demise, and this meant, effectively, that he still controlled the Senate. The ones who had voted him out had learnt that they couldn't have everything at once. As a Socialist MP had told me wearily, 'It's not perfect. But we are living through a transition from dark to light.'

'*Zorro!*' said Alex loudly, and stopped the pickup. It was a fox, an animal rarely spotted in Chile, and it stood on the road with a hare in its mouth, silhouetted in front of a snowy mountain bisected by a thin waterfall. We entered rainforest soon after that, and the Queulat national park, where we got out to walk down a steep and muddy cliff path to the Padre García waterfall, spectacular even by Chilean standards and exuding a thick jungular smell of wet and rotting vegetation. It felt good. Droplets clung to the burnt orange trumpets of the waterfall flowers like to a car after rain, and humming birds skated over the bamboo.

A perfectly triangular glacier hung between two mountain peaks to the east, bright white and blue against a cloudless sky, and the byzantine slopes of the mountains below it were sprayed with deep pink magellanic fuchsias.

There were rivers everywhere, and Mark and Alex discussed their troutiness earnestly. But we pushed on northwards, leaving the Carretera Austral just before sunset, and headed east in search of the Figueroa river. First we had to cross the Rosselot. The Ministry of Public Works had obligingly provided a wooden platform attached by chains to two overhead cables and operated by a pair of dour locals; the current propelled it, us and the pickup to the opposite bank. Eighteen miles up the valley a handwritten sign told us we couldn't go any further: the road was under construction right up to the Argentinian border. A man came out of an operations hut, and once we forced him to admit that it was in fact possible to continue some way further up this road, he was persuaded to radio the chief in Coyhaique and let us petition our case. The chief was cross because we interrupted his dinner. 'You can go through,' his voice eventually crackled, 'at nine o'clock tomorrow morning.'

It was very black and very cold, so we decided to return to the nearest village to spend the night in a guesthouse. When we got back to the Rosselot the pontoon bridge was floating on the opposite bank. We mentally limbered up to get the tents out. Suddenly the platform began to move: the operators had seen our headlights from their cottages, and reluctantly came to our rescue.

In the morning the mud streets of the village were touched with frost, and as we sat waiting for the pickup to warm up, watching a man guiding a flock of sheep down the road, I reflected that waking up in a tent wouldn't have been much fun. We crossed on the pontoon while men with wide-brimmed hats pulled down over their ears led their horses to drink at the sepulchral bank of the dark green water. Against the blue mist, thin rivulets of smoke trickled from chimney pipes on steep shingle roofs.

The river valley cut through rainforest burgeoning with ferny undergrowth, the silence punctuated by the musical prattle of the chucao, a smallish bird with a vertical tail, its trill part of the daily background noise. We followed the Figueroa upstream, along sheer banks of colossal evergreens. Mark and Alex tried to fish, but only found diminutive brook and brown trout; they were both convinced we had to move even further upstream, to the next lake, so we picked laboriously through the forest on the closed road, eventually confounded by an intractable mound of earth. Dynamite exploding ahead made the windows rattle. The two men were bitterly disappointed. We cooked sausages later over a fire near a small bridge, and watched a black mink grubbing among a pile of stones. Mark and Alex hated minks; they were an introduced menace, and destroyed the ecosystem of the riverbank.

The pontoon operators narrowed their eyes when they saw us again. We crossed, drove away quickly and continued examining rivers to the north until we reached the upper limit of the Eleventh Region; the mountains seemed to be getting even higher. My companions were restless, because they were longing to fish; they both suddenly decided they didn't want to camp. They were tired of camping, by the end of the season. Mark was soon going back to the UK for six months. They were very close. Alex was the butt of all the jokes at the Sheraton, but it belied a deeply felt friendship, most of all between these two I was travelling with. When I heard Alex talk in English, I heard Mark's inflection and Mark's idiom.

We stopped, later, at cabins rented out by a friend of Alex' in a clearing at the northern tip of Lake Risopatrón. The two of them fished from a rowing boat for a couple of hours at dusk while I read in the long grass, and they returned transformed; the sight of rainbow trout on the end of their lines had made everything all right.

They had found fish, we were all relaxing, and besides that the owner of the cabins was a gourmet. She made everything herself, from unsalted butter to crisp cheese bread, goose liver pâté, wild raspberry compotes and coconut cake, and she smoked her own salmon. There was no question of moving on after just one day.

We ate a great deal, drank far too much wine, and we fished. I was the gillie, rowing them up and down the lake. My scabies left me. We kept a woodburning stove going in the cabin, and a supply of wine cartons outside. I wrote out the words to Sylvio Rodríguez songs sitting in the car, and ran the battery down, eyed by a flock of fat white geese. I looked up at the mountains a lot, and thought how much I was going to miss them.

Mark and Alex dropped me at Puyuhuapi, a strangely prosperous village with wooden shingle houses and a carpet factory. The carpet factory was actually a shingle house too, and its products, hand woven on magnificent looms, were famous. Many of the residents of the village had German names; it was founded by Germans in 1935, and until the advent of the Carretera Austral in the 1980s it had been entirely cut off. There were rumours, in other places in the region, about where the money had come from, and a man in Coyhaique told me a long tale about a war criminal who had lived alone at the end of a fjord to the north. My informant also said that one of the Puyuhuapi elders had been Hitler's chauffeur, but I thought that was unlikely.

We said goodbye after one last lunch together and I waved them off, forcing a smile. I had arranged to stay that night at a hotel owned by a Santiago-based company who had invited me to visit the Laguna San Rafael and its glacier, the most famous in Chile, in their catamaran the next day. The hotel was on the other side of a stretch of water, and a launch arrived to take me there; it was a luxurious place, built around thermal springs and peopled with bejewelled Argentinians. I tried to heave myself through this abrupt transition, but despite the comfort I felt miserable. I was tired, my knuckles were bleeding from rowing Alex all morning, my scabies had risen like Lazarus, a carton of wine had exploded in the carpetbag over the only decent clothes I had left, and, most of all, I missed Mark and Alex. It had been one of the best trips; it was hard to imagine that I had only known the pair of them for a matter of weeks. Dawdling in such good company in one of the most beautiful regions of the world had caused all my anxieties to disappear.

I tried to sleep, but couldn't, so I swam in one of the thermal pools, in the open air overlooking the water and forest. It made me feel much better, until an Argentinian told me that exertion in hot water causes heart attacks.

By seven the next morning I was cruising the fjords again, this time in high style on board a very grand catamaran called the *Patagonia Express*. I was the only press guest: the other passengers were Argentinian tourists from the hotel. We stopped at Puerto Aguirre, an isolated fishing village I had spied from the top deck of the *Evangelista*. The locals had built the tiny houses of their cemetery on the slope of the island opposite, ferrying the dead across their own Styx.

The catamaran was delightful. There was nothing to do except sit at the bar and watch the scenery float past, and as it was a free bar and the barman had a neat line in cocktails, this was very agreeable. He shook his cocktails with panache. His speciality was a kind of Chilean *cuba libre*; I quickly forgot the name, but it had the word Patagonia in it. The

Argentinians sat down at tables in the dining area and the men produced enough photographic equipment to open a Dixons concession on board while the women read *Good House-keeping*. The barman told me his name was Norman. He was wearing a white polyester shirt, and he looked remarkably like Douglas Hurd, even sporting the ice-cream cone quiff. The cocktails got stronger as we approached the glaciers, and in the lagoon itself, almost landlocked and one of only three places in the world where three plates meet, strangely sculpted blue icebergs appeared, and Norman added more ice to the cocktail jug in appreciation. The icebergs were as small as manhole covers and as big and pointy as the Matterhorn. The glacier San Rafael, the famous glacier, looked like a rough blue tide between the brown and green jagged mountains. It stretches over twenty miles back into the interior, is more than one-and-a-half miles wide, and it moves up to 200 feet a day. I had developed a passion for these glaciers. I believe Darwin did, too, in his understated, English way: '... they may be likened to great frozen Niagaras; and perhaps these cataracts of blue ice are to the full as beautiful as the moving ones of water.'

The *Patagonia Express* dropped anchor directly opposite the ice-cliffs. I cannot say it was beautiful; it was beyond all that. I stood on deck in the painfully cold air watching icebergs calve into the still water. The falling blocks boomed in the silence, like blasts of dynamite on some distant planet. It was impossible not to think of Coleridge's vision of ice in *The Ancient Mariner* ('The ice did split with a thunder fit'); even Norman's eye glittered obligingly.

Some of us strapped on lifejackets and climbed into a Zodiac. The tallest ice cliffs, at least 180 feet high, revealed themselves to be cleft with deep blue caverns of cold air stretching back into the inner world of the earth. Gulls with black spindly legs landed on ice floes, and under the water I could see spectral outlines of secret things. We motored through the pack-ice along all one-and-a-half miles of the shining glacier. It radiated coldness. A crewman shouted and pointed behind us, and we turned our heads to see a tower of ice the size of a multi-storey carpark plunging into the lagoon, the foundations bouncing upwards with ostentatious languor as the top disappeared.

Back on board Norman offered round a tray of large whiskies on rocks chipped from the glacier which he alleged were 30,000 years old and might well have been. An Argentinian with two Nikons round his neck made a fulsome speech thanking the crew for bringing us to this 'unworldly' place and then insisted that I make one too, 'on behalf of the foreigners'. There are gradations of foreign, of course, and compared with me the Argentinians and Chileans felt united. The glacier experience had made me sentimental, and as I was the only fully qualified foreigner on board and no one understood English I recited Yeats' 'Had I the heavens' as if it were a formal speech, which rather spoilt it, but everyone clapped. As we moved away from San Rafael the Argentinians took photographs of me on deck as if I were as rare a phenomenon as the glacier itself. I had been consorting with Norman for some time, and I lounged inscrutably against the rail in dark glasses as if I spent my life being photographed by tourists.

The sky condensed into a blue, grey and white miasma, and yellow rays beamed through like a Blake painting, diffusing themselves through titanic icebergs. It was hard to leave that place, but Norman eased the pain. As the stars came out an Argentinian bank manager tried to point out formations and constellations. People were always doing that, and I hated it; I didn't need sordid terrestrial labels bringing the stars under control. Giving them shapes from our world (the Plough; the Hunter) robbed them of their otherness. They belonged to the land of the imagination, the most beguiling country of them all. I had spent many nights alone with the Chilean stars, and I wasn't going to let a bank manager turn them into agricultural implements.

The catamaran docked at Chacabuco at midnight, disgorging the Argentinians into a hotel. Several of them tried to persuade me to check in, worried about letting me loose in Patagonia, but I had a plan to make it over to Coyhaique that night and surprise Mark and Alex. It was time for me to abandon the far south and return to the civilization of Puerto Montt, as I had to start thinking about getting back to Santiago. I could take a plane easily enough from Balmaceda to Puerto Montt, and Coyhaique was en route to Balmaceda.

I wound up having to take a taxi to Coyhaique, and I climbed through the window of the Sheraton at one-thirty in the morning. Alex was sitting watching the Oscars ceremony on television, and Mark was asleep in bed, his jeans dangling onto the floor from one ankle (he hadn't managed to get his boot off). It was a great reunion, which merited several cartons of wine, though in fact it was only two days since we had split up. I dreamt that Douglas Hurd was standing on an iceberg with a cocktail shaker in his hand, and the next morning I disappeared for good, on a bus to Balmaceda, whence a plane took me to Puerto Montt. It flew low, and the late afternoon sun turned the multitudinous rivers into gold ribbons between brown crepey mountains. The glaciers rippled, like folds of glossy cloth, and out to the west the archipelago throbbed, suffused in an amber glow.

Unable to resist one last little trip in the three days I had allocated myself before I travelled back up to Santiago, I stayed the night at my usual guesthouse in Puerto Montt and went to the bus station early the next morning, aiming hopefully for Río Negro, a village more commonly known by the name of its local volcano, Hornopirén. I picked out the right queue immediately: the further away from an urban centre a bus is heading, the rougher the aspect of the people waiting to get on it. Teeth are an especially good guide. (In Japan, the further you travel from Tokyo, the shorter people get.) I got on, anyway. Buses are downgraded, as their roadworthiness and comfort diminish, according to the conditions of the route, and from the look of the bent metal hulk marked 'Hornopirén' I inferred that I was in for a long, hard journey.

The road was extremely bad, but the sun shone on the old alerce trees, and when the bus drove on to a ferry a sweaty man in a cook's hat dispensed chipped mugs of Nescafé on deck from a grimy galley the size of a telephone box.

Five hours after leaving Puerto Montt the bus stopped with a weary grating of its brakes at a small village on an estuary overlooked by the volcano. People in Puerto Montt often spoke of this volcano – proprietorially, as if of all the volcanoes in the country, they were bound by some special relationship to this one. I found a hotel next to one of the sawmills. It was just the kind I liked: polished wood floor, plank walls, brightly coloured window frames, an erratic electricity supply, a woodburning stove batting out the heat in the spacious kitchen and a view from my room of oxen tied up on the shore, silhouetted against the wooded islands in the estuary. There were no other guests, and I liked that too.

I spent the afternoon walking to the volcano; it took about six hours to get there and back. It was a sharp, sunny day, and the air was wonderfully clear. There was snow on the grey mountains, but the fabled volcano in front of them was green. It was small, by Chilean standards, and it was glowing very faintly, as if dimly lit from within. I passed two or three wooden houses. A little girl in an embroidered frock ran out of one of them asking if I wanted to buy *küchen*. For some odd reason it was her little face which suddenly made me very aware that the journey was ending soon and that rural Chile was slipping away from me. I wanted to spray mental fixative over my memories.

When I got back to the village the water had drained from the estuary and the owner of the hotel invited me to eat with the extensive family in the big kitchen. During the meal I was initiated into a secret of Chilean Spanish.

'The wires are all corroded in the fuse box,' said Mrs Hotel to her husband. 'We'll have to get the *gasfiter* in.'

'What,' I said, 'does the gas man fix the electrics?'

'No,' she said, 'I'm talking about the electric *gasfiter*.'

'So,' I said, 'if the plumbing goes wrong you call the plumbing *gasfiter*?'

'That's right.'

'And if the gas . . .'

But I already knew the answer.

Later, I sat on the jetty and read by torchlight. I was reading about Hayek, the conservative economist whose book lent its name to the Chilean constitution. He argued that the preservation of economic freedom is logically and philosophically more important that the preservation of the institutions of democracy. Many foreign governments endorsed the dictatorship by behaving as if the iron fist of military rule were a matter of minor or at least secondary importance. During an official visit to Chile in October 1980, Cecil Parkinson, then British Minister of Trade, said this: 'There's a good deal of similarity between the economic policies of Chile and those of Great Britain.'

Only when asked later by a journalist what the chief differences were did he comment,

'Our experience takes place in a democratic context, and that of Chile was undertaken by an authoritarian regime.'

*

283

After two ascetic days at Hornopirén I returned to Puerto Montt, still unprepared for an even more abrupt change of environment: Santiago, where I planned to stay for five weeks. I went straight to the train station to buy a ticket on the Santiago sleeper. The opening of a Puerto Montt-Santiago rail link in the second decade of the century was perceived as an event of great historical significance, and it's still the only passenger service which travels up and down the country rather than across. It hasn't picked up much speed over the years, contriving to take twenty-four hours to reach Santiago, which, considering that it travels on good track all the way, is quite an achievement for a journey of about six hundred and fifty miles. I thought this famous old rail journey would provide a quiet and undemanding way to end an odyssey. Two factors were to emerge which meant it didn't quite work out like that.

The first was that Chris Sainsbury had been commissioned to write a piece on the train for a book being published in the UK entitled *Train Journeys of the World*, and he suggested we travel together. I was delighted at the prospect of his company, though it did mean the journey wouldn't be very quiet. The second was that one of the faxes waiting for me at the public fax office in Puerto Montt was from Mr Fixit in Santiago. He was inviting me to stop off at Los Lingues on my way back for a lunch party, and by great coincidence this party was taking place the next day. I telephoned him and arranged to get off the train at San Fernando, two hours or so before Santiago and ten minutes from Los Lingues. This was all very well, but it turned out that we arrived in San Fernando at four-thirty in the morning.

If I was going to commit the social gaffe of turning up early for a party, I might as well do it in style.

The PR department of the Chilean Railway, keen to extract maximum mileage from the illustrious reputation of their oldest and longest service, claim that Puerto Montt is the most southerly train station in the world; Chris told me, however, that there was a little steam line further south in Argentina.

When I arrived at this station the train was waiting. It looked awful. The carriages, painted blue and yellow and looking confusingly Swedish, were rusty and didn't match. I asked a guard on the platform how old the train was.

'*Muchos años, muchos.*'

The inside was more encouraging. Built in Germany between the wars, our carriage was upholstered in dark polished wood, heavy puke-coloured velvet and chunky silver fittings. We had a compartment to ourselves with a copper basin encased in a teak surround, a fawn carpet and an angular 1930s lightfitting with two of the four shades missing. The windows were small, and there was a fan.

There was hardly anyone on the train, and the staff started playing cards in the bar before we had even pulled out of the station. Many of the original carriages had been replaced (the regular derailments had something to do with this), but the train's charm clung on; there was a spirit about it. The bathroom was dimly lit, and had a stately old shower with cork walls. The links between carriages were loose, and they swung around dangerously, causing the doors of the train to flap open.

We settled in, arranging our things around the compartment. It took an hour to get to the top of the hill outside Puerto Montt. I already wanted to see the glaciers again, and I knew in my heart that I almost certainly never would, which touched me with a deep sadness; I padded tragically along the empty corridors like a character in an Agatha Christie novel. We reached the shores of Lake Llanquihue, and the scenery looked tame after the landscape of the Carretera Austral; it made me feel tamed, and I didn't like it.

*

I was sitting, in the middle of the afternoon, with my feet up in the compartment, reading *The Road to Oxiana*. We stopped with such frequency, and for such extended periods, that I had failed to notice that the train had been stationary for a long time even by its own impressive standards. Chris suddenly rushed in from the bar.

'Where's my camera? We've hit a cow.'

I went to the door and saw staff prodding around on the line ahead. Portions of the cow lay on the embankment. Chris got off and set about his task with vigour. I suggested that readers of *Train Journeys of the World* might not want to look at photographs of cattle guts sprayed over the hedgerows; but he carried on.

The journey continued. When the train stopped, it did not glide to a halt, it slammed on its brakes, and everything shot forward. You risked your life stepping between carriages on the way to the bar, and Chris solved this problem by staying in the bar all the time.

By lunchtime the passenger count had reached double figures; the staff still outnumbered us, and they remained defiantly in the bar, which was also the restaurant car, presided over by an imperial chef wearing a tall white hat. The other restaurant staff wore white jackets and black bootlace ties, and the whole team spent a good portion of the journey eating. Just after the ticket collector and a waiter had sat down to a vat of mussels the train lurched to a stop at Antilhue, where women were selling floral grave wreaths on the platform. Six of the crew alighted and engaged in protracted negotiations. The train seemed to run entirely for the benefit of the staff.

There was another gringo on the grain, and we invited him to join us for a drink. He was a Dutch chemistry teacher, and he was in a terrible state because the hotel he had been staying at in Puerto Montt had caught fire. He had been writing postcards in his room and smelt burning, and when he opened the door he was confronted by a wall of smoke.

At Temuco (210 miles in ten hours) the chef got off to put money on the horses, and the train changed from diesel to electric.

We pulled into San Fernando two hours late, and I called Germán, who arrived heroically soon after, music screaming out of the car speakers. We went to a café and drank pints of coffee; it was good to see him again. When we got to Los Lingues servants were marching along garden paths bearing tables and baskets of flowers, cars and vans were delivering amplifiers and oysters, small knots of singers and musicians were practising in corners, stableboys were brushing down horses and in the kitchens teams of cooks and assistants were rolling pastry for *empanadas*, basting suckling pigs and squeezing sacks of lemons for pisco sours. Besides feeling light-headed from lack of sleep, the abrupt contrast of this luxuriant excess with my experiences of the past two months had a curious effect. It made me feel as if I were standing outside of my body and watching myself walk through the hacienda.

They gave me my old room. Don Germán and Doña Marie Elena embraced me as we crossed on a footpath, much too polite to comment on my general appearance. I noticed that nobody smelt of fish. I had a bath, wondering if my clothes would contaminate the room, and stayed in until the water was cold. I was rather unprepared for this occasion, mentally and physically. Rowena's cocktail dress had been lurking in a binliner at the bottom of the carpetbag since I was last at Los Lingues, so I got it out and gave it a shake. It had looked a lot nicer when she gave it to me.

The great and the good of Santiago were at this party, bright of plumage in their designer gear. I felt, at first, like Alice in

Wonderland, but the sybarite within me soon dealt with any lingering feelings of detachment. The pisco sours tasted good. A famous Chilean saxophonist played to us during cocktails on the lawn. It was a long way from a wet tent in Patagonia.

I woke up feeling rested, though with a slight headache, stretched out in an eighteenth-century bed on copious lace pillows. Yellow stripes of sunlight slid through the cracks in the shutters, and beyond the splashes of the fountain I heard people arriving for mass in the hacienda chapel. I got up for the service, and sat on a dark wooden pew at the back next to the maid who looked after my room. Her mother was in charge of the laundry, and her three brothers groomed the horses. Generations of the same families had worked on the estate and been baptized, married and mourned in its chapel; the turbulence of modern Chilean history had not obliterated the sense of cyclical permanence which imbued the hacienda like a kind of unreconstructed Tolstoyan feudalism.

Chapter Fifteen

Love many; trust few – and always paddle your own canoe.

Billy Two Rivers, Canadian Mohawk Chief

I arrived in Santiago just in time to take Simon and Rowena out for dinner, as they were about to fly to London for two months' home leave; they were getting married. Sitting in a smart restaurant in a city made me feel as if I had returned to reality, and that was sad. It was good to see Simon and Rowena again though. They had generously insisted that I stay in their flat while they were gone. Beatriz was coming in three times a week to clean, so I was excellently set up. But for the first day or two, once they had left, I wandered disconsolately around the huge, empty flat, looking through the oversize plate glass windows at the traffic and the smog.

I spread out everything I had accumulated on the kitchen floor. There wasn't much. The outstanding feature was a handsome collection of children's drawings. I had often made friends with children, and they had regularly offered me a specially drawn picture as a parting gift; I always liked them to draw their village or town. As I had asked each child to write the place where the picture was drawn in the corner, I was able to line them up geographicall, a string of young Chilean auto-images. They had drawn a llama with a triangular body; an approximation of a salt flat; a bush with bunches of grapes dangling from it; a bed with four stick people sleeping in it (that was from Santiago); a man fishing; a sophisticated attempt at *cochayuyo* (leathery thongs of seaweed); a person in a poncho and a wide-brimmed hat on a horse; an iceberg (I only recognized it because it was blue) – but every one included a row of upside down 'v's with a blob of colour at the tip representing snow. The children had unified their collective portrait as faithfully as the high-altitude colours on the maps.

I began making telephone calls to names I had been given or contacts I had established, planning the five weeks ahead. One invitation had been waiting at the flat for me when I got back to Santiago. It was from Paul Mylrea, the Reuters bureau chief, and his wife Frances Lowndes, whom I had met at a dinner when I first arrived in Chile. They were inviting me to a party at their home in Santiago on the night of the UK general election. I was very pleased, as, like many others, I was inclined to think that the British public were about to elect their first Labour government for thirteen years, and I wanted to celebrate with people who not only knew where Britain was, but also appreciated the significance of this great victory.

A Reuters terminal in the house would enable us to have the results as soon as they were announced, and the congenial time difference meant that the first ones would be in by eight o'clock. I made a cake and wrote 'Labour' on it in almonds, and when I arrived at seven everyone was in good spirits and the party was already lively.

By nine we were quiet. By ten we were depressed. At eleven-thirty I took a taxi home from the funereal remnants of what should have been a party. At least God gave us a small earthquake that night, out of sympathy. My bed began to vibrate, and I dreamt that I was at the Hotel Valdivia.

The Columban Sisters I had met in the north had given me the number of their colleagues in the slums of the capital, and when I called them I found that they already knew about me.

'We were expecting you,' said a cheerful Irish voice. 'Come over, and stay as long as you like.'

I took three buses and ended up in a part of town where all the houses looked temporary and which seemed to go on for ever, through miles of identical squalor. Within two hours of closing the door on my newly acquired penthouse I was ringing the bell on the iron gate of a clean and neat two-storey brick house surrounded by high railings.

'Welcome,' said a white-haired nun who came out to unpadlock the gate. We drank a quick cup of tea with the other nuns and left in a hurry, as it was Palm Sunday, and mass was about to begin.

We bought crosses made of bunches of herbs from a table in the church courtyard; the modern building was sweet with delicate blue rosemary flowers. It was very crowded, and the priest walked round sprinkling water from an orange plastic washing-up bowl. I was amazed to see a group of guitarists and to recognize most of the hymns as Spanish translations of choruses I had heard in Pentecostal churches in Britain. The congregation waved their crosses enthusiastically and we processed around the block, the guitarists swaying like troubadours and pounding out 'Jesus Christ Superstar' among the spent glue tubes on the broken roads.

I stayed in the slums for ten days, moving from house to house wherever I was invited to spread my sleeping bag. In the poky shops (there were no supermarkets) I wasn't surprised to see people purchasing single cigarettes; I had observed this

291

practice many times in southern Europe. They caught me out, however, when they counted their peso coins to buy one teabag and three matches. Much later, I learnt that the single teabag routine had been used by the opposition parties in the 1988 election campaign. They had made a television commercial showing a Chilean woman buying one teabag in a corner shop.

Nobody lived in a cardboard box. All the houses I visited had sanitation. Acute poverty is less visible in urban Chile than in the shanty towns of Brazil and Peru – but it is no less deadly. Chronic unemployment and chronic overcrowding lead to endemic social dysfunction and endemic misery; I didn't have to look far to see that. Substance abuse, alcohol abuse, drug-related crime and wife-beating were commonplace. Petty thieving to finance addiction was simply a part of daily life. The nuns told me that in one chapel the toilets had been stolen three times and that they had to take the taps off the sinks when they locked up. The local drugrunning ringleader was in prison standing trial for murdering a mourner at a funeral party, so at least life was quieter; the nuns had learnt to be grateful for such things.

According to the United Nations, 5 million Chileans (almost 40 per cent of the population) live in poverty, and 1.7 million in 'absolute poverty'. In that suburb there was no hospital, and one chemist serviced many thousands of people. There was no school for the over-fourteens; those sufficiently dedicated had to take long bus journeys into the centre of the city.

What they enjoyed in abundance were off-licences, and these remained open till three in the morning (the chemist shut at nine-thirty in the evening). There were also plenty of bars, though few of them were legal: most people drank in dens called *clandestinos*. Two or three times I was invited into one of these stygian rooms smelling of wine and marijuana. I never saw another woman there; women were part of the despair the men were erasing. Although I was always made welcome, I felt uncomfortable in the *clandestinos*, as if I had strayed too far into their vortex of poverty.

I talked to some of the young people about politics, but they had no passion; they were tired before their time. A decade or two earlier those communities had been power-houses of political energy. No one had any confidence in politics anymore; the junta's programme of depoliticization might have ultimately failed, but to a certain extent it had succeeded in weakening the general will to resist, and along with Chile's imported consumer culture it had stifled the imaginations of the disaffected youth.

I stayed for three days with a young woman called Evelyn. One of the nuns had introduced us. Evelyn was a committed member of the local church, and she was open, good-natured and always cheerful; the latter quality was particularly hum-bling as the youngest of her three children had gone blind at the age of one. Pablito was three now, and he was always with her. She didn't have any money, as her husband had been unemployed for six years. He skulked around the house during the day doing what Evelyn called d-i-y but which looked to me like nothing. The family lived in a lean-to on the side of Evelyn's in-laws' small brick house. One day she took me to her church to meet the priest.

'He's like you – Australian, or North American, I forget which. Most of the priests we get round here are foreign. Chileans don't like the job. The foreign ones help us a lot, you know, they don't just do churchy things, they get involved in our lives and problems. Then the bishops get nasty about it – they think we're being too political. What do I care about the bishops?'

The priest was an Australian in his thirties, and looked like a teddy bear. I asked him why there were so many foreign priests.

'A lot of reasons. After Cuba the Pope made a formal request to orders abroad asking them to send 10 per cent of their priests to Latin America. It's caused a lot of trouble – suspicions and that. There's been years of argument about where foreign money to the Church comes from, too. I mean, besides the fact that here you have an institution in a critically dependent situation, you also had self-confessed CIA front organizations working with groups within the Church.'

'So it's a political thing – the left don't like you?'

'No, it's more complicated than that. Frankly, nobody's keen on foreign priests. The right hate us too. The military regime got stuck into the popular South American pastime of expelling us left, right and centre. Just get on with the job as long as you can, that's my view.'

Evelyn was dusting the trestle table altar. We had brought little Pablito along in his oversize pushchair, and he was gurgling in a corner. Father Tony was arranging tables for catechism classes.

'Don't you ever feel you're taking on an impossible task, I mean amid all this suffering?'

'I don't think macro. I play my little role. I'll never leave them now. Eh, Evelyn?' He switched to Spanish. 'We do OK, don't we?'

I offered to take the children to the park. She was pitifully thrilled. She had a week's washing to do, by hand and in cold water. We had to take a bus to get to the park, and she tried to press the children's fare on me. The park was a small, scrubby piece of wasteland with a few tufts of yellow grass. There were some old tyres scattered around which other children were crawling in and out of, and Pablito's brother and sister joined in immediately, while I attempted to keep him amused with 'This Little Piggy' though I had trouble finding a cultural equivalent for roast beef.

All three of them fell asleep on the bus back. Pinned to the seat by their bodies, I tried to work out how I felt about being in the slum. First of all I felt alienated; I believe that emanated from disgust at my rich and privileged life. I also felt despair. Nobody except the likes of Father Tony was ever going to do anything for them – and there were few like him. Their lives were never going to get any easier, or less anguished, or more comfortable. The power of despair to diminish struck me very hard during that bus journey.

Once the two eldest children were running along their street, bursting to tell their mother what they had been doing, I thought, conversely, that being with Evelyn gave me hope for the human spirit. I suspect now that hope was my bourgeois luxury.

I went back to the Sisters for Easter, but to another house in another suburb. On Saturday evening, after the vigil and procession, the congregation built a fire outside the church and stood round it holding candles. We crowded into the diminutive building for mass, the priest's voice competing with the beat of a neighbouring disco. Three babies were baptized, and afterwards sponge cake and Fanta were dispensed next to the altar. One set of parents invited a group of us back to their home for a meal – they must have been saving up for it all year – and after we had eaten the tables were cleared away and we danced until the sky was light.

Before I left on Easter Sunday I joined a private communion service at a missionary house. The priest was Irish, as were the three Sisters present, so mass was said in English. The man didn't offer me the host, Ninevite that I was.

Over the weeks in Santiago, installed again in my football-pitch sized flat, I spent a lot of time with Germán, often together with his cousin Felipe and my friends Ken Forder and Sylvie Bujon, whom I had met during my first few days in

Chile after a mutual friend in London had put us in touch. Sylvie was a French journalist, and her husband Ken was a political officer at the US Embassy. They were about my age, and they were easy-going and fun. Sylvie was very bright, very stylish and typically French in her habits, but Ken wasn't typical of his country at all – he was the kind of person who rose above nationality. He was an unusual diplomat, in that he was frank, open and relaxed, and did not defend the United States with the Pavlovian zeal of some of his colleagues. They both had a well-developed sense of humour, they were sensitive, and generous hosts, and we had some very good times together.

We often went to Spandex, my favourite nightclub in Santiago, which was open on Fridays only and located in a cavernous old theatre in the centre of town. It was a great place to go at one or two in the morning after doing something else, and, as in all good nightclubs, it was perfectly acceptable to have a nap on one of the many sofas if you felt tired. Spandex exemplified counterculture, and it was full of eccentrics; I couldn't help wondering where these people were during the day, as I seldom saw anyone like them on the streets.

'Probably working as minor civil servants, or librarians,' said Ken.

Most of the nightclubs in the city were located in the *barrio alto*, lair of the rich, and were peopled with glamorous society types and wealthy poseurs. The *nouveau riche* syndrome in Santiago was repellent. It was particularly unpalatable when observed among the young: men and women of twenty who had lived almost all their lives under Pinochet and whose aspirations were to own a Landrover and eat in Pizza Hut, their cellular phones at their side, worshipping at their dual shrines of conformism and ostentation. Anyway, Spandex was different. Small podia were provided for solo dancing performances by anyone who felt the urge, and the evening was punctuated by the occasional floor show. These shows seemed to be based on the concept of cramming as many taboos into one act as possible. We saw men dressed up as nuns acting out a ritual which involved simulated oral sex and shooting up (not simultaneously), and a bizarre dance by three people dressed up as rabbits stretching condoms between their teeth. I didn't care much for the acts, but I enjoyed Spandex very much, as its laid-back flavour and sense that you could do anything or nothing without being watched were unusual qualities for a nightclub.

I never made it to closing time, though; the latest I managed was five, when it was still pulsating with energy. One night we ran into some Frenchmen there whom I knew; they were botanists, and had been working in Chile for eight months. I had first met them in the north, and had seen them socially two or three times in the capital. They were leaving for Paris the next morning, and had booked a private bus to take them and their friends from home to the airport so the party could continue for as long as possible.

After Spandex we went to their flat and had pisco sours for breakfast; the bus, inevitably, failed to turn up. Undaunted, a botanist strode out onto Apoquindo, one of the main streets of Santiago (it was rush hour by now), leapt on to a bus and offered the driver approximately twenty pounds in cash to collect everyone from the house and proceed to the airport. 'Everyone off!' shouted the driver without a moment's hesitation, and the disgruntled and besuited passengers disembarked into the polluted morning air.

The buses of Santiago are a phantasmagoria. Over a thousand *per hour* travel in each direction along the city's major artery at peak time. It is difficult to understand what Pinochet's total deregulation meant for the city. A transport economist at the Catholic University told me that average

297

vehicle ownership among bus-service operators is two, and that as there are several large fleets this means that many people own just one clapped-out bus which they loan to a hapless driver who works on commission. It isn't surprising that both congestion and pollution stand at record levels. As the autumn set in, the newspapers filled up with stories of increased air pollution. The winters are the worst, and after I returned from Chile almost every letter I received from Santiago included a paragraph about respiratory or other problems suffered by my correspondents as a direct result of the murderous air. During those few months alone, contaminant levels exceeded World Health Organization limits on fifty days, sometimes reaching ten times the readings of cities such as Los Angeles, and a prominent biochemist I had met wrote telling me that the intake of particles was akin to smoking between sixty and eighty cigarettes a day but details were being suppressed to avoid public panic.

Ken had access to a flat in Viña del Mar, the biggest coastal resort in Chile and a stereotypical playground of the rich and famous, and the three of us stayed there one weekend. It was less than two hours from Santiago, and we only slept there, as we spent our time in neighbouring Valparaíso, unlike most normal people in Chile who find Viña so desirable that if they can't afford its hideous prices they stay in sleazy Valpo and commute the other way.

There were some great bars in Valparaíso which didn't appear to have changed for thirty years. In our favourite a woman in her fifties in a crocheted cardigan sang the South American equivalent of Edith Piaf accompanied by a pianist with Brylcreemed hair and a nylon shirt and an accordionist with a wooden leg. Between numbers all three stared morosely at the audience. They hated us. Later on the woman was replaced by a man who looked like Einstein in an ill-fitting grey suit. He clutched the microphone to his face as he sang his angst-ridden songs, squeezing his eyes tight and occasionally rushing outside to the pavement, returning through another door. Besides ten small round tables there was an enormously long zinc bar at which a motley collection of eccentrics lingered, waited on by inscrutable staff in dinner jackets with shiny elbows, all as much a part of the place as the tarnished gilt mirrors. It was a typical Valparaíso style, redolent of spivs, hard times and the society of the South American urban underclass before it was subsumed in an electronic superculture.

When we returned to the car, our carguarder failed to appear. Often the quality of this 'work' is less than satisfactory. When I was out with a British diplomat once we returned to his vehicle and the carguarder accepted his cash with a cheerful, '*está bien!*' (Everything OK!). It was only when we drove off that we noticed the offside wing mirror hanging by a wire. It was unusual to find that the man had abandoned his post, as generally the guarders spring out of nowhere at the scent of cash. We drove towards Viña and two miles on there was our man, weaving among the traffic, indiscriminately demanding money from passing motorists.

I managed to get up to the Andes one last time. I went for the day from Santiago. The poplars were glowing yellow against the evergreens – my first autumnal Easter. It didn't feel a bit like autumn: as Darwin wrote in one of his poetic moments, when he was very near where I was then, '... that pensive stillness was absent, which makes the autumn in England indeed the evening of the year.'

The bus followed the river Maipo, and the landscape changed abruptly to bare rock streaked with mineral deposits. We stopped to let off a passenger next to a memorial to Pinochet's survival when he was ambushed in 1976. FMRP terrorists had hidden behind the rocks and waited for the general and his entourage, but the bullets hit the wrong people. To a certain extent it did him good, as it weakened the opposition, the various factions of which were already embroiled in disputes which threatened the United Accord they had signed in an attempt to present a single, democratic alternative to the junta. He made people suffer for it, anyway.

There was even a glacier ahead. It was mostly very beautiful up there, but every so often an expanse of slag or the apparatus of a hydroelectric power station made it look very ugly – as ugly as it had been beautiful. The bus driver was a lively character, and when he found out that I was English he shouted 'Las Malvinas!'; I was really getting tired of that. There was talk of the royal family, and an inspection of my passport fuelled speculation, as I was christened Sara Diana, that all British citizens are named after royalty.

I sat in a thermal pool later. It overlooked the white water of the Volcán river, and was itself overlooked by multi-coloured mountains and a band of higher snowscapes. The water was opaque ochre, and a dozen Chileans lounged contentedly at the edge.

The days slipped away from me. People started calling from London, saying, 'When are you coming home?' and familiar faces began marching across the landscape of my dreams. On my last Friday I climbed Santa Lucía hill in the centre of the city in the late afternoon ready for the thirty minutes or so when the sky turned salmon pink. I always made a point of stopping to observe this; half the sky became a slow gradation of colour from dark to light, the glow concentrating behind the black hills. When there were clouds, they formed a ridged panoply of blue and pink.

The next evening I had a dinner party for four people who had been particularly helpful to me. There were in their late thirties, and their money was very old. They certainly knew how to party: the first guest left at a quarter to five, despite the fact that at three o'clock there was an earthquake. As we were on the thirteenth floor it was quite noticeable (the glasses clinked together, anyway), but they brushed it aside – 'It's only a baby one!' One of them brought me an envelope of cocaine as a present, proudly presenting it as 'the best' as if he had produced a bottle of vintage Krug.

Ken and Sylvie threw a farewell party for me. I had a long history of having parties the night before I left on big trips, and it was always a mistake, so we decided to hold this one on my penultimate night, to be sensible. Germán and his cousin Felipe were the first to arrive. They turned up in suits and ties, looking immaculate. Ken, Sylvie and I were wearing jeans.

'Why didn't you tell me it was casual?' hissed Germán later.

'We usually only mention it when it isn't,' I said.

But it was all right. The party was great. Felipe made a speech in Spanish, I replied in English, and Germán, exuberant and generous, finished off.

'And for her last night,' he announced, 'I invite you all to my house for champagne and oysters tomorrow.'

Being sensible had its advantages.

The next day – my last – was Labour Day, so Ken, Sylvie and I drove to Zapallar, summer residence of the seriously rich. All the heavyweight politicians disappear to elaborate houses on the coast north west of the city at the weekend; even the leader of the Chilean Communists has a house in Zapallar. The streets exuded money, class and exclusion. I had heard Zapallar called 'the Southampton of Chile,' a baffling comparison (I had obviously missed something in Hampshire) until I discovered that the Southampton in question was the one in upstate New York. We ate swordfish and dozed off our hangovers on the beach. It occurred to me as I was lying there that it was a bank holiday, and I wondered where Mr Fixit was going to get oysters and champagne. Fortunately it wasn't my problem, and I went to sleep.

When I got to his house that evening two servants were arranging hundreds of oysters on large plates on the dining room table, and the fridge was loaded with champagne.

'Where did you get all this?' I asked him.

'I called the suppliers we use for the hacienda on their home numbers and told them if they didn't send it all round I'd stop buying from them.'

The plane to Rio was delayed for three hours, which meant that I would miss my next two connections. I felt exhausted, miserable, hungover and desperate, and I hadn't even left yet. The airport was brightly lit, even in the early morning, and the grime and litter of the concourse stood out in sharp focus, as did the anxiety and fatigue of the passengers who eddied pathetically around the coffee bar, which was out of coffee.

I found a red plastic seat and sat on it, my feet resting on the carpetbags. There was nothing I had ever wanted to do less than leave Chile. With my eyes closed, to still the sick misery of that moment, I called up the memory of a birthday lunch on the shore of a bright blue lake – a bottle of warm champagne, the crisp, still air, the saffron steppe and purple mists of Patagonia, the trail of ducks breaking the surface of the water, the ponderous curlicues of smoke rising from the rim of a volcano, the trill of the chucao and the sweet taste of the box-leafed barberry, the shadows of a flock of black-necked swans on an Andean mountain – and after a few minutes the calm elation of that day came to me again, and I knew I would make it come many times over the months and years which would be known as 'after Chile', so I wasn't really leaving at all.

Select Bibliography

Kenneth R. Andrews, *Drake's Voyages: A Reassessment of their Place in Elizabethan Maritime Expansion*, London, 1967

Michael Alford Andrews, *The Flight of the Condor*, London, 1982

Harold Blakemore, 'Chile', in *Latin America: Geographical Perspectives*, Harold Blakemore & Clifford T. Smith (eds), London, 1971, 1983

――――, *British Nitrates and Chilean Politics: 1886–1896*, London, 1974

E. Lucas Bridges, *The Uttermost Part of the Earth*, London, 1948

Sheila Cassidy, *Audacity to Believe*, London, 1977

Elsa M. Chaney, 'Old and New Feminists in Latin America: the Case of Peru and Chile', in *Journal of Marriage and the Family*, vol. 35, no. 2 (1973)

Pamela Constable and Arturo Valenzuela, *A Nation of Enemies*, New York, 1991

William V. D'Antonio and Frederick B. Pike (eds), *Religion, Revolution and Reform*, London, 1964

Charles Darwin, *Voyage of the Beagle*, London, 1839

Nathaniel Davis, *The Last Two Years of Salvador Allende*, Ithaca, 1985

Alonso de Ercilla, *La Araucana*, Santiago, 1969

José Donoso, *The Boom in Spanish American Literature: A*

Personal History, New York, 1977

Judith Laikin Elkin, *Jews of the Latin American Republics*, Chapel Hill, 1980

Seymour M. Hersh, *Kissinger: the Price of Power*, New York & London, 1983

Alistair Horne, *Small Earthquake in Chile*, London 1972, 1990

Brian Loveman, 'Military Dictatorship and Political Opposition in Chile 1973–86', in *Journal of Inter-American Studies*, vol. 28, no. 3 (1986)

———, *Chile: The Legacy of Hispanic Capitalism*, New York, 1979, 1988

Gabriel García Márquez, *Clandestine in Chile*, Cambridge, 1989

R. L. Mégroz, *The Real Robinson Crusoe*, London 1939

Andrea T. Merrill (ed), *Chile, A Country Study*, Washington, DC, 1982

Gabriela Mistral, *Antología Poética*, Santiago, 1974

Theodore H. Moran, *Multinational Corporations and the Politics of Dependence*, Princeton, 1974

David E. Mutchler, *The Church as a Political Factor in Latin America, with Particular Reference to Colombia and Chile*, New York, 1971

Pablo Neruda, *Confieso que he vivido: Memorias*, 1974

Jan Read, *Chilean Wine*, London, 1987

Eric Shipton, *Tierra del Fuego: the Fatal Lodestone*, London, 1973

Brian H. Smith, *The Church and Politics in Chile*, Princeton, 1982

Julian H. Steward (ed), *Handbook of South American Indians*, vols I & II, New York, 1957

Jacobo Timerman, *Chile: Death in the South*, London, 1987

Arturo and J. Samuel Valenzuela, *Chile: Politics and Society*, New Brunswick, 1976